Neil Somerville

What the Year of the Rabbit holds in store for you

Your Chinese Horoscope 2011

TO ROS, RICHARD AND EMILY

HarperElement
An Imprint of HarperCollins*Publishers*
77–85 Fulham Palace Road
Hammersmith, London W6 8JB

www.harpercollins.co.uk

and *HarperElement* are trademarks of
HarperCollins*Publishers* Limited

Published by HarperElement 2010

1

A catalogue record for this book is
available from the British Library

ISBN 978-0-00-735409-2

Printed and bound in Great Britain by
Clays Ltd, St Ives plc

CONTENTS

———◆◆◆———

ABOUT THE AUTHOR

Neil Somerville is one of the leading writers in the West on Chinese horoscopes. He has been interested in Eastern forms of divination for many years and believes that much can be learned from the ancient wisdom of the East. His annual book on Chinese horoscopes has built up an international following and he is also the author of *What's your Chinese Love Sign?* (Thorsons, 2000), *Chinese Success Signs* (Thorsons, 2001) and *The Answers* (Element, 2004).

Neil Somerville was born in the year of the Water Snake. His wife was born under the sign of the Monkey, his son is an Ox and daughter a Horse.

ACKNOWLEDGEMENTS

In writing *Your Chinese Horoscope 2011* I am grateful for the assistance and invaluable support that those around me have given.

I would also like to acknowledge Theodora Lau's *The Handbook of Chinese Horoscopes* (Harper & Row, 1979; Arrow, 1981), which was particularly useful to me in my research.

In addition to Ms Lau's work, I commend the following books to those who wish to find out more about Chinese horoscopes: Kristyna Arcarti, *Chinese Horoscopes for Beginners* (Headway, 1995); Catherine Aubier, *Chinese Zodiac Signs* (Arrow, 1984), series of 12 books; E. A. Crawford and Teresa Kennedy, *Chinese Elemental Astrology* (Piatkus Books, 1992); Paula Delsol, *Chinese Horoscopes* (Pan, 1973); Barry Fantoni, *Barry Fantoni's Chinese Horoscopes* (Warner, 1994); Bridget Giles and the Diagram Group, *Chinese Astrology* (HarperCollins*Publishers*, 1996); Kwok Man-Ho, *Complete Chinese Horoscopes* (Sunburst Books, 1995); Lori Reid, *The Complete Book of Chinese Horoscopes* (Element Books, 1997); Paul Rigby and Harvey Bean, *Chinese Astrologics* (Publications Division, South China Morning Post Ltd, 1981); Ruth Q. Sun, *The Asian Animal Zodiac* (Charles E. Tuttle Company, Inc., 1996); Derek Walters, *Ming Shu* (Pagoda Books, 1987) and

The Chinese Astrology Workbook (The Aquarian Press, 1988); Suzanne White, *The New Astrology* (Pan, 1987), *The New Chinese Astrology* (Pan, 1994) and *Chinese Astrology Plain and Simple* (Eden Grove Editions, 1998).

As we march into a new year
we each have our hopes, our ambitions and our dreams.

Sometimes fate and circumstance will assist us,
sometimes we will struggle and despair,
but march we must.

For it is those who keep going,
and who keep their aspirations alive,
who stand the greatest chance of securing what they want.

March determinedly,
and your determination will, in some way, be rewarded.

Neil Somerville

INTRODUCTION

The origins of Chinese horoscopes have been lost in the mists of time. It is known, however, that oriental astrologers practised their art many thousands of years ago and even today Chinese astrology continues to fascinate and intrigue.

In Chinese astrology there are 12 signs named after 12 different animals. No one quite knows how the signs acquired their names, but there is one legend that offers an explanation. According to this legend, one Chinese New Year the Buddha invited all the animals in his kingdom to come before him. Unfortunately, for reasons best known to the animals, only 12 turned up. The first to arrive was the Rat, followed by the Ox, Tiger, Rabbit, Dragon, Snake, Horse, Goat, Monkey, Rooster, Dog and finally Pig. In gratitude, the Buddha decided to name a year after each of the animals and that those born during that year would inherit some of the personality of that animal. Therefore those born in the year of the Ox would be hardworking, resolute and stubborn, just like the Ox, while those born in the year of the Dog would be loyal and faithful, just like the Dog. While it is not possible that everyone born in a particular year can have all the characteristics of the sign, it is incredible what similarities do occur, and this is partly where the fascination of Chinese horoscopes lies.

In addition to the 12 signs of the Chinese zodiac there are five elements and these have a strengthening or moderating influence upon the signs. Details about the effects of the elements are given in each of the chapters on the signs.

To find out which sign you were born under, refer to the tables on the following pages. As the Chinese year is based on the lunar year and does not start until late January or early February, it is particularly important for anyone born in those two months to check carefully the dates of the Chinese year in which they were born.

Also included, in the appendix, are two charts showing the compatibility between the signs for personal and business relationships and details about the signs ruling the different hours of the day. From this it is possible to locate your ascendant and, as in Western astrology, this has a significant influence on your personality.

In writing this book I have taken the unusual step of combining the intriguing nature of Chinese horoscopes with the Western desire to know what the future holds, and have based my interpretations upon various factors relating to each of the signs. Over the years in which *Your Chinese Horoscope* has been published I have been pleased that so many have found the sections on the forthcoming year of interest and hope that the horoscope has been constructive and useful. Remember, though, that at all times you are master of your own destiny.

I sincerely hope that *Your Chinese Horoscope 2011* will prove interesting and helpful for the year ahead.

THE CHINESE YEARS

Rat	18 February	1912	to	5 February	1913
Ox	6 February	1913	to	25 January	1914
Tiger	26 January	1914	to	13 February	1915
Rabbit	14 February	1915	to	2 February	1916
Dragon	3 February	1916	to	22 January	1917
Snake	23 January	1917	to	10 February	1918
Horse	11 February	1918	to	31 January	1919
Goat	1 February	1919	to	19 February	1920
Monkey	20 February	1920	to	7 February	1921
Rooster	8 February	1921	to	27 January	1922
Dog	28 January	1922	to	15 February	1923
Pig	16 February	1923	to	4 February	1924
Rat	5 February	1924	to	23 January	1925
Ox	24 January	1925	to	12 February	1926
Tiger	13 February	1926	to	1 February	1927
Rabbit	2 February	1927	to	22 January	1928
Dragon	23 January	1928	to	9 February	1929
Snake	10 February	1929	to	29 January	1930
Horse	30 January	1930	to	16 February	1931
Goat	17 February	1931	to	5 February	1932
Monkey	6 February	1932	to	25 January	1933
Rooster	26 January	1933	to	13 February	1934
Dog	14 February	1934	to	3 February	1935
Pig	4 February	1935	to	23 January	1936

Rat	24 January	1936	to	10 February	1937
Ox	11 February	1937	to	30 January	1938
Tiger	31 January	1938	to	18 February	1939
Rabbit	19 February	1939	to	7 February	1940
Dragon	8 February	1940	to	26 January	1941
Snake	27 January	1941	to	14 February	1942
Horse	15 February	1942	to	4 February	1943
Goat	5 February	1943	to	24 January	1944
Monkey	25 January	1944	to	12 February	1945
Rooster	13 February	1945	to	1 February	1946
Dog	2 February	1946	to	21 January	1947
Pig	22 January	1947	to	9 February	1948
Rat	10 February	1948	to	28 January	1949
Ox	29 January	1949	to	16 February	1950
Tiger	17 February	1950	to	5 February	1951
Rabbit	6 February	1951	to	26 January	1952
Dragon	27 January	1952	to	13 February	1953
Snake	14 February	1953	to	2 February	1954
Horse	3 February	1954	to	23 January	1955
Goat	24 January	1955	to	11 February	1956
Monkey	12 February	1956	to	30 January	1957
Rooster	31 January	1957	to	17 February	1958
Dog	18 February	1958	to	7 February	1959
Pig	8 February	1959	to	27 January	1960
Rat	28 January	1960	to	14 February	1961
Ox	15 February	1961	to	4 February	1962
Tiger	5 February	1962	to	24 January	1963
Rabbit	25 January	1963	to	12 February	1964
Dragon	13 February	1964	to	1 February	1965
Snake	2 February	1965	to	20 January	1966
Horse	21 January	1966	to	8 February	1967

Goat	9 February	1967	to	29 January	1968
Monkey	30 January	1968	to	16 February	1969
Rooster	17 February	1969	to	5 February	1970
Dog	6 February	1970	to	26 January	1971
Pig	27 January	1971	to	14 February	1972
Rat	15 February	1972	to	2 February	1973
Ox	3 February	1973	to	22 January	1974
Tiger	23 January	1974	to	10 February	1975
Rabbit	11 February	1975	to	30 January	1976
Dragon	31 January	1976	to	17 February	1977
Snake	18 February	1977	to	6 February	1978
Horse	7 February	1978	to	27 January	1979
Goat	28 January	1979	to	15 February	1980
Monkey	16 February	1980	to	4 February	1981
Rooster	5 February	1981	to	24 January	1982
Dog	25 January	1982	to	12 February	1983
Pig	13 February	1983	to	1 February	1984
Rat	2 February	1984	to	19 February	1985
Ox	20 February	1985	to	8 February	1986
Tiger	9 February	1986	to	28 January	1987
Rabbit	29 January	1987	to	16 February	1988
Dragon	17 February	1988	to	5 February	1989
Snake	6 February	1989	to	26 January	1990
Horse	27 January	1990	to	14 February	1991
Goat	15 February	1991	to	3 February	1992
Monkey	4 February	1992	to	22 January	1993
Rooster	23 January	1993	to	9 February	1994
Dog	10 February	1994	to	30 January	1995
Pig	31 January	1995	to	18 February	1996
Rat	19 February	1996	to	6 February	1997
Ox	7 February	1997	to	27 January	1998

Tiger	28 January	1998	to	15 February	1999
Rabbit	16 February	1999	to	4 February	2000
Dragon	5 February	2000	to	23 January	2001
Snake	24 January	2001	to	11 February	2002
Horse	12 February	2002	to	31 January	2003
Goat	1 February	2003	to	21 January	2004
Monkey	22 January	2004	to	8 February	2005
Rooster	9 February	2005	to	28 January	2006
Dog	29 January	2006	to	17 February	2007
Pig	18 February	2007	to	6 February	2008
Rat	7 February	2008	to	25 January	2009
Ox	26 January	2009	to	13 February	2010
Tiger	14 February	2010	to	2 February	2011
Rabbit	3 February	2011	to	22 January	2012

NOTE

The names of the signs in the Chinese zodiac occasionally differ, although the characteristics of the signs remain the same. In some books the Ox is referred to as the Buffalo or Bull, the Rabbit as the Hare or Cat, the Goat as the Sheep and the Pig as the Boar.

For the sake of convenience, the male gender is used throughout this book. Unless otherwise stated, the characteristics of the signs apply to both sexes.

WELCOME TO THE
YEAR OF THE RABBIT

Whether nibbling the grass in a lush green meadow, living on a hillside or kept as a family pet, there is an air of contentment about the Rabbit. Little seems to trouble him and he just gets on with life in a quiet and peaceable manner. And while a lot can happen in a Rabbit year, it can touch the lives of all of us in a positive and inspiring way. This is a time which favours the family and encourages learning and personal growth as well as the commemoration of major events.

Politically, Rabbit years are times of diplomacy and negotiation. In this one, in view of some of the tensions and warring going on, many of the world's leaders will be examining ways forward, exploring options and trying to reach consensus. Over the year some carefully negotiated agreements will be forged which will not only bring peace to some troubled regions but also help in reducing carbon emissions, decommissioning weapons and tackling world economic issues. The year will see a succession of summits and, as a result, the strengthening of ties between world leaders and nations.

Interestingly, previous Rabbit years have seen the formation of the Entente Cordiale between Britain and France, the establishment of a hotline between Moscow and Washington, the ending of the Vietnam War and, in 1987, the INF treaty between America and the Soviet Union being signed, which paved the way for the destruction of all land-based medium- and short-range missiles. It was in that same Rabbit year that Soviet President Mikhail Gorbachev introduced *glasnost*, the policy of openness that was to transform life in the Soviet Union and later have a great impact on events in Eastern Europe. What happens in 2011 can be equally far-reaching.

Economically, many countries will see slow but steady growth. To help, many governments will offer financial incentives to encourage investment and stimulate growth as well as reduce unemployment. Also, after the lessons of the banking crisis, tighter controls will be in force and the policy of many a fiscal body and government will be cautious encouragement. There will be gains to be had in many of the stock markets around the world, with some notable rallies. However, these may be followed by some sharp corrections and investors cannot afford to lower their guard during the year.

Several industries are likely to fall under the spotlight this year, especially in the alternative energy sector. Much attention will be focused on finding new ways to harness the world's resources, including new research projects and encouragement for wind farms, wave power and solar energy.

The Rabbit year is also likely to be marked by some medical breakthroughs, not only in the treatment, even conquering of certain diseases, but also in their early diagnosis and prevention. The Rabbit year's emphasis on research can lead to some momentous findings as well as the introduction of life-changing procedures. It was a previous Rabbit year that saw the first successful kidney transplant and the invention of the iron lung.

Another feature of the Rabbit year is that it strongly favours culture, and some artists and performers will push the boundaries and create some extraordinary pieces. The year will also see some major touring exhibitions, which will allow more people to appreciate artwork and historic artefacts. In addition many countries will hold important festivities and celebrations during the year, both in commemorating achievements and promoting trade and industry. It was sixty years ago that the Festival of Britain was held in the UK, an event considered a landmark at the time.

There will also be considerable focus over the year on education. Governments will be keen to increase funding to schools as well as provide grants and incentives for those entering further education or vocational training. In many countries there will also be measures to increase the number of apprenticeship and work placement schemes. Education and training will certainly be high on the agenda of many a government.

With the year's emphasis on personal development, many people will be giving some consideration to their lifestyle. Whether by attending to their well-being, taking up new interests or enrolling on a course or study programme, they will find the Rabbit year favours personal growth and the opportunities will be there – but they *do* need to be grasped.

The Rabbit year also favours family values and quite a few people will be making sure that more quality time is spent with their loved ones. Here again this can be a year for personal reappraisal and as a result many will bring their lifestyle into better balance. Relationships, too, are favourably aspected and this can be a year for finding or renewing love and starting a family as well as appreciating loved ones.

Overall, the Year of the Rabbit will be a full and interesting one. A lot will happen on the world stage and even though there will be dangers, tensions and tragic moments, there will also be reason for hope. It is a year for discussion, diplomacy and, importantly, personal growth. As George Eliot, born under the sign of the Rabbit, noted, 'It's them that take advantage that get advantage i' this world.'

To benefit in the Year of the Rabbit it is a case of taking advantage of opportunities, particularly to make more of yourself and your personal strengths. While some signs will fare better than others, the Rabbit year is a promising and encouraging one. Use it well and I wish you every success and good fortune.

YOUR CHINESE
HOROSCOPE 2011

18 FEBRUARY 1912 ～ 5 FEBRUARY 1913   *Water Rat*

5 FEBRUARY 1924 ～ 23 JANUARY 1925   *Wood Rat*

24 JANUARY 1936 ～ 10 FEBRUARY 1937   *Fire Rat*

10 FEBRUARY 1948 ～ 28 JANUARY 1949   *Earth Rat*

28 JANUARY 1960 ～ 14 FEBRUARY 1961   *Metal Rat*

15 FEBRUARY 1972 ～ 2 FEBRUARY 1973   *Water Rat*

2 FEBRUARY 1984 ～ 19 FEBRUARY 1985   *Wood Rat*

19 FEBRUARY 1996 ～ 6 FEBRUARY 1997   *Fire Rat*

7 FEBRUARY 2008 ～ 25 JANUARY 2009   *Earth Rat*

THE
RAT

THE PERSONALITY OF THE RAT

To see,
and to see what others do not see.
That is true vision.

The Rat is born under the sign of charm. He is intelligent, popular and loves attending parties and large social gatherings. He is able to establish friendships with remarkable ease and people generally feel relaxed in his company. He is a very social creature and is genuinely interested in the welfare and activities of others. He has a good understanding of human nature and his advice and opinions are often sought.

The Rat is a hard and diligent worker. He is also very imaginative and is never short of ideas. However, he does sometimes lack the confidence to promote his ideas and this can often prevent him from securing the recognition he deserves.

The Rat is very observant and many Rats have made excellent writers and journalists. The Rat also excels at personnel and PR work and any job that brings him into contact with people and the media. His skills are particularly appreciated in times of crisis, for the Rat has an incredibly strong sense of self-preservation. When it comes to finding a way out of an awkward situation, he is certain to be the one who comes up with a solution.

The Rat loves to be where there is a lot of action, but should he ever find himself in a very bureaucratic or restrictive environment he can become a stickler for discipline and routine. He is also something of an opportunist and is constantly on the lookout for ways in which he can improve his wealth and lifestyle. He rarely lets an opportunity go by and can become involved in so many plans and schemes that he sometimes squanders his energies and achieves very little as a result. He is also rather gullible and can be taken in by those less scrupulous than himself.

Another characteristic of the Rat is his attitude towards money. He is very thrifty and to some he may appear a little mean. The reason for this is purely that he likes to keep his money within his family. He can be most generous to his partner, his children and close friends and relatives. He can also be generous to himself, for he often finds it impossible to deprive himself of any luxury or object he fancies. He is very acquisitive and can be a notorious hoarder. He also hates waste and is rarely prepared to throw anything away. He can be rather greedy and will rarely refuse an invitation to a free meal or a complimentary ticket to a lavish function.

The Rat is a good conversationalist, although he can occasionally be a little indiscreet. He can be highly critical of others – for an honest and unbiased opinion, the Rat is a superb critic – and will sometimes use confidential information to his own advantage. However, as he has such a bright and irresistible nature, most people are prepared to forgive him his slight indiscretions.

Throughout his long and eventful life the Rat will make many friends and will find that he is especially well suited to those born under his own sign and those of the Ox, Dragon and Monkey. He can also get on well with those born under the signs of the Tiger, Snake, Rooster, Dog and Pig, but the rather sensitive Rabbit and Goat will find him a little too critical and blunt for their liking. The Horse and Rat will also find it difficult to get on with each other – the Rat craves security and will find the Horse's changeable moods and rather independent nature a little unsettling.

The Rat is very family orientated and will do anything to please his nearest and dearest. He is exceptionally loyal to his parents and can himself be a very caring and loving parent. He will take an interest in all his children's activities and see that they want for nothing. He usually has a large family.

The female Rat has a kindly, outgoing nature and involves herself in a multitude of different activities. She has a wide circle of friends, enjoys entertaining and is an attentive hostess. She is also conscientious about the upkeep of her home and has good taste in home furnishings. She is most supportive to the other members of her family and, due to her resourceful, friendly and persevering nature, can do well in practically any career she chooses.

Although the Rat is essentially outgoing, he is also a very private individual. He tends to keep his feelings to himself and while he is not averse to learning what other people are doing, he resents anyone prying too closely into his own affairs. He also does not like solitude and if he is alone for any length of time he can easily get depressed.

The Rat is undoubtedly very talented, but he does sometimes fail to capitalize on his many abilities. He has a tendency to become involved in too many schemes and chase after too many opportunities at once. If he can slow down and concentrate on one thing at a time, he can become very successful. If not, success and wealth can elude him. But, with his tremendous ability to charm, he will rarely, if ever, be without friends.

THE FIVE DIFFERENT TYPES OF RAT

In addition to the 12 signs of the Chinese zodiac there are five elements and these have a strengthening or moderating influence on the signs. The effects of the five elements on the Rat are described below, together with the years in which they were exercising their influence. Therefore those Rats born in 1960 are Metal Rats, those born in 1912 and 1972 are Water Rats, and so on.

Metal Rat: 1960
This Rat has excellent taste and certainly knows how to appreciate the finer things in life. His home is comfortable and nicely decorated and he likes to entertain and mix in fashionable circles. He has considerable financial acumen and invests his money well. On the surface he appears cheerful and confident, but deep down he can be troubled by worries that are quite often of his own making. He is exceptionally loyal to his family and friends.

Water Rat: 1912, 1972
The Water Rat is intelligent and very astute. He is a deep thinker and can express his thoughts clearly and persuasively. He is always eager to learn and is talented in many different areas. He is usually very popular, but his fear of

loneliness can sometimes lead him into mixing with the wrong sort of company. He is a particularly skilful writer, but he can get sidetracked very easily and should try to concentrate on just one thing at a time.

Wood Rat: 1924, 1984

The Wood Rat has a friendly, outgoing personality and is popular with his colleagues and friends. He has a quick, agile brain and likes to turn his hand to anything he thinks may be useful. His one fear is insecurity, but given his intelligence and capabilities, this fear is usually unfounded. He has a good sense of humour, enjoys travel and, due to his highly imaginative nature, can be a gifted writer or artist.

Fire Rat: 1936, 1996

The Fire Rat is rarely still and seems to have a never-ending supply of energy and enthusiasm. He loves being involved in some form of action, be it travel, following up new ideas or campaigning for a cause in which he fervently believes. He is an original thinker and hates being bound by petty restrictions or the dictates of others. He can be forthright in his views but can sometimes get carried away in the excitement of the moment and commit himself to various undertakings without thinking through all the implications. Yet he has a resilient nature and with the right support can go far in life.

Earth Rat: 1948, 2008

This Rat is astute and very level-headed. He rarely takes unnecessary chances and while he is constantly trying to improve his financial status, he is prepared to proceed slowly and leave nothing to chance. He is probably not as adventurous as the other types of Rat and prefers to remain in familiar territory rather than rush headlong into something he knows little about. He is talented, conscientious and caring towards his loved ones, but at the same time can be self-conscious and worry a little too much about the image he is trying to project.

PROSPECTS FOR THE RAT IN 2011

The Year of the Tiger (14 February 2010–2 February 2011) will have been a busy one for the Rat and he may have felt uneasy with its pace and level of change. The Rat likes action but it has to be on his terms, and events during the year could have caused him some anxiety and soul-searching. And in the remaining Tiger months he will need to be wary.

One of the Rat's greatest strengths is his ability to get on well with others and in the closing months of the Tiger year he should make the most of his opportunities to meet others and consult them over his ideas and plans. This is no time for him to be too independent in outlook or go it alone. In particular, if he is in a dilemma over a decision or work situation, by discussing it with his family and those able to advise, he will be able to benefit from their suggestions. August and December could see an increase in social activity.

The Rat will also need to keep careful control of his spending and, where possible, plan for more substantial purchases. As there will be chances for many Rats to travel in the closing months of the year, early provision for this could help.

Work-wise, the Rat will need to remain alert and be prepared to adapt to any changes introduced. Tiger years can be demanding, but Rats are resourceful and it will still be possible for many to make headway. Overall, the Tiger year does require the Rat to be on his mettle, but it will not be without its opportunities or rewards.

The Year of the Rabbit starts on 3 February and will be an interesting one for the Rat. During it he can make useful progress but the emphasis of the Rabbit year is on patience and persistence and the Rat must not act in haste or expect speedy results. It is very much a case of adapting to the times and proceeding slowly, carefully and methodically.

This is particularly the case in the Rat's work. During the year many Rats will find their experience serving them well, with their advice often being sought and greater and more specialist responsibilities being offered. Although some situations may be demanding, by rising to the challenge and showing himself willing, the Rat can do himself considerable good.

A helpful development will be the opportunities the Rat will have to work closely with colleagues as well as meet others connected with his industry. Some contacts made during the year could offer particularly useful support and advice.

This also applies to those Rats who are keen to move on from their present position or are seeking work. By talking to others and obtaining advice, they may well find their manner and background impressing others and leading to possibilities worth considering. April, June, September and November could see some encouraging developments.

Over the year all Rats should also take advantage of any training they are offered or, if seeking work, any initiatives and refresher courses that are available. By being willing and using any chances to further their skills and knowledge, they will not only be demonstrating their commitment but also widening their options for the future. Progress may not be swift, but the Rabbit year does reward initiative.

The Rat will, however, need to be careful in financial matters. Although in some areas he may be thrifty, he can also be indulgent and he does need to keep careful control of his outgoings and avoid too many unplanned purchases. This is a year for financial discipline. Also, if considering any large expenditure, he would do well to check the terms and obligations as well as make cost comparisons. Where outgoings are concerned, this is no year for rush or taking risks.

With his sociable nature, the Rat always sets much store by his relations with others and both domestically and socially this will be a busy and eventful year. Domestically, 2011 will bring some notable events, possibly an addition to the family, a wedding or another special cause for celebration. Loved ones will often look to the Rat for support and advice, as well as help in arranging certain matters, and his skills will be much appreciated, but throughout the year he does need to be aware of the views of others. To be too dogmatic over certain issues or not show sufficient consideration could bring problems and misunderstandings.

Fortunately Rats are usually very thoughtful, but this is a year for awareness and good communication.

The Rat will also welcome the support of friends during the year and whether meeting for a chat, enjoying shared interests or attending a function or other occasion, he will often appreciate the times he goes out. There will also be good opportunities for him to get to know others over the year and his personable nature will help him add to his social circle and, in some cases, make a significant new friendship. May, August and November to mid-January will see the most social activity.

A further benefit of the year will be the way in which the Rat is able to give some time to his own personal development. This can be through skills he acquires in his work, interests he pursues or activities he sets himself. By following up his ideas and opportunities, he can take much satisfaction from what he does. Many Rats are skilled communicators and for those who enjoy writing, this is another activity which can bring pleasure this year as well as be a satisfying outlet for their creativity.

Generally during the Rabbit year the Rat will need to remain alert, consult others and consider his actions carefully. This is no time for rush or being too single-minded. However, by making the most of his opportunities, especially to further his skills and interests, he can make reasonable headway and enjoy many of his activities. And domestically and socially there will be some memorable occasions to enjoy.

The Metal Rat

This can be a reasonable year for the Metal Rat, although throughout he will need to show patience. He may be keen for plans to go ahead and results to come through, but situations cannot be rushed. This is a slower-paced year than some, but it will certainly not be without its benefits.

At work many Metal Rats will be content to remain in their present position and concentrate on the duties they know well. The skills they have built up and their in-house knowledge can serve them well and make this an often satisfying time. In addition many could be given other responsibilities or targets to meet and, while often challenging, this can give them greater incentive as well as add new interest to their role.

The Metal Rat will also be helped by the good working relations he has with those around him and whenever possible he should continue to build on his contacts. Also, while he may be expert in his present role, he should make the most of any chances to develop his knowledge and skills. By taking advantage of any training that is available and keeping informed about developments in his industry, he will find the knowledge he gains and initiative he shows can be of present *and* future value.

For Metal Rats who are keen to move on from their present role or seeking work, the Rabbit year can proceed in curious ways. For months nothing may happen and then all of a sudden several interesting opportunities may come at once. April, June, September and November could see some important developments, but key to so much in the Rabbit year is patience. Results *will* come, but they will need waiting and striving for. However, with the Metal

Rat's prospects showing an upturn next year, what he accomplishes now can be a contributing factor in his later success, and it is well worth him persevering.

A positive aspect of the year will be the way the Metal Rat is able to develop certain interests. Although sometimes his free time will be limited, by setting some aside for pursuits he enjoys he will not only derive much personal satisfaction from what he does but could also find new ideas and possibilities opening up. For Metal Rats who enjoy creative activities, it would be worth making more of their talents, as Rabbit years very much favour creativity.

The Metal Rat is usually careful in money matters and in the Rabbit year he needs to remain his cautious and vigilant self. With several substantial expenses during the year, including family and accommodation costs, he should watch his outgoings and, whenever possible, make advance provision for certain outlays. He also needs to be careful when dealing with paperwork, including matters relating to tax or benefits, and keep receipts and guarantees safe. A mistake or lost document could be to his disadvantage. Metal Rats, take note and do be thorough and careful in financial matters.

Many Metal Rats will see considerable activity in their home life over the year and for some this could include a family celebration. Here the Metal Rat's organizational ability will prove a real asset. Those close to him will also often be grateful for his advice, support and ability to empathize. However, no year is ever free of its strains and if differences of opinion do arise or pressures lead to irritability, the Metal Rat needs to recognize and deal with these as best he can. Without care, something that starts out in a small way could escalate and undermine the rapport he enjoys with those around him. Metal Rats, again take note. Domestically this can be a pleasing and potentially exciting year, but it is also one to be mindful *and* aware.

This also applies to the Metal Rat's social life. Over the year he will enjoy many of the events he attends, but he does need to remain his attentive self. Misunderstandings may arise and the Metal Rat may become concerned by something he hears. At such times he should act, find out what is really happening and, where possible, smooth over any disagreements. For the most part his social life will be pleasurable and problem free, but throughout the year he does need to be alert and aware of the views of others. This also applies to those Metal Rats enjoying new romance. This is no time to take the feelings of another for granted. Relationships will need to be nurtured and the more attentive the Metal Rat is, the better.

As with the general nature of the year, some months will be quiet socially while others will see a flurry of invitations and opportunities to go out. The second half of the year will be busier than the first, with May, August and mid-November to mid-January likely to be the liveliest and more interesting months.

Although the slow-moving nature of the Rabbit year may sometimes frustrate the Metal Rat, by being patient and using his time and opportunities to advantage, he can still gain a lot from it. Developing his skills can bring him particular satisfaction and his achievements will prepare him for the more substantial successes that await in 2012. In his home life there could be important events to enjoy and by being attentive and giving time to others, he will find his relations with others can be positive, meaningful and often special. Overall, a quietish year, but one which can be of considerable value in the longer term.

TIP FOR THE YEAR
Seize any opportunities to develop your skills and knowledge and spend time furthering your personal interests. These can be satisfying and often lead to other possibilities. Also, give time to others. You have great personal skills and should use your gifts well.

The Water Rat

This will be a significant year for the Water Rat. Although some parts of it may be quiet, what he is able to set in motion could have considerable long-term value. Also, many Water Rats will have the chance to develop new skills and ideas and their accomplishments will be of present *and* future benefit.

In his work the Water Rat will often have the chance to further his position, possibly as colleagues move on and positions become available or new initiatives and ways of working are introduced. By being willing and adaptable, he will not only have the opportunity to gain new experience but also to widen his scope for the future. Also, with the in-house knowledge many Water Rats will now have acquired, if they have ideas they feel could be helpful, they should put these forward. By being involved and using their knowledge and experience to advantage, they will not only be showing commitment but also underlining their potential. Taking the initiative will reward many Water Rats well this year.

Many will choose to remain with their present employer and build on their position and skills, but for those who are anxious to move on or are seeking work, the Rabbit year can have interesting developments in store. Obtaining a position will require considerable time and effort, but by being persistent and widening the scope of what they are prepared to consider, many Water Rats will be successful in setting their career off in a new direction. This is very much a year to be open to possibility. April, June, September and November could see some interesting work developments.

Another positive aspect of the year will be the chance the Water Rat will have to get to know and work with others. With his easy manner, he will impress quite a few new people and do his reputation a lot of good. Also, if he is seeking a position or is ever in a dilemma over a work situation, he should be forthcoming and talk to those with the knowledge and experience to help. This is not a time for being too independent in approach. Support, contact and initiative are very much the order of the day – and year.

The Water Rat has an enquiring mind and if there is a subject that catches his attention over the year, he should aim to find out more. Similarly, if there is a project he would like to tackle, he should make time for it. Both practical and creative pursuits can bring him much satisfaction during the year and, as with so much that is started in 2011, also be of value in the future.

With the pressures and various activities of the year the Water Rat should also try to take a holiday and give himself a proper break. Even if he is not able to travel very far, a change of scene and rest from his usual routine can do him a lot of good. Also, if he receives invitations to meet up with family or friends, he should do his best to go. The second half of the year could bring some interesting and sometimes unexpected travel opportunities.

This will also be an interesting year socially and the Water Rat could be invited to a variety of events. Again, if he makes the time to go, he can not only enjoy himself but also benefit in other ways, whether through meeting others, having the chance to relax or, in some cases, getting new ideas. May, August and November to mid-January could be the busiest months socially, but throughout the year the Water Rat can do himself a lot of good by being active and following up invitations.

His domestic life will also be busy and the Water Rat will do much to help and advise both younger and more senior relations. There could also be good reason for a family celebration or get-together during the year, with the Water Rat often instrumental in making arrangements. In many a household he will play a pivotal and appreciated role. However, at all times he will need to be attentive to those around him and aware of their views. An oversight or assumption could cause problems. Water Rats, take note and do consult others. September and December could see some interesting domestic developments.

With many demands on his resources, in financial matters the Water Rat will need to stay disciplined. In order for certain plans to go ahead, he needs to budget carefully as well as keep a watch on his general level of spending. He should also be thorough when dealing with financial paper-work and prompt in returning forms and dealing with important correspondence. Financially, this is a year for vigilance.

Overall, however, the Year of the Rabbit will be a generally pleasant and constructive one for the Water Rat. It will give him some excellent chances to develop his skills and benefit from opportunities. He will be supported and encouraged by those around him and if he uses his time well, his actions can be to both his present and future advantage.

TIP FOR THE YEAR
Spend time with family and friends and appreciate your interests. By keeping your lifestyle in balance you will get far more out of the year as well as prepare the way for the interesting opportunities that lie ahead, particularly in 2012.

The Wood Rat
This will be a year of important developments for the Wood Rat, with his personal life often memorable, possibly due to an addition to the family, the decision to get married or, if currently unattached, meeting someone who will quickly become special. On a personal level this can be a busy and eventful year.

Also, with his ability to relate well to others, the Wood Rat will find himself in increasing demand, with many opportunities to go out and socialize. Whether meeting up with others through his work, his interests or his existing friendships, this will be an active and interesting year. For Wood Rats who have had recent relationship problems or are feeling lonely, perhaps having moved to a new area, the Rabbit year can see a brightening in their situation and their positive actions and personable nature can reward them well.

Naturally no year is without its problems and while the Wood Rat's relations with others will be positive, he does still need to be attentive. A lapse or *faux pas* could come to be regretted. Those Wood Rats in a well-established relationship should give time to their partner and be open and communicative. This is no year to make assumptions or take the feelings of another for granted. Fortunately most Wood Rats are considerate and aware, but extra attention this year can make an appreciable difference. May, August and mid-November to early January will see the most social opportunities.

Another important feature of the year will be the chance the Wood Rat will have to further his interests and if there is a subject or activity that appeals to him, he should follow it up. Some Wood Rats may become intrigued by a completely new activity. For those who enjoy creative pursuits it would also be worth promoting their ideas, as they could enjoy an encouraging response. Rabbit years do favour creativity.

In his work the Wood Rat could find this a slow-moving year, with the results of his efforts taking some while to filter through. While this may occasionally be frustrating, the Wood Rat can still derive much value from what he is able to do. This includes gaining experience in different areas of his work as well as getting himself better known. By making the most of this time, when opportunities do arise he will often be well placed to benefit.

Most Wood Rats will remain with their present employer over the year, while those who decide to make a change or are seeking work would do well to widen the range of positions they are prepared to consider and, if eligible, take advantage of retraining opportunities. Their quest will take time and persistence and many Wood Rats will eventually be offered a position that is different from what they were doing previously. While initially this may be something of a challenge, what the Wood Rat is able to achieve this year can often be a significant platform that he can build on in the future. April, June, September and November could see some interesting possibilities, but whenever the Wood Rat sees an opening that appeals to him, he should act. Opportunities can arise unexpectedly throughout the year.

In financial matters, the Wood Rat will need to remain disciplined. With his existing commitments and some additional personal expenses, he will find that careful budgeting is required. Fortunately his often thrifty nature will help, but Wood Rats, as with all Rats, can give way to moments of extravagance. While the Wood Rat and his loved ones will enjoy an often pleasing lifestyle this year, it is still a time for watchfulness and control. Also, if the Wood Rat enters into any financial agreement, he needs to check the terms and obligations. In financial matters, this is no year to be lax.

Overall, the Rabbit year may be slow moving in parts but the skills the Wood Rat is able to acquire can often be personally satisfying as well as help to open up future possibilities. And on a personal level, this can be a meaningful time with important developments.

TIP FOR THE YEAR

Avoid rush. Set about your activities carefully and make the most of the present. The positive actions you take and abilities you demonstrate can reward you well, although maybe not straightaway. Also, make the most of your personable nature by using your chances to meet others and add to your social circle. With care, this can be a valuable year with long-term benefits.

The Fire Rat

Although on the surface this may seem a quiet year for the Fire Rat, what he undertakes now can have far-reaching consequences. The importance of the Rabbit year should not be underestimated.

Fire Rats born in 1996 will find much of their time will be devoted to studying and education. With exams and coursework to prepare for, the more organized and disciplined they are, the better. There could also be some interesting developments in store as they take certain subjects or skills to new levels. In some cases they could become particularly inspired by some work they do and this could indicate areas it would be worth specializing in later or even taking up as a future career.

Also, by taking up opportunities to extend their skills, especially in areas such as music, drama or sport, many Fire Rats will not only derive increasing pleasure from what they do but also find other possibilities beginning to open up. As far as personal development is concerned, this can be an important year and by making the most of the facilities and tuition available to him, the young Fire Rat can get a tremendous amount back from the effort he now puts in.

It is also important that he remains open to new ideas. In some cases his interests or skills could take him in a new direction or lead to other activities that appeal to him. By being prepared to follow these up – and here his adventurous nature can help – he can make the developments of the year significant. The Rabbit year is one of considerable potential, but opportunities do need taking.

The Fire Rat will be well supported in most of what he does throughout the year and should listen carefully to the advice he is given. Although he may have his own thoughts and inclinations, by being receptive he could be alerted to other options or helped with decisions he needs to make. Also, if he has any personal or educational problems, by talking about these he gives others the chance to help and advise.

The Fire Rat will particularly value the support of some very close friends over the year and will not only enjoy sharing interests but also thoughts and confidences. New activities he takes up can also bring him into contact with others and lead to some helpful new friendships.

Although the Fire Rat will often be very much involved with his own activities and studies, he should also aim to contribute to his home life. Whether assisting with certain tasks or just being open and talking to those around him, he will find his involvement and input can make a difference as well as lead to better understanding and rapport. The more involved he is, the better.

For Fire Rats born in 1936 this can also be an interesting year, although throughout they will need to consult closely with others. Whether discussing ideas or plans they may be considering or concerns and problems they may have, by being open and willing to talk, these Fire Rats will often be helped and reassured. This is no year for going it alone or being too independent (or obtuse) in attitude.

Also, while the Fire Rat may be keen for certain plans to come to fruition, especially if related to his accommodation, he will need to show patience over the year. This is not a time favouring rush. In the Rabbit year it is often the case of moving plans forward when the time is right rather than hurrying things through. However, while the slow-moving nature of the year may occasionally frustrate the Fire Rat, it can have its benefits, as delays can lead to better decisions or allow the Fire Rat to benefit from sales and other favourable buying opportunities.

Throughout the year the Fire Rat will derive considerable satisfaction from his interests, with creative pursuits often bringing especial pleasure. Sharing what he does with his friends and loved ones can also bring more enjoyment and meaning to his activities.

He will also delight in some of the travel opportunities that arise and, whether visiting relations or taking a short break, will again enjoy the chance to see places new to him and the social opportunities his travels can often bring.

On a more cautionary note, he does need to be thorough when dealing with money matters and to check any important correspondence and forms he receives and question anything that concerns him. To delay or make assumptions could be to his disadvantage. Fire Rats, take note.

Whether born in 1936 or 1996, the Fire Rat can find the Rabbit year an encouraging one and by making the most of his ideas and opportunities, he can get a lot of value and personal satisfaction from what he does. If he is open to new possibilities and listens closely to others, interesting developments can take place which can be to his benefit. The Rabbit year may not be one of swift events, but it can be constructive and its benefits far-reaching.

TIP FOR THE YEAR
Make the most of your opportunities. With willingness, backed by support, a lot can open up for you. Effort and commitment can reward you well both now and in the future.

The Earth Rat

The Earth Rat tends to be more cautious than some of the other types of Rat, preferring to proceed carefully and in a measured way. This approach will serve him well this year and he will enjoy some interesting and pleasing personal developments.

As the Rabbit year starts it will be to the Earth Rat's advantage to give some thought to what he wants to see happen over the next 12 months. This could involve his work situation, accommodation or personal interests he is keen to pursue, but whatever his ideas, by thinking them through and talking them over with his loved ones, he will find he has more specific aims to work towards and will be able to direct his energies more effectively. Also, as many Earth Rats will discover, Rabbit years do not favour rush, and adapting to the rhythm of the year will bring far better results.

One factor in the Earth Rat's favour will be the support and advice he receives from those around him. When considering ideas or making decisions, he will find the process of talking things through will clarify his preferences in his own mind as well as give him the chance to benefit from the suggestions of others. This is no year to be too independent-minded.

One area in which particular care is needed is finance and if the Earth Rat receives correspondence that is unclear or causes him concern, it is important that he seeks advice, perhaps from a helpline. Similarly, with any large transaction or obligation he may take on, he should check the terms and conditions. The extra attention he gives to his finances can help prevent mistakes and sometimes save unnecessary outlay.

Many Earth Rats will be keen to proceed with certain accommodation plans during the year, possibly replacing equipment or adding new comforts to their home. Here again, the Earth Rat needs to remain alert. Purchases should not be rushed, and if he takes his time, he may not only be better pleased with his eventual choices but also benefit from some advantageous offers. For Earth Rats who decide to move, again the Rabbit year can be slow moving, with sales, purchases and moves often protracted.

For those in work the Rabbit year can be a generally satisfying one, particularly as the Earth Rat may have more chance to concentrate on his area of expertise. When pressures or problems arise, colleagues will often be keen to draw on his experience as well as admire his resourceful approach. During the year many Earth Rats will find their skills in demand and while they will often be content to remain in their present role, their work can give them a sense of achievement.

Some may, though, decide to take advantage of retirement options or reduce their working commitments. Although this may be something they have been looking forward to for some time, such a change can impact their lives in several ways. To help, these Earth Rats should give serious thought to what it is they now want to do. With carefully considered plans, they can find the Rabbit year can mark the start of an exciting new chapter. As with so much this year, the more the Earth Rat can plan ahead, the better he will fare.

Earth Rats who are interested in altering their working commitments or keen to take on another role could also benefit from ideas they have or opportunities that arise. With resourcefulness, good advice and initiative, they can make the Rabbit year a time of interesting possibilities.

The Earth Rat will also derive much satisfaction from his interests and by setting himself specific aims or projects will be pleased with what he is able to get underway. This is a year which rewards focus and dedication. Another important feature of it will be the opportunities that open up for the Earth Rat, and whether attracted by locally run courses and new activities or joining with others to try out new pursuits, by being open to what is offered, he can greatly benefit.

Throughout the year the Earth Rat will also value the good friendships he has. Not only will he enjoy meeting up with his friends but he can also benefit from their support and goodwill. Many Earth Rats will find their interests will bring them into contact with others and for those keen to extend their social circle this can be a pleasing and interesting year. May, June, August and the closing months of the Rabbit year are likely to be the most active socially.

The Earth Rat's domestic life can also be rewarding, and by sharing his thoughts, he will find many plans developing well, even if sometimes slowly. Not only can he benefit from the support he is given over the year but he will also do much to advise and assist others, including helping to arrange some important family occasions. Domestically, this can be a full and pleasing year, but the key will be good liaison and co-operation.

The Earth Rat would also do well to try and go away with his loved ones over the year. A break can do everyone a lot of good and if the Earth Rat considers his destination carefully, he will particularly enjoy the places he visits and activities he carries out.

Much will go in the Earth Rat's favour this year but, as with any year, problems can still arise. When they do, the Earth Rat does need to consult others and find a solution or amicable arrangement. To ignore problems could lead to them escalating or leave them lingering unsatisfactorily in the background. The Earth Rat's tactful and thoughtful manner can be very useful this year, but at times of concern he does need to be active, involved and forthcoming.

Overall, the Year of the Rabbit is one for going ahead with plans, and with the Earth Rat's careful approach and the support of others, he will be satisfied with how he is able to develop his ideas and interests. This may not be a year for swift developments, but it can be a quietly satisfying one.

TIP FOR THE YEAR
Give yourself some time, especially to develop your personal interests. The skills you use and ideas you follow

up can bring you a great deal of pleasure. Also, be open to new activities. These can develop in an often interesting and advantageous manner.

FAMOUS RATS

Ben Affleck, Ursula Andress, Louis Armstrong, Lauren Bacall, Dame Shirley Bassey, Kathy Bates, Irving Berlin, Silvio Berlusconi, Kenneth Branagh, Marlon Brando, Charlotte Brontë, Jackson Browne, George H. W. Bush, Glen Campbell, David Carradine, Jimmy Carter, Aaron Copland, Cameron Diaz, David Duchovny, Noël Edmonds, T. S. Eliot, Eminem, Colin Firth, Clark Gable, Liam Gallagher, Al Gore, Hugh Grant, Lewis Hamilton, Thomas Hardy, Prince Harry, Haydn, Charlton Heston, Buddy Holly, Mick Hucknall, Henrik Ibsen, Jeremy Irons, Samuel L. Jackson, Jean-Michel Jarre, Scarlett Johansson, Gene Kelly, Avril Lavigne, Jude Law, Gary Lineker, Lord Andrew Lloyd Webber, Ian McEwan, Katie Melua, Claude Monet, Richard Nixon, Ozzy Osbourne, Sean Penn, Terry Pratchett, Ian Rankin, Lou Rawls, Burt Reynolds, Jonathan Ross, Rossini, William Shakespeare, Donna Summer, James Taylor, Leo Tolstoy, Henri Toulouse-Lautrec, Spencer Tracy, the Prince of Wales, George Washington, the Duke of York, Emile Zola.

6 FEBRUARY 1913 ~ 25 JANUARY 1914	*Water Ox*
24 JANUARY 1925 ~ 12 FEBRUARY 1926	*Wood Ox*
11 FEBRUARY 1937 ~ 30 JANUARY 1938	*Fire Ox*
29 JANUARY 1949 ~ 16 FEBRUARY 1950	*Earth Ox*
15 FEBRUARY 1961 ~ 4 FEBRUARY 1962	*Metal Ox*
3 FEBRUARY 1973 ~ 22 JANUARY 1974	*Water Ox*
20 FEBRUARY 1985 ~ 8 FEBRUARY 1986	*Wood Ox*
7 FEBRUARY 1997 ~ 27 JANUARY 1998	*Fire Ox*
26 JANUARY 2009 ~ 13 FEBRUARY 2010	*Earth Ox*

THE
OX

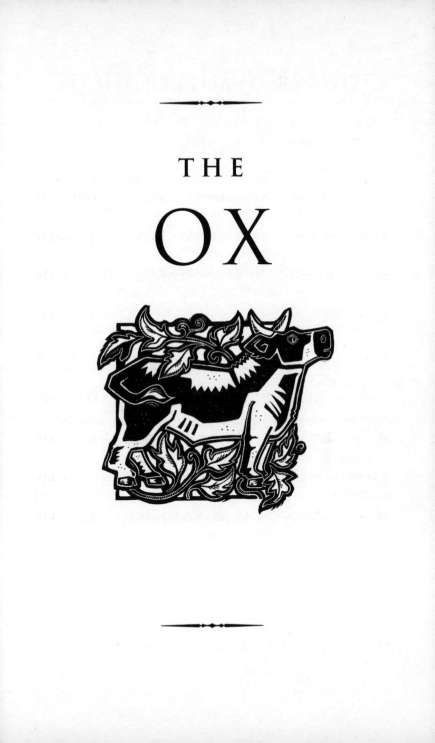

THE PERSONALITY OF THE OX

The more considered the way,
the more considerable the journey.

The Ox is born under the signs of equilibrium and tenacity. He is a hard and conscientious worker and sets about everything he does in a resolute, methodical and determined manner. He has considerable leadership qualities and is often admired for his tough and uncompromising nature. He knows what he wants to achieve in life and, as far as possible, will not be deflected from his ultimate objective.

The Ox takes his responsibilities and duties very seriously. He is decisive and quick to take advantage of any opportunity that comes his way. He is also sincere and places a great deal of trust in his friends and colleagues. He is, nevertheless, something of a loner. He is a quiet and private individual and often keeps his thoughts to himself. He also cherishes his independence and prefers to set about things in his own way rather than be bound by the dictates of others or influenced by outside pressures.

The Ox tends to have a calm and tranquil nature, but if something angers him or he feels that someone has let him down, he can have a fearsome temper. He can also be stubborn and obstinate and this can lead him into conflict with others. Usually he will succeed in getting his own way, but should things go against him he is a poor loser and will take any defeat or setback extremely badly.

The Ox is often a deep thinker and rather studious. He is not particularly renowned for his sense of humour and does not take kindly to new gimmicks or anything too innovative. He is too solid and traditional for that and prefers to stick to the more conventional norm.

His home is very important to him and in some respects he treats it as a private sanctuary. His family tends to be closely knit and the Ox will make sure that each member does their fair share around the house. He tends to be a hoarder, but he is always well organized and neat. He also places great importance on punctuality and there is nothing that infuriates him more than to be kept waiting, particularly if it is due to someone's inefficiency. The Ox can be a hard taskmaster!

Once settled in a job or house the Ox will quite happily remain there for many years. He does not like change and he is also not particularly keen on travel. He does, however, enjoy gardening and other outdoor pursuits and he will often spend much of his spare time out of doors. He is usually an excellent gardener and whenever possible will make sure he has a large area of ground to maintain. He usually prefers to live in the country than the town.

Due to his dedicated and dependable nature the Ox will usually do well in his chosen career, providing he is given enough freedom to act on his own initiative. He invariably does well in politics, agriculture and in careers that need specialized training. He is also very gifted artistically and many Oxen have enjoyed considerable success as musicians or composers.

The Ox is not as outgoing as some and it often takes him a long time to establish friendships and feel relaxed in another person's company. His courtships are likely to be long, but once he is settled he will remain devoted and loyal to his partner. He is particularly well suited to those born under the signs of the Rat, Rabbit, Snake and Rooster. He can also establish a good relationship with the Monkey, Dog, Pig and another Ox, but he will find that he has little in common with the whimsical and sensitive Goat. He will also find it difficult to get on with the Horse, Dragon and Tiger – the Ox prefers a quiet and peaceful existence and those born under these three signs tend to be a little too lively and impulsive for his liking.

The female Ox has a kind and caring nature and her home and family are very much her pride and joy. She always tries to do her best for her partner and can be a most conscientious and loving parent. She is an excellent organizer and a very determined person who will often succeed in getting what she wants in life. She usually has a deep interest in the arts and is often a talented artist or musician.

The Ox is a very down-to-earth character. He is sincere, loyal and unpretentious. He can, however, be rather reserved and to some he may appear distant and aloof. He has a quiet nature, but underneath he is very strong-willed and ambitious. He has the courage of his convictions and is often prepared to stand up for what he believes to be right, regardless of the consequences. He inspires confidence and trust and throughout his life he will rarely be short of people who are ready to support him.

THE FIVE DIFFERENT TYPES OF OX

In addition to the 12 signs of the Chinese zodiac there are five elements and these have a strengthening or moderating influence on the signs. The effects of the five elements on the Ox are described below, together with the years in which they were exercising their influence. Therefore those Oxen born in 1961 are Metal Oxen, those born in 1913 and 1973 are Water Oxen, and so on.

Metal Ox: 1961

This Ox is confident and very strong-willed. He can be blunt and forthright in his views and is not afraid of speaking his mind. He sets about his objectives with a dogged determination, but he can become so involved in his various activities that he can be oblivious to the thoughts and feelings of those around him, and this can sometimes be to his detriment. He is honest and dependable and will never promise more than he can deliver. He has a good appreciation of the arts and usually has a small circle of very good and loyal friends.

Water Ox: 1913, 1973

This Ox has a sharp and penetrating mind. He is a good organizer and sets about his work in a methodical manner. He is not as narrow-minded as some of the other types of Ox and is more willing to involve others in his plans and aspirations. He usually has very high moral standards and is often attracted to careers in public service. He is a good judge of character and has such a friendly and persuasive manner that he usually experiences little difficulty in securing his objectives. He is popular and has an excellent way with children.

Wood Ox: 1925, 1985

The Wood Ox conducts himself with an air of dignity and authority and will often take a leading role in any enterprise in which he becomes involved. He is very self-confident and is direct in his dealings with others. He does, however, have a quick temper and has no hesitation in speaking his mind. He has tremendous drive and willpower and an extremely good memory. He is particularly loyal and devoted to the members of his family and has a most caring nature.

Fire Ox: 1937, 1997

The Fire Ox has a powerful and assertive personality and is a hard and conscientious worker. He holds strong views and has very little patience when things do not go his way. He can also get carried away in the excitement of the moment and does not always take into account the views of those around him. He nevertheless has many leadership qualities and will often reach positions of power, eminence and wealth. He usually has a small group of loyal and close friends and is very devoted to his family.

Earth Ox: 1949, 2009

This Ox sets about everything he does in a sensible and level-headed manner. He is ambitious but also realistic in his aims and is often prepared to work long hours in order to secure his objectives. He is shrewd in financial and business matters and is a very good judge of character. He has a quiet nature and is greatly admired for his sincerity and integrity. He is also very loyal to his family and friends and his views are often sought.

PROSPECTS FOR THE OX IN 2011

The Ox will often have felt uncomfortable with the developments and fast pace of the Tiger year (14 February 2010–2 February 2011). It will have been a demanding time, with many Oxen facing increased pressures and difficult decisions. However, while the aspects in the Tiger year may be mixed, there is good reason for the Ox to take heart, for his prospects are more encouraging in the next Chinese year.

In what remains of the Tiger year the Ox will need to proceed carefully. In his work he should concentrate on his specific duties and also take note of the developments going on around him. This is no time for him to be too independent in approach. For Oxen who are considering a change or are seeking a position, September and November could see some interesting possibilities.

In financial matters the Ox will need to be vigilant and take his time when making more substantial purchases as well as watch his outgoings. Risks or haste could lead to regret.

With a lot likely to be on his mind, the Ox also needs to be forthcoming and share his thoughts with those around him. This will be far better than brooding or keeping any anxieties to himself. Both family and friends will be keen to advise and support. In addition, by playing his usual active part in home life, he will particularly appreciate some of the occasions that take place towards the end of the year. Similarly, in his social life, if he takes up invitations and spends time with his friends, he will not only enjoy himself but can also do himself considerable good, particularly as this will give him the chance to relax and unwind.

The Tiger year may be challenging, but it will not be without its pleasures, and the more the Ox joins with others (and watches his independent tendencies), the more he is likely to gain from it.

The Year of the Rabbit begins on 3 February and will be a much improved one for the Ox. Rather than feeling buffeted by events and the pace that characterizes the Tiger year, he will be able to focus on his objectives and achieve some positive results. Admittedly, the Rabbit year will still have its problems, but overall this can be a far more satisfying and constructive time for the Ox.

For Oxen who are starting the Rabbit year dissatisfied, at a low ebb or disappointed with recent progress, this is very much a time to draw a line under what has happened and to look ahead. With a positive 'can do' approach, the Ox will find more opening up for him.

This will be especially the case at work, and many Oxen will feel that the time is now right to take their skills further and explore new options. For quite a few, developments in their current place of work could give them the opening they want. By keeping alert and indicating their desire to progress, many will be able to make important – and sometimes overdue – headway. Any new roles and duties will also involve the Ox learning new skills and adapting to different ways of working, but by showing commitment and resolve, he can do himself and his reputation much good.

For Oxen who are keen to take their career in another direction, as well as those seeking work, again the Rabbit year can have encouraging developments in store. To benefit, these Oxen will need to be active in making enquiries as well as consider other ways in which they could use their strengths, but by chance, almost as if by fate taking a hand, an opening could arise which is not only suitable but gives these Oxen an exciting and often inspiring new challenge. Mid-March to early June and October could see some interesting developments, but whenever opportunities arise the Ox needs to act swiftly and emphasize his qualities and experience.

The progress the Ox makes at work can also lead to an increase in income, but money matters still need to be handled carefully. The Ox does need to budget for his commitments and try to reduce any borrowings. He should also be careful if he becomes involved in a more informal arrangement, including lending to another person, as problems and misunderstandings could arise. In money matters this is a year for caution and careful management.

On a personal level, however, the Rabbit year has much to offer. For Oxen enjoying romance this is set to grow stronger as the year progresses, while for the unattached, a chance meeting can often become meaningful and new love add excitement to the year. Oxen who would welcome more company can do much to help their position by taking up activities which will allow them to meet others. Sometimes a locally run course or a social or interest group could be what they need. The action they take can often reward them well. March, April, July and September could offer some fine opportunities to meet others as well as be active times socially.

The Ox's home life can also keep him busy during the year. With his practical nature, he may well decide to improve his home in some way, perhaps redecorating certain rooms, sorting and tidying up particular areas and, for the gardener, enjoying time outdoors. Practical activities, especially those that can be shared, can bring the Ox much pleasure this year.

He will also do a lot to support loved ones during the year. Someone close to him could experience some difficulty and the support, encouragement and assistance the Ox is able to give may be of more value than he may realize. In turn, should a problem arise which he himself does not feel competent to deal with, he should seek advice. He may be keen to do his best, but if the situation warrants expert advice, he should feel able to call upon it. Oxen, do remember this. Personally, this can be a satisfying year, but do be prepared to draw on the assistance of others if required.

Overall, the Year of the Rabbit is an encouraging one for the Ox and by looking to make progress, using his time well and seizing his opportunities, he can make headway as well as enjoy some pleasing personal developments.

The Metal Ox

This will be an important year for the Metal Ox and with it marking his fiftieth birthday he will be keen to get this new decade off to a positive start. As he has demonstrated so often, when he sets himself specific aims, his hard work and focus usually secure what he wants, and so it will be this year. This is no time to be fettered by recent disappointments (the previous Tiger year in particular could have been an awkward one) but to concentrate on the present *and* look determinedly ahead.

As 2011 begins the Metal Ox could find it particularly helpful to draw up some plans for the year. With thoughts in mind he will find his efforts opening up some fresh possibilities and rewarding him in often special ways. The Rabbit year can be an interesting one and also have some surprises in store.

The Metal Ox's relations with others will be especially important this year. His loved ones will often be keen to mark his fiftieth birthday in fine style and not only will he be the centre of attention but often touched by the affection shown him. However, it will not only be his birthday and other family occasions that will be meaningful, but the support and assistance he receives throughout the year. In turn, he should talk openly about his activities and plans and listen closely to advice given. In some cases, new possibilities could arise as a result. This is very much a year that favours a co-operative rather than independent approach.

In his home life the Metal Ox will also be pleased with some of the activities that take place, including practical projects and activities shared with his loved ones. He will also take a fond interest in the activities of those around him and the advice and practical support he gives to younger and more senior relations will be welcomed, particularly if they are facing problems or anxieties. The Metal Ox has many redoubtable qualities and he will not let them down.

This will also be an interesting year as far as his social life is concerned. He will have the chance to meet new people and form important new friendships and sometimes, for the unattached, find romance. This is a year that favours activity and the Metal Ox will enjoy and often benefit from his chances to meet others. March, April, July and September could be the most active months socially.

The Metal Ox should also give some time to his own interests over the year, as these help keep his lifestyle in balance. To mark his fiftieth year, he could also be tempted to try something new. By carefully thinking through his ideas and then taking action, he can make this a constructive and personally beneficial time. In addition, if he is keen to travel and has a particular destination in mind, by making enquiries he could find his travels adding another exciting strand to the year.

As far as his work is concerned, the Rabbit year holds interesting possibilities. Although progress may not be swift or opportunities plentiful, there will still be some good chances for the Metal Ox to move forward. These could be in his existing place of work as more senior positions or other responsibilities become available. The Metal Ox will often be well placed to benefit, and with determined action and the willingness to put himself forward, he can make important headway.

There will, though, be some Metal Oxen who will feel they have accomplished all they can in their present role and be keen to switch to something different. For these Metal Oxen, as well as those seeking work, the Rabbit year can have encouraging developments in store. Obtaining a new position may not be easy, but by keeping alert and thinking of different ways in which they could use their experience – talking to employment agencies could give them interesting thoughts to consider – they could be offered an interesting new challenge. This is a year to be open to possibility. Mid-March to early June and October could be important months work-wise.

In order to go ahead with his plans, the Metal Ox will need to be disciplined in money matters and keep a close watch on his outgoings. Also, when entering into agreements he needs to check the terms and details and to be particularly careful if lending to someone. Without increased vigilance, problems could arise. Metal Oxen, take note and in money matters do be thorough and careful.

Overall, the Rabbit year can be an important one for the Metal Ox. It will not only bring some special times but also some opportunities to develop. Whether in his work or his personal interests, by being forward thinking and acting on his aims, the Metal Ox will find his energy and focus leading to a lot opening up for him. A positive and encouraging year.

TIP FOR THE YEAR

Decide on your aims for the year. Once your attention is directed on these, interesting developments can follow. Also, value your relations with others. These can help make this important year all the more successful.

The Water Ox

There is a Chinese proverb which states, 'With aspirations you can go anywhere; without aspirations you can go nowhere.' As a determined Ox, the Water Ox certainly has aspirations and the Rabbit year will encourage him and reward him well.

In his work this is a year of important developments. For Water Oxen who have been languishing in their present role or are feeling disappointed with their recent progress, the Rabbit year can provide the chance they have been hoping for. Sometimes this could arise as colleagues move on, creating vacancies and promotion opportunities, or the Water Ox could be alerted to a position which is different from what he has been used to but which he is well suited for. Opportunities can arise suddenly in the Rabbit year and the Water Ox can also help his position by taking up any available training courses and following developments within his industry. In 2011 he should remember 'With aspirations you can go anywhere' and should keep those aspirations firmly alive with initiative and action.

For Water Oxen seeking work, again the year can bring interesting possibilities. However, to benefit, these Water Oxen should not be too restrictive in the type of work they are prepared to consider. By looking at various options and considering different ways in which they can use their strengths, they could be alerted to an often ideal opportunity. Some might decide to retrain and certainly for many this can be a year of some very interesting options which can give their career and self-esteem a considerable boost. Mid-March to early June and October could see significant developments.

The headway the Water Ox makes in his work can also lead to an increase in income, but money-wise this is a year for care. The Water Ox's commitments are likely to be considerable and he should not relax his usual disciplined approach to finance. He should be particularly careful if lending to another person and if he has concerns over any money-related matter during the year, he should seek advice and clarification.

His relations with others, however, will be important and often special. In his home life this can be a busy time, with the Water Ox actively helping those with decisions that need taking, assisting and encouraging those in education and perhaps also supporting someone in need. He can be of inestimable help to others over the year.

He will also spend time on practical projects. Many Water Oxen will redecorate some rooms and undertake other home improvements during the year. Their projects could take longer than intended but will be satisfying when complete. Also, while the Water Ox may be content to tackle a lot single-handedly, it is important that he draws on the assistance of others where necessary and is open and forthcoming about his own activities and concerns. He will do a lot for others this year but should give them the chance to reciprocate too.

Although the Water Ox will have many commitments it is also important that he allows himself time for rest and relaxation. Personal interests that allow him to unwind can do him a lot of good. Also, if sedentary for much of the day, he would do well to consider appropriate exercise or activities that can help his well-being. To be at his best, it would be worth giving thought to his lifestyle, quality of diet and general level of exercise.

He should also not neglect his social life. By meeting up with friends and going to events that appeal to him, he can again do himself a lot of good as well as benefit from the support that others can give, sometimes in unexpected ways.

This is also a special year for affairs of the heart and for Water Oxen who are alone and would perhaps welcome romance, a chance encounter could add an exciting element to their lives. Chance does play a big part this year. For socializing and meeting others March, April, July and September to mid-October can be busy and important months.

Overall, the Water Ox has much in his favour this year. With his friendly, straightforward manner, determination and good judgement, he will be able to make his strengths count as well as benefit from the encouraging aspects that prevail. This is a year for progress and action, but also to be alert to the excellent and often fortuitous chances the Rabbit year can bring.

TIP FOR THE YEAR
Pay attention to your relations with others. Some people you know can be particularly instrumental in your progress this year, whether through giving advice and support, making suggestions or alerting you to opportunities. Shared interests and activities can also be pleasurable.

The Wood Ox
This is a year of considerable potential for the Wood Ox, with interesting possibilities opening up and some special times to look forward to. However, it is also a year requir-

ing action. To make things happen the Wood Ox will need to make some important decisions and be prepared to move forward. Fortunately, one of the hallmarks of the Wood Ox character is his determination, and with belief and initiative, he can get a lot out of this year.

The aspects for his personal life are especially favourable and Wood Oxen with a partner will often have exciting plans to share and will do much to help and encourage one another. For those who are parents, or become parents this year, the time they spend with babies or young children can be especially rewarding. Many will also busy themselves making improvements to their home and will enjoy seeing their plans take shape. This can be a satisfying and often exciting time.

The Wood Ox will also benefit from the assistance given by family members and close friends. Not only will they be keen to support and advise him but if he needs greater assistance (especially if a young parent) or practical help with any undertaking, the time and help others give can make an appreciable difference. Whenever the Wood Ox feels under strain or in need of a helping hand, he should ask.

Also, while a lot in his personal life can go well, he may become concerned about a loved one who is experiencing difficulties. If he is prepared to listen and offer support, his care and good sense will be of more value than he may realize.

The Wood Ox will appreciate his social life during the year and those who have to move because of work or other changing circumstances will find the Rabbit year can give them the chance to establish a new social circle. Here again this can be a personally significant time and by being active, the Wood Ox can benefit a great deal from what happens.

For those who are currently alone, the Rabbit year is especially encouraging and many unattached Wood Oxen will meet their future partner over the year. Sometimes romance can start in an unexpected way, with chance playing an important part. March, April, July and September could see the most social activity, but throughout the Rabbit year the Wood Ox should take advantage of opportunities to go out and meet others.

He should also make sure he sets time aside over the year to enjoy his interests and recreational pursuits. With his commitments, sometimes these can get neglected, but they are nevertheless important ways of keeping his lifestyle in balance and also give him the chance to enjoy certain skills or activities. Sometimes they have the added benefit of bringing him into contact with others or giving him additional exercise. If there is a subject that appeals to him this year, it would be worth him finding out more. The Rabbit year can open up some important possibilities for him, some of which can be to his longer-term benefit.

This can also be an interesting year as far as work prospects are concerned. For Wood Oxen who have remained in the same position for some time, the Rabbit year will bring the opportunity to take on greater and often more satisfying responsibilities. If the Wood Ox keeps alert for suitable opportunities, he will find his experience and background can make him a strong candidate. Again this is a year favouring decisive and determined action.

The Wood Ox can also help his prospects by being an active member of any team and taking advantage of any training available to him. By demonstrating his commitment and using his people skills well, he can underline his potential.

The Rabbit year can also present some good opportunities for those Wood Oxen currently seeking work. By widening the scope of what they are prepared to consider and making a special effort with their applications, many will find their persistence rewarded. Some could also benefit from openings created by government initiatives. Mid-March to early June, late September and October could be active months for work matters.

The progress the Wood Ox makes in his work can also lead to an increase in income, but financially this is a year for care. The Wood Ox will need to control his spending and make advance provision for some of his plans, including any deposits he may be required to put down. Here his disciplined nature can be of considerable help, but should he have any concerns about a financial matter, it would be worth him seeking additional advice.

In spite of this need to watch his outgoings, he should still try to take a holiday at some time over the year and so give himself a break. Even if he decides not to travel too far, a change of scene can do him a lot of good as well as give him some all-important fun.

Overall, the Year of the Rabbit is one of interesting possibility, and by being active and willing, the Wood Ox will have some opportunities to make progress as well as some special times to enjoy. There will be a lot in his favour this year and it rests with him to use his talents well.

TIP FOR THE YEAR

Believe in yourself. Act positively and build on your strengths. You can achieve a lot this year. Also, value the special relationships you have with those around you. These can be rewarding and significant times.

The Fire Ox

This will be a satisfying year for the Fire Ox and will give him the chance to further his ideas and plans. With a willing attitude, he can achieve a great deal this year.

For Fire Oxen born in 1997 this will be a significant year educationally. As they move to more advanced work they will need to be disciplined in their studying and make the most of their opportunities. What they do now can give them a solid foundation for the next few years. This is not a time to waste.

Also, the Fire Ox will find that by putting in the effort, he will often derive more satisfaction from what he does. This not only includes the progress he makes in his studies but also the new skills he acquires. In some cases what he learns now could particularly inspire him and encourage him to do more. Whether this is with computer skills, sport or more creative activities, the chances will be there for the Fire Ox to make progress, and the more receptive he is, the more he can take from the present time.

He will also derive considerable pleasure from the interests he pursues and the aims he sets himself over the year. If he wants to take a particular hobby further, he will find that if he works on his objectives, he will not only accomplish more but often see new possibilities opening up. The

Rabbit year is an encouraging one and by being active the Fire Ox can gain a lot personally from his activities.

He will also value the good friendships he has. Not only can shared interests bring a lot of fun but there will also be chances to swap ideas as well as give and receive support. Although, as an Ox, the young Fire Ox may take his time making friends, once he has done so he enjoys a strong rapport with them. This year, as he gets to do more, his social circle is set to increase.

The Fire Ox should also be forthcoming over the year and be prepared to talk to those at home as well as his tutors, particularly if he has any concerns. By being open, he will allow those around him to advise and support him more. At home, he can also help rapport and understanding by helping more with certain activities. And should a close relation experience problems or be under pressure this year, any extra he is able to do will be particularly appreciated.

Many Fire Oxen will also have the opportunity to travel this year and whether this is connected with their education or a personal interest, they will often enjoy the chance to see areas new to them.

Overall, the Rabbit year holds considerable promise for the young Fire Ox, but it rests with him to make the most of it. With commitment and a willingness to learn, he can get a lot of satisfaction from what he does and the progress he makes. As an ambitious Fire Ox, he also knows that what he does now can prepare him for opportunities that lie ahead, and the benefits of his actions can be far-reaching.

For Fire Oxen born in 1937 this can also be an interesting year. However, to get the most from it, the Fire Ox will need to decide on his aims and plans for the year. This will allow him to better direct his time and energy. His ideas could concern alterations he would like to make to his home, projects to carry out in his garden (if he has one) or ways of developing his interests and furthering his knowledge, but whatever he decides upon, once he sets plans in motion, he will often become thoroughly absorbed in them. The Fire Ox also has an enquiring mind and if there are subjects that are intriguing him, he should follow them up. With good use of his time, he can make this a pleasing and constructive year.

This will also be a busy year for family matters. As always the Fire Ox will take a keen interest in the activities of younger relations and over the year will offer much useful support and advice. The rapport he has with some of his loved ones can, despite a considerable gap in years, often be special. While he will do a lot to help others, he too will be glad of the help and support he receives and if anything is troubling him at any time or he would welcome additional assistance, he needs to be forthcoming and ask. In addition, if any complex matter is concerning him during the year, rather than keeping it to himself he should seek the advice of someone qualified to assist. While this is an encouraging year, the Fire Ox should remember that help is at hand should he need it.

In money matters he should remain his careful and vigilant self. This includes watching his outgoings and making provision for his commitments and plans. Also, he should be wary of risk or entering into agreements without checking the full implications. When dealing with his finances, he needs to be disciplined, alert and prepared to question anything that is unclear.

Many Fire Oxen will have travel opportunities over the year and whenever possible the Fire Ox should take advantage of invitations he receives or offers that appeal to him, whether these involve visiting friends and relations or going away for a holiday or short break.

Whether born in 1937 or 1997, the Fire Ox will be offered considerable scope by the Rabbit year and by setting about his activities in a determined and willing way, he will often be pleased with what he is able to accomplish. He should also be open to the opportunities that will come his way, for these can be to his benefit. Overall, a satisfying and constructive year.

TIP FOR THE YEAR

Act on your dreams and hopes. Once you make a start, you can both enjoy what you do and look forward to the benefits that can follow on from your actions. Also, develop new interests and skills and enjoy the rapport you have with those around you.

The Earth Ox

This will be a year of important decisions for the Earth Ox. Although he may be feeling buffeted by recent events, the Rabbit year will give him more chance to regain the initiative and determine his own way forward. In addition many Earth Oxen will be helped by the support of those around them as well as benefit from some moments of good fortune. For many this is a year of considerable promise.

For Earth Oxen in work there will be both chances and choices. With staff movements and changes underway there will be opportunities for many Earth Oxen to take on more work and/or move to another position. Sometimes the change involved could be quite a wrench, particularly if the Earth Ox has been in the same position for some time, but for those who are keen to take on new challenges and use their talents in other ways, the Rabbit year can present some interesting opportunities. For many this will be a year of important decisions.

Whether the Earth Ox decides to move elsewhere or remain where he is, he will need to keep alert and follow developments closely. This is no time to immerse himself so much in his own activities that he risks becoming isolated or remaining unaware of certain proposals. In 2011 all Earth Oxen need to keep informed and involved.

For Earth Oxen who are feeling staid or discontented where they are, again the Rabbit year can present some interesting choices. Some Earth Oxen may have the opportunity to take retirement, and should this tempt them, they should study the implications and take appropriate advice. Others may decide to look for alternative positions as well as consider different ways in which they could use their experience. Making a change may not be easy, but some ideas the Earth Ox has could indicate an exciting way forward. Mid-March to early June and October could see important work developments.

Throughout the year the Earth Ox will be encouraged by the support and advice he is given and whenever he is considering his options, he should talk to those around him and make sure any concerns and questions are addressed. As an Earth Ox, he may be independent-minded, but this is no time for acting alone or keeping thoughts to himself. Earth Oxen, do take note.

The Earth Ox also needs to be thorough when dealing with financial matters, especially when handling important paperwork or entering into any agreements. Again, if in doubt, he should seek advice and clarification. In the Rabbit year he should avoid haste, risk or acting against his better judgement.

With the year's emphasis on personal development, the Earth Ox should also set some time aside to enjoy and further his interests. This includes adding to his knowledge as well as going to special events. Some Earth Oxen could be tempted by courses available in their area or online. By doing something positive and pursuing something they enjoy, they can make this a satisfying time.

The Earth Ox is often selective in his socializing and prefers to keep things relatively low key. However, if he receives invitations or sees events that appeal to him, he should try to go, as his social life and some of the interests he pursues can bring variety and balance to his lifestyle and do him good. Earth Oxen who are alone and would welcome the chance to make new friends should also make every effort to go out more and perhaps consider joining local societies and interest groups. The Earth Ox's relations with others are well aspected this year and for the unattached there are good prospects for new friendships and romance. March, April, July and September could see the most social activity.

The Earth Ox's domestic life is also likely to be active, with some excitement concerning the activities and success of a younger relation. Whenever arrangements need making, the Earth Ox's organizational skills will be particularly valued, and his loved ones will often be grateful for his foresight and attentiveness. He will also be the driving force behind certain plans and decisions this year and whether these involve travel, home alterations or major purchases, his initiative can lead to a lot happening.

However, while a lot can go well this year, problems and difficulties can still raise their head. When they do, co-operation is the order of the day and the Earth Ox should join with those around him to give time and attention to the situation. This is a year favouring combined effort.

Overall, the Rabbit year can be an important one for the Earth Ox, particularly in view of some of the choices that will open up for him. By drawing on the advice and support available to him and following his instincts, he will generally be pleased with how he fares.

TIP FOR THE YEAR
You can do well this year, but do take your time when making decisions and follow your instincts. Also, draw on the willingness of others to advise and support. Developing your interests can reward you well.

FAMOUS OXEN

Lily Allen, Hans Christian Andersen, Peter Andre, Gemma Arterton, Johann Sebastian Bach, Warren Beatty, Kate Beckinsale, David Blaine, Napoleon Bonaparte, Susan Boyle, Jeff Bridges, Albert Camus, Jim Carrey, Charlie Chaplin, George Clooney, Natalie Cole, Bill Cosby, Tom Courtenay, Tony Curtis, Diana, Princess of Wales, Marlene Dietrich, Walt Disney, Patrick Duffy, Jane Fonda, Edward

Fox, Michael J. Fox, Peter Gabriel, Elizabeth George, Richard Gere, Ricky Gervais, William Hague, Handel, King Harald V of Norway, Adolf Hitler, Dustin Hoffman, Hal Holbrook, Anthony Hopkins, Billy Joel, King Juan Carlos of Spain, John Key, B. B. King, Keira Knightley, Mark Knopfler, Burt Lancaster, Kate Moss, Alison Moyet, Carey Mulligan, Eddie Murphy, Jack Nicholson, Leslie Nielsen, Barack Obama, Gwyneth Paltrow, Oscar Peterson, Paula Radcliffe, Robert Redford, Lionel Richie, Wayne Rooney, Tim Roth, Rubens, Meg Ryan, Amanda Seyfried, Jean Sibelius, Bruce Springsteen, Meryl Streep, Lady Thatcher, Alan Titchmarsh, Scott F. Turow, Vincent van Gogh, Zoë Wanamaker, Sigourney Weaver, the Duke of Wellington, Arsène Wenger, W. B. Yeats.

26 JANUARY 1914 ⌒ 13 FEBRUARY 1915   *Wood Tiger*

13 FEBRUARY 1926 ⌒ 1 FEBRUARY 1927   *Fire Tiger*

31 JANUARY 1938 ⌒ 18 FEBRUARY 1939   *Earth Tiger*

17 FEBRUARY 1950 ⌒ 5 FEBRUARY 1951   *Metal Tiger*

5 FEBRUARY 1962 ⌒ 24 JANUARY 1963   *Water Tiger*

23 JANUARY 1974 ⌒ 10 FEBRUARY 1975   *Wood Tiger*

9 FEBRUARY 1986 ⌒ 28 JANUARY 1987   *Fire Tiger*

28 JANUARY 1998 ⌒ 15 FEBRUARY 1999   *Earth Tiger*

14 FEBRUARY 2010 ⌒ 2 FEBRUARY 2011   *Metal Tiger*

THE
TIGER

THE PERSONALITY OF THE TIGER

It's
the zest,
the enthusiasm,
the giving the little bit more,
that makes the difference.
And opens up so much.

The Tiger is born under the sign of courage. He is a charismatic figure and usually holds very firm views. He is strong-willed and determined and sets about most of his activities with tremendous energy and enthusiasm. He is very alert and quick-witted and his mind is forever active. He is a highly original thinker and is nearly always brimming with new ideas or full of enthusiasm for some new project or scheme.

The Tiger adores challenges and loves to get involved in anything that he thinks has an exciting future or that catches his imagination. He is prepared to take risks and does not like to be bound either by convention or the dictates of others. He likes to be free to act as he chooses and at least once during his life he will throw caution to the wind and go off and do the things he wants to do.

The Tiger does, however, have a somewhat restless nature. Even though he is often prepared to throw himself wholeheartedly into a project, his initial enthusiasm can soon wane if he sees something more appealing. He can also be rather impulsive and there will be occasions in his life when he acts in a manner he later regrets. If he were to think things through or be prepared to persevere in his various activities, he would almost certainly enjoy a greater degree of success.

Fortunately the Tiger is lucky in most of his enterprises, but should things not work out as he hoped, he is liable to suffer from severe bouts of depression and it will often take him a long time to recover. His life often consists of a series of ups and downs.

He is, however, very adaptable. He has an adventurous spirit and rarely stays in the same place for long. In the early stages of his life he is likely to try his hand at several different jobs and he will also change his residence fairly frequently.

The Tiger is very honest and open in his dealings with others. He hates any sort of hypocrisy or falsehood. He is also well known for being blunt and forthright and has no hesitation in speaking his mind. He can be rebellious at times, particularly against any form of petty authority, and while this can lead him into conflict with others, he is never one to shrink from an argument or avoid standing up for what he believes is right.

The Tiger is a natural leader and can rise to the top of his chosen profession. He does not, however, care for anything too bureaucratic or detailed, and he does not like to obey orders. He can be stubborn and obstinate and throughout his life he likes to retain a certain amount of independence in his actions and be responsible to no one but himself. He likes to consider that all his achievements are due to his own efforts and he will not ask for support from others if he can avoid it.

Ironically, despite his self-confidence and leadership qualities, he can be indecisive and will often delay making a major decision until the very last moment. He can also be sensitive to criticism.

Although the Tiger is capable of earning large sums of money, he is rather a spendthrift and does not always put his money to its best use. He can also be most generous and will often shower lavish gifts on friends and relations.

The Tiger cares very much for his reputation and the image that he tries to project. He carries himself with an air of dignity and authority and enjoys being the centre of attention. He is very adept at attracting publicity, both for himself and the causes he supports.

The Tiger often marries young and he will find himself best suited to those born under the signs of the Pig, Dog, Horse and Goat. He can also get on well with the Rat, Rabbit and Rooster, but will find the Ox and Snake a bit too quiet and serious for his liking, and he will be highly irritated by the Monkey's rather mischievous and inquisitive ways. He will also find it difficult to get on with another Tiger or a Dragon – both partners will want to dominate the relationship and could find it difficult to compromise on even the smallest of matters.

The Tigress is lively, witty and a marvellous hostess at parties. She takes great care over her appearance and is usually most attractive. She can be a very doting mother and while she believes in letting her children have their freedom, she makes an excellent teacher and will ensure that her children are well brought up and want for nothing. Like her male counterpart, she has numerous interests and likes to have sufficient independence and freedom to go off and do the things she wants to do. She has a most caring and generous nature.

The Tiger has many commendable qualities. He is honest, courageous and often a source of inspiration to others. Providing he can curb the wilder excesses of his restless nature, he is almost certain to lead a fulfilling and satisfying life.

THE FIVE DIFFERENT TYPES OF TIGER

In addition to the 12 signs of the Chinese zodiac there are five elements and these have a strengthening or moderating influence on the signs. The effects of the five elements on the Tiger are described below, together with the years in which they were exercising their influence. Therefore those Tigers born in 1950 and 2010 are Metal Tigers, those born in 1962 are Water Tigers, and so on.

Metal Tiger: 1950, 2010
The Metal Tiger has an assertive and outgoing personality. He is very ambitious and while his aims may change from time to time, he will work relentlessly until he has obtained what he wants. He can, however, be impatient for results and become highly strung if things do not work out as he would like. He is distinctive in his appearance and is admired and respected by many.

Water Tiger: 1962
This Tiger has a wide variety of interests and is always eager to experiment with new ideas or satisfy his adventur-

ous nature by going off to explore distant lands. He is versatile, shrewd and has a kindly nature. He tends to remain calm in a crisis, although he can be annoyingly indecisive at times. He communicates well with others and through his many capabilities and persuasive nature usually achieves what he wants in life. He is also highly imaginative and is often a gifted orator or writer.

Wood Tiger: 1914, 1974

The Wood Tiger has a friendly and pleasant personality. He is less independent than some of the other types of Tiger and more prepared to work with others to secure a desired objective. However, he does have a tendency to jump from one thing to another and can easily become distracted. He is usually very popular, has a large circle of friends and invariably leads a busy and enjoyable social life. He also has a good sense of humour.

Fire Tiger: 1926, 1986

The Fire Tiger sets about everything he does with great verve and enthusiasm. He loves action and is always ready to throw himself wholeheartedly into anything that catches his imagination. He has many leadership qualities and is capable of communicating his ideas and enthusiasm to others. He is very much an optimist and can be most generous. He has a likeable nature and can be a witty and persuasive speaker.

Earth Tiger: 1938, 1998

This Tiger is responsible and level-headed. He studies everything objectively and tries to be scrupulously fair in all his dealings. Unlike other Tigers, he is prepared to specialize in certain areas rather than get distracted by other matters, but he can become so involved in what he is doing that he does not always take into account the opinions of those around him. He has good business sense and is usually very successful in later life. He has a large circle of friends and pays great attention to both his appearance and his reputation.

PROSPECTS FOR THE TIGER IN 2011

With his energy, personality and ideas, the Tiger will have been able to make a lot happen during his own year (14 February 2010–2 February 2011) and will have seen some interesting developments in many areas of his life. The closing months of the year will continue to be busy, with the Tiger generally faring well.

Relations with others are particularly favourably aspected and many Tigers will find themselves in increasing demand as the year draws to a close. There could be domestic arrangements to make, relations to meet up with and parties and other social events to go to. For the unattached, affairs of the heart can add some excitement to this time. December and January can be particularly active and special months.

Many Tigers will have seen significant changes in their work over the year and the closing months will give them the chance to familiarize themselves with their new role.

For those seeking work or hoping to move elsewhere, this is a time to keep alert for openings and to act quickly when anything arises that interests them.

With his generally active lifestyle, the Tiger will also need to keep a close watch on his spending at this time. Particularly when socializing or shopping, he could find he has spent far more than anticipated. In order to go ahead with certain plans, some advance budgeting could be helpful. Also, with many Tigers having the chance to travel towards the end of the year, setting funds aside for this will allow them to enjoy their time away all the more.

The Tiger year can certainly be a full and eventful one for the Tiger and by seizing his opportunities, he can gain a lot from it. And on a personal level his own year can give rise to some splendid occasions.

The Year of the Rabbit begins on 3 February and will give the Tiger an excellent chance to make headway. It is a year favouring development and progress and the Tiger can enjoy some fine personal achievements.

At work the Tiger will often find himself encouraged to make more of particular strengths and skills. Sometimes he will be given more specialist work or new objectives to concentrate on as well as have the chance of additional training. Although some of what is asked of him can bring increased pressure, by taking advantage of what is offered the Tiger can not only make good headway but also open up other possibilities for the longer term. For many Tigers this is a year when they will reach another stage in their career, with their previous commitment being both recognized and rewarded.

Most Tigers will have chances to progress with their present employer and will benefit from their in-house knowledge and proven skills, but for those who feel opportunities are limited where they are or are seeking work, the Rabbit year again holds interesting prospects. To benefit fully, these Tigers should consider other ways in which they can use their skills. With some innovative thinking (and the Tiger does have many fine ideas) as well as consultation with employment agencies and other contacts, they could identify new areas which particularly appeal to them. Also, when making applications, if they find out about the responsibilities involved and stress what they can bring to the position, they can do much to strengthen their chances. The Rabbit year can bring fresh possibilities for the Tiger and it rests with him to act quickly and effectively. The months from April to early July and September could see some particularly good opportunities, but in general this is very much a year to keep alert and informed, build on skills and take the initiative. For the determined Tiger, the Rabbit year can be important and successful.

Another interesting aspect of the year will be the recreational possibilities that open up for the Tiger. By pursuing activities he enjoys, he can reinforce the constructive nature of the present time. Interests that allow him to get out of doors and take additional exercise could particularly appeal, as could developing new ideas and more creative activities. Whatever the Tiger decides to do, his inventive and adventurous streak can serve him well this year.

His financial position can also see an improvement and many Tigers will benefit from a rise in income or receive funds from another source. However, to make the most of this upturn the Tiger does need to manage his finances well. This includes looking to reduce borrowings as well as budgeting ahead. Care and good control can lead to more satisfactory purchases as well as plans going ahead and certain pressures easing. This is a year when it will reward the Tiger to be disciplined, careful and prudent.

With his active and outgoing nature the Tiger is able to get on well with many people and over the year his social life can bring him considerable pleasure. There will be good opportunities for him to meet others, with some important new friendships being made. Existing romances, especially those started in the Tiger year, can often become more meaningful, while many Tigers who are currently unattached will have excellent opportunities to meet others. This can be a special year for affairs of the heart, with quite a few Tigers settling down with a partner or getting married. The period from May to August and November could see the most social activity, although throughout the year the Tiger will have opportunities to go out and occasions to look forward to.

He will also derive much contentment from his home life during the year. Although he and members of his family will often be busy, if he makes sure quality time is spent together and there is good communication and co-operation, everyone can benefit. Sometimes suggestions the Tiger puts forward could be particularly appreciated, whether for improvements in the home or for activities everyone can enjoy. His contribution to home life can certainly bring pleasure to his loved ones this year. With the Rabbit year's emphasis on personal development, some Tigers may also decide to start a new interest or self-improvement activity with a loved one, with each helping and motivating the other. This is a year favouring shared pursuits.

Although the aspects are supportive, no year is without its problems or pressures, and when any difficulties do arise, the Tiger should be careful not to act too precipitously. By allowing himself time to collect his thoughts, consider possibilities and talk over situations, he may defuse tensions and find solutions to problems. The Rabbit year favours measured responses, and time and patience will help at some of the more awkward moments of the year.

Generally, the Year of the Rabbit is a positive one for the Tiger and will allow him to move forward. It is a time to act on his ideas and seize his opportunities. He will generally be well supported, with his home and social life being particularly important to him. Overall, a satisfying year and one especially favouring personal growth.

The Metal Tiger

This can be a constructive year for the Metal Tiger, although it will require good planning. With some ideas and hopes in mind, the Metal Tiger will be able to get a lot out of the next 12 months, but if he proceeds in too *ad hoc* a manner, time and some good opportunities could be lost. As 2011 starts all Metal Tigers should consider setting themselves some objectives for the year and having something definite to work towards.

As personal development is favourably aspected this year, if there is a skill the Metal Tiger would like to learn or improve, or a subject that has been intriguing him, this is an ideal time to follow this up. Self-improvement activities could be especially satisfying, with the Metal Tiger exploring ways he can use his new knowledge. Some Metal Tigers will also decide to give some attention to their wellbeing and, with proper guidance, will be pleased with the changes they make.

For Metal Tigers who are particularly keen to meet others, it could be well worth considering joining groups, enrolling on courses and going to interest-related events. With his keen and enterprising nature, the Metal Tiger will nearly always have something to look forward to, but May to early September and November are likely to be the busiest months socially. Also, during the year the Metal Tiger could have the chance to help a very good friend, and the support he gives can be significant. Many of those around him value his judgement and over the year he can demonstrate what a true friend he is.

The Rabbit year can also spring its surprises and some of these could be travel related. The Metal Tiger may see a last-minute offer that particularly appeals to him or be tempted to travel to a special event. If so, he should seize his opportunities. In addition, if there is a particular destination he is keen to visit or something he specifically wants to do, by making enquiries and keeping alert he could benefit from some ideal offers.

He will also enjoy his home life over the year, with shared activities bringing him particular pleasure. Again, if he acts on his ideas, he can make this a satisfying and constructive time. There could also be some family highlights during the year, with an achievement or anniversary to mark.

Although the Metal Tiger will enjoy a lot of the year, as with any year there will be pressures and problems to address. Rather than keep these to himself, he should talk them over with his loved ones and, if appropriate, seek professional advice. He should also be wary of acting on any complicated matter too quickly. Facts, implications and sometimes obligations will need to be checked and clarified. When problems arise, the Metal Tiger will need to be thorough and avoid haste.

This also applies to financial matters. The Metal Tiger should study any financially-related forms carefully and question anything which is unclear. This is a year for care and keeping alert. In addition, if he makes advance provision for some of his plans and keeps a watchful eye on spending, he will find he is able to go ahead with much more as well as benefit from some favourable buying opportunities.

For Metal Tigers in work this will be a busy year, with many facing a heavier workload and new pressures. However, while demanding, it will offer the Metal Tiger an excellent chance to add to his experience. Many Metal Tigers could find their in-depth knowledge particularly valued as colleagues seek their advice or they guide and instruct more junior staff. The Rabbit year can be an exacting one but give the Metal Tiger the opportunity to display and develop his strengths.

For Metal Tigers seeking work, the Rabbit year can present a number of choices. Sometimes these could involve adapting and using their skills in new ways or taking on a temporary position with a view to seeing how it develops, but by remaining open to possibility, many could succeed in taking on an interesting new role. April to early July and September could see important work developments.

Metal Tigers who retire this year can also make this a constructive time. By giving careful thought to what they now want to do and getting their plans underway, they can see the year developing in an encouraging manner.

Overall, the Rabbit year holds promising prospects for the Metal Tiger and by acting on his ideas and opportunities, he will often derive much satisfaction from what he is able to do and the benefits that follow on. An interesting and favourable year.

TIP FOR THE YEAR
Think through what you want to achieve and talk your ideas over with those around you. With some clear ideas and the support of others, you can accomplish a great deal this year and also benefit from opportunities.

The Water Tiger

This will be a positive year for the Water Tiger and while it may lack the activity of some, he will often be pleased with the progress he makes. For many Water Tigers this can be an encouraging and personally satisfying time.

With the year's emphasis on personal development, if there are any particular skills the Water Tiger feels it could be useful to learn or improve on, he should make enquiries and see what is possible. By looking to develop *and* doing something definite about it, he will often benefit from the knowledge he acquires. New skills could be one of the most important legacies of the Rabbit year.

As far as personal interests are concerned, the Water Tiger could also find it helpful to see what courses, interest groups and amenities are available in his area. With positive action backed by enthusiasm, he can make this a particularly rewarding time. The Water Tiger also has talents as a communicator, and any Water Tigers who enjoy writing should set time aside to enjoy their skills and creativity. In the Rabbit year the Water Tiger should use his strengths and chances wisely.

With the year favouring personal improvement, if the Water Tiger feels he is lacking sufficient exercise or his diet could be improved, it would be worth him seeking advice on the best way to proceed. Appropriate changes can make a noticeable difference, including improving energy levels.

The Water Tiger will value the help and support he is given over the year and, particularly when considering a new activity or project, he should talk over his ideas with those around him. Similarly, by being forthcoming over any concerns he may have, he will enable others to better understand and advise.

In his home life, with often busy lifestyles and different schedules to work around, the Water Tiger will need to ensure there is good co-operation and everyone does their fair share around the home. Also, despite the activity of the year, setting time aside for shared pursuits will not only help rapport and understanding but also add to the quality of home life.

Another feature of the year will be the support the Water Tiger is able to give to both younger and more senior relations, and although he may not want to appear interfering, his assistance can make a difference. The Water Tiger's people skills will be much in evidence this year.

He will also find this an active and pleasing year socially. With the year's emphasis on self-development, it is possible he will meet others who have embarked on a self-improvement activity or who share his interests (and sometimes problems), and this can lead to new friendships being made. For the unattached, affairs of the heart are also well aspected. Late April to August and November could see the most social activity.

In the Water Tiger's work, there will be excellent chances to develop his skills. Often these will be with his present employer, with him being encouraged to make more of his specialist skills and being well placed for greater responsibilities. Admittedly, the headway many Water Tigers make this year will be modest rather than substantial, but a key benefit of the Rabbit year will be the experience the Water Tiger gains. This can prepare him well for future opportunities.

For Water Tigers who are seeking work or would like a change from what they are currently doing, the Rabbit year can be an excellent time to evaluate their position and consider the direction they would now like their career to take. With careful thought and some guidance, many could discover new possibilities to pursue, possibly involving retraining. For quite a few Water Tigers this is a year to take stock, consider what they now want to do and be prepared to adapt and learn. Opportunities could arise at almost any time, but April to early July and September could see some important work developments.

Many Water Tigers can look forward to an increase in earnings this year, but all will need to be disciplined in their spending and allow for their commitments and plans. Without care, anything extra could quickly be spent and not always in the best way. This is a year for good control and careful budgeting.

Overall, the Year of the Rabbit can be an interesting one, but the Water Tiger does need to act. With willingness and enthusiasm, he can make progress, but if he takes a more laid-back approach, valuable time and opportunities could be lost. Water Tigers, take note and do build on what this year offers.

TIP FOR THE YEAR
Be willing to learn and venture forward. You have a lot to offer and the positive action you take now can stand you in good stead as well as widen your options for the future. Use this year well, for its lessons and benefits can be far-reaching.

The Wood Tiger

There is a Chinese proverb that could be helpful for the Wood Tiger this year: 'There is no trick to a bountiful harvest – simply work your hoe with diligence.' In the Rabbit year the Wood Tiger can accomplish a great deal, but it will require discipline *and* diligence.

In his work the Rabbit year can see some significant developments. For those Wood Tigers who are employed in relatively large organizations, vacancies could arise in other departments and by applying and indicating their desire to progress, they can make encouraging headway and in the process gain valuable new experience.

For those who feel opportunities are limited where they are or who would welcome new challenges, this is also a time to look at other possibilities and actively make enquiries. Once they start they will be setting important (and unstoppable) wheels in motion. The year will see many Wood Tigers having to adapt to new situations and learn new skills. While these may be initially daunting, the Wood Tiger will welcome the chance to prove himself in new ways. The trick in the Rabbit year is to show resolve and willingness.

A factor in the Wood Tiger's favour is the good working relations he enjoys with so many. Senior colleagues could prove particularly helpful in putting in recommendations, encouraging his career progression or providing him with positive references. In the Rabbit year the Wood Tiger should continue to make the most of his people skills and, if applicable, consider joining a professional body connected with his industry. Getting himself better known will not only give him more connections but also help his long-term prospects. What is achieved this year can be significant.

For Wood Tigers seeking work, the Rabbit year can again bring some interesting opportunities. These may differ from what the Wood Tiger is used to but give him an excellent chance to widen his experience. One of the key features of the Rabbit year is that it favours personal development and any new skills the Wood Tiger can gain can be a major legacy of the year. April to early July and September could see some good opportunities, but throughout the year all Wood Tigers should keep alert for chances to pursue. This is a time for resolve and initiative.

The progress many Wood Tigers are able to make at work can bring an increase in income and some will also benefit from an additional sum during the year. However, while many can look forward to an improvement in their fortunes, all Wood Tigers will need to remain disciplined and prudent in their spending. With care and good management, they will be able to improve their situation over the year; if not, any gains could be frittered away.

The Rabbit year can also bring some travel opportunities and even if some Wood Tigers do not actually travel too far in distance, a change of scene and break from routine can do them a lot of good. Sometimes chances to go away can appear at short notice, but wherever possible the Wood Tiger should try to take them up.

As far as his personal interests are concerned, the Rabbit year can be an immensely satisfying one. Although the Wood Tiger's free time may be limited, by setting some aside for activities he enjoys, he can develop certain ideas and skills. The Rabbit year holds considerable potential for the Wood Tiger and his personal interests are another outlet for his talents and creativity.

For many Wood Tigers their work and interests will also have a pleasing social element and be a good way to meet others. As with so much this year, by making the most of situations, the Wood Tiger stands to benefit. And for the unattached, the Rabbit year can present some fine romantic opportunities.

The Wood Tiger's domestic life is also set to be busy and eventful. During the year there will be many demands on his time and he may despair of all that is being asked of him, but by remaining organized, deciding on priorities and using his time effectively, he will not only be able to cope but also accomplish a great deal. Throughout the year it is also important that he is forthcoming about his plans and concerns. This is a year for sharing with others.

Overall, the Rabbit year is very much a time for the Wood Tiger to build on his skills and strengths and look to move forward. With resolve and willingness, he can make this an interesting and fulfilling year. Throughout, he will be helped by the support and goodwill of those around him and his relations with others will be an important and encouraging factor in his progress.

TIP FOR THE YEAR
You have great people skills – use them well. With support, you will find your prospects – and year – will be so much better.

The Fire Tiger

The Fire Tiger will have seen a lot happen in recent years. He will have had personal successes and gained much valuable experience, but he will also have had disappointments and regrets. In 2011 he is set for a rewarding year which will give him the chance to build on his strengths and enjoy positive developments in several areas of his life.

His personal life could be particularly special this year, with some exciting developments to look forward to. Some Fire Tigers may become parents or see the realization of some long-held hopes, including marriage, a move to more suitable accommodation or the achievement of a personal objective. A lot can go the Fire Tiger's way this year, but he does need to act determinedly. This is a year for initiative and for setting plans in motion. As Virgil wrote, 'Fortune favours the bold,' and to get the most from the year the Fire Tiger will need to be bold *and* believing.

He will be helped by the support he receives and will find that by sharing activities and pooling ideas and energy, more will get to happen, and more quickly. In addition if the Fire Tiger has any concerns or doubts, it is important that he talks to others and gets clarification and advice. More senior relations may also do much to assist him over the year.

In addition to the positive developments in the Fire Tiger's personal life, his social life can bring him much pleasure. Once again he will appreciate the camaraderie of good friends and welcome the chance to talk over news and run over ideas. Some of his personal interests may also have a strong social element and the Fire Tiger will enjoy going to events and meeting other enthusiasts. This is very much a year for action.

The Rabbit year also favours affairs of the heart and for Fire Tigers who are unattached or have recently experienced some personal difficulty, this can be a year of exciting developments, with many meeting someone special by chance. Love, whether existing or new, can add a sparkle to many a Fire Tiger's year. Mid-April to August and November could see the most social activity.

Another feature of the year will be the travel opportunities it brings and whether going away for a short break or taking a main holiday, the Fire Tiger will often delight in visiting places new to him. Whenever time and finance permit, he should take his chances to travel.

The Rabbit year can also see some important developments at work. For Fire Tigers who are already established in a certain career, there will be excellent chances to build on their skills and take on greater responsibilities. Some senior colleagues could be particularly instrumental in helping the Fire Tiger's career development. For many Fire Tigers, this is a year that will give them the opportunity to prove themselves in new ways and add to their experience and reputation. It may be one for more steady rather than major advance, but it will mark an important stage in the Fire Tiger's development.

For Fire Tigers who decide to move on from where they are or are seeking work, the Rabbit year can again bring some good opportunities. Often these will require the Fire Tiger to adapt existing skills and learn new ones, but by being willing and showing commitment, he can not only improve his present situation but also prepare himself for future opportunities. Effort and flexibility, backed by the Fire Tiger's keen and enthusiastic nature, can prove a winning combination this year. April to early July, September and early October could see some good work opportunities and even if some applications do not go the Fire Tiger's way, his determination and persistence will prevail. He knows he has a lot to offer and this is a year to believe in himself and to put himself forward.

With the developments of the year and his often active lifestyle, he will, however, need to be careful in money matters. Over the year there will be many demands on his resources and he needs to manage his outgoings wisely. This is not a time for proceeding too hurriedly or succumbing to too many impulse purchases. Accommodation in particular could be a major expense, especially as quite a few Fire Tigers will move over the year. The Fire Tiger can make his money go a long way this year, but he does need to be prudent and disciplined.

Overall, the Year of the Rabbit can be a special and pleasing one for the Fire Tiger. His relations with others are very favourably aspected with many Fire Tigers enjoying the love of another, finding romance and seeing some personal hopes fulfilled. It is also an excellent year for personal development and the new skills and knowledge the Fire Tiger acquires can have present *and* long-term value. With willingness, support and determination, he can make this an important and frequently exciting year.

TIP FOR THE YEAR

Be prepared to learn and develop. What you do now will be an investment in yourself and your future. Also value those around you. They can be both special and helpful to you. Listen to them.

The Earth Tiger

This will be a pleasing and rewarding year for the Earth Tiger, although to get the full benefit from it, he will need to remain focused. Trying to do too much could lead to less satisfactory outcomes. The Rabbit year is one for steady and committed effort.

For Earth Tigers born in 1998 this will be an important year in their education. During it they will continue to build on their knowledge and study subjects in further depth. What they learn now can open up fresh possibilities and allow them to do more as well as discover new strengths. The more creative Earth Tigers will often take especial delight in furthering their talents, while those who prefer more physical or practical pursuits will again have some excellent chances to build on their skills. This is very much a year for the Earth Tiger to make the most of the facilities and opportunities available.

However, while important progress can be made this year, it will require effort and discipline. Also, the Earth Tiger does need to manage his time well. With so many possible distractions (including the internet and/or playing games), he does need to set time aside for uninterrupted study and concentrate on what he needs to do. The Rabbit year rewards focus and application.

The Earth Tiger will value the support he is given and if he has problems or feels he is floundering in certain subjects, he should let others know. If he is forthcoming, those around him will be better able to assist.

With his active and outgoing nature, he can also look forward to many enjoyable times with his friends. Shared interests can provide a lot of fun, although on some occasions the Earth Tiger may need to watch his exuberance. To over-exert himself, take risks or get carried away in the excitement of the moment could lead to problems. Earth Tigers, take note and do not be too reckless.

The Earth Tiger could also find his circle of friends increasing as a result of his various activities and many will make what will prove a strong and enduring new friendship. The Earth Tiger's relations with others can bring him a great deal of pleasure this year.

With his active nature, the Earth Tiger will often want to buy things and spend his money on certain activities. Over the year there will certainly be many temptations, but here again self-discipline will often lead to better outcomes. Whenever possible the Earth Tiger should be careful not to spend too much on a whim but to think through his purchases.

Overall, this can be a pleasing year for the young Earth Tiger and by using his time well he will be able to do a great deal. As the Chinese proverb reminds us, 'Achievement comes from diligence and nothing is gained by fooling around.' The Earth Tiger will have good fun this year, but to do himself justice he also needs to make it a year of application.

For Earth Tigers born in 1938 this is again a year for deciding on plans and activities. With some purposeful aims, the more senior Earth Tiger can achieve a lot.

One area which many of these Earth Tigers will give attention to will be their home. Their plans could include adding new comforts, replacing equipment and smartening certain rooms. Some may also decide to sort through storage areas. Although they will be keen to embark on such projects, they could take longer and be more disruptive than envisaged and the Earth Tiger will need to allow time for their completion.

Some of his plans will also involve making choices and deciding on purchases. Here again he should not act too hurriedly. By taking his time, thinking over his requirements and considering what is available, he will not only make more appropriate selections but sometimes also benefit from favourable buying opportunities. He may be eager, but this is not a year for undue haste.

The Earth Tiger also needs to be thorough in financial matters. When entering into agreements or dealing with tax, pension or benefit matters, he should check the small print and seek advice on anything which is unclear. An oversight could be to his disadvantage. Earth Tigers, take note.

In all his activities, the Earth Tiger also needs to fully involve others. He may have clear ideas about what he wants, but this is a year for co-operation rather than inde-pendent-mindedness, and the more consultation there is, the better the eventual result will be.

The Rabbit year favours personal development and the Earth Tiger can derive much pleasure from his interests and the ways in which he can use his knowledge. If there is a project he would like to set himself, he could find this gives him something positive to focus on and keeps him pleasantly occupied.

He will also find himself in demand over the year. Not only will he follow the activities of family members with fond interest but those close to him will value his support and advice. Shared activities, whether of a practical nature or more enjoyable pursuits, including travel, can also be special and will mean a lot to the Earth Tiger.

For Earth Tigers who are alone and would welcome greater company, the Rabbit year holds promising prospects. To help, these Earth Tigers would do well to consider starting a new activity or joining a special interest group. By taking advantage of opportunities available in their area, they will not only have more chance to socialize but also to make new friendships. In addition, their travels can often have a good social element.

Whether born in 1938 or 1998, the Earth Tiger can make this a pleasing and fulfilling year by concentrating on his aims and seizing his opportunities. And he will be considerably helped by the support and goodwill of others.

TIP FOR THE YEAR
Focus on your goals. With effort, you can accomplish a lot this year as well as reap some fine personal benefits.

FAMOUS TIGERS

Paula Abdul, Amy Adams, Kofi Annan, Sir David Attenborough, Queen Beatrix of the Netherlands, Victoria Beckham, Beethoven, Tony Bennett, Tom Berenger, Chuck Berry, Usain Bolt, Jon Bon Jovi, Sir Richard Branson, Matthew Broderick, Garth Brooks, Mel Brooks, Isambard Kingdom Brunel, Agatha Christie, Charlotte Church, Phil Collins, Robbie Coltrane, Sheryl Crow, Tom Cruise, Penelope Cruz, Charles de Gaulle, Leonardo DiCaprio, Emily Dickinson, David Dimbleby, Dwight Eisenhower, Queen Elizabeth II, Enya, Roberta Flack, Frederick Forsyth, Jodie Foster, Megan Fox, Lady Gaga, Crystal Gayle, Buddy Greco, Germaine Greer, Ed Harris, Hugh Hefner, William Hurt, Ray Kroc, Shia LaBeouf, Stan Laurel, Jay Leno, Matt Lucas, Groucho Marx, Karl Marx, Marilyn Monroe, Demi Moore, Alanis Morissette, Rafael Nadal, Robert Pattinson, Jeremy Paxman, Marco Polo, Beatrix Potter, Renoir, Kenny Rogers, the Princess Royal, Dame Joan Sutherland, Dylan Thomas, Liv Ullman, Jon Voight, Julie Walters, H. G. Wells, Oscar Wilde, Robbie Williams, Dr Rowan Williams, Tennessee Williams, Sir Terry Wogan, Stevie Wonder, William Wordsworth.

14 FEBRUARY 1915 ～ 2 FEBRUARY 1916   *Wood Rabbit*

2 FEBRUARY 1927 ～ 22 JANUARY 1928   *Fire Rabbit*

19 FEBRUARY 1939 ～ 7 FEBRUARY 1940   *Earth Rabbit*

6 FEBRUARY 1951 ～ 26 JANUARY 1952   *Metal Rabbit*

25 JANUARY 1963 ～ 12 FEBRUARY 1964   *Water Rabbit*

11 FEBRUARY 1975 ～ 30 JANUARY 1976   *Wood Rabbit*

29 JANUARY 1987 ～ 16 FEBRUARY 1988   *Fire Rabbit*

16 FEBRUARY 1999 ～ 4 FEBRUARY 2000   *Earth Rabbit*

3 FEBRUARY 2011 ～ 22 JANUARY 2012   *Metal Rabbit*

THE
RABBIT

THE PERSONALITY OF THE RABBIT

Whenever
Wherever
With whoever.
Always I try to understand.
Without this one flounders.
But with understanding,
at least you have a chance.
A good chance.

The Rabbit is born under the signs of virtue and prudence. He is intelligent, well mannered and prefers a quiet and peaceful existence. He dislikes any sort of unpleasantness and will try to steer clear of arguments and disputes. He is very much a pacifist and tends to have a calming influence on those around him. He has wide interests and usually a good appreciation of the arts and the finer things in life. He also knows how to enjoy himself and will often gravitate to the best restaurants and nightspots in town.

The Rabbit is a witty and intelligent speaker and loves being involved in a good discussion. His views and advice are often sought by others and he can be relied upon to be discreet and diplomatic. He will rarely raise his voice in anger and will even turn a blind eye to matters that displease him just to preserve the peace. He likes to remain on good terms with everyone, but he can be rather sensitive and takes any form of criticism very badly. He will also be the first to get out of the way if he sees any form of trouble brewing.

The Rabbit is a quiet and efficient worker and has an extremely good memory. He is very astute in business and financial matters, but his degree of success often depends on the conditions that prevail. He hates being in a situation which is fraught with tension or where he has to make sudden decisions. Wherever possible he will plan his various activities with the utmost care and a good deal of caution. He does not like to take risks and does not take kindly to change. Basically, he seeks a secure, calm and stable environment, and when conditions are right he is more than happy to leave things as they are.

The Rabbit is conscientious and because of his methodical and ever-watchful nature he can often do well in his chosen profession. He makes a good diplomat, lawyer, shopkeeper, administrator or priest, and he excels in any job where he can use his superb skills as a communicator. He tends to be loyal to his employers and is respected for his integrity and honesty, but if he ever finds himself in a position of great power he can become rather intransigent and authoritarian.

The Rabbit attaches great importance to his home and will often spend a lot of time and money maintaining and furnishing it and fitting it with all the latest comforts – the Rabbit is very much a creature of comfort! He is also something of a collector and there are many Rabbits who derive much pleasure from collecting antiques, stamps, coins, *objets d'art* or anything else which catches their eye or particularly interests them.

The female Rabbit has a friendly, caring and considerate nature, and will do all in her power to give her home a happy and loving atmosphere. She is also very sociable and enjoys holding parties and entertaining. She has a great ability to make the maximum use of her time and although she involves herself in numerous activities, she always manages to find time to sit back and enjoy a good read or a chat. She has a great sense of humour, is very artistic and is often a talented gardener.

The Rabbit takes considerable care over his appearance and is usually smart and well turned out. He also attaches great importance to his relations with others and matters of the heart are particularly important to him. He will rarely be short of admirers and will often have several serious romances before he settles down. He is not the most faithful of signs, but he will find that he is especially well suited to those born under the signs of the Goat, Snake, Pig and Ox. Due to his sociable and easy-going manner he can also get on well with the Tiger, Dragon, Horse, Monkey, Dog and another Rabbit, but he will feel ill at ease with the Rat and Rooster, as both these signs tend to speak their mind and be critical in their comments and the Rabbit just loathes any form of criticism or unpleasantness.

The Rabbit is usually lucky in life and often has the happy knack of being in the right place at the right time. He is talented and quick-witted, but he does sometimes put pleasure before work and wherever possible will opt for the easy life. He can at times be a little reserved and suspicious of the motives of others, but generally will lead a long and contented life and one which – as far as possible – will be free of strife and discord.

THE FIVE DIFFERENT TYPES OF RABBIT

In addition to the 12 signs of the Chinese zodiac there are five elements and these have a strengthening or moderating influence on the signs. The effects of the five elements on the Rabbit are described below, together with the years in which they were exercising their influence. Therefore those Rabbits born in 1951 and 2011 are Metal Rabbits, those born in 1963 are Water Rabbits, and so on.

Metal Rabbit: 1951, 2011

This Rabbit is capable, ambitious and has very definite views on what he wants to achieve in life. He can occasionally appear reserved and aloof, but this is mainly because he likes to keep his thoughts to himself. He has a quick and alert mind and is particularly shrewd in business matters. He can also be very cunning in his actions. He has a good appreciation of the arts and likes to mix in the best circles. He usually has a small but very loyal group of friends.

Water Rabbit: 1963

The Water Rabbit is popular, intuitive and keenly aware of the feelings of those around him. He can, however, be rather sensitive and tends to take things too much to heart. He is very precise and thorough in everything he does and has an exceedingly good memory. He tends to be quiet and at times rather withdrawn, but he expresses his ideas well and is highly regarded by his family, friends and colleagues.

Wood Rabbit: 1915, 1975

The Wood Rabbit is likeable, easy-going and very adaptable. He prefers to work in a group rather than on his own and likes to have the support and encouragement of others. He can, however, be rather reticent in expressing his views and it would be in his own interests to become a little more open and let others know how he feels on certain matters. He usually has many friends, enjoys an active social life and is noted for his generosity.

Fire Rabbit: 1927, 1987

The Fire Rabbit has a friendly, outgoing personality. He likes socializing and being on good terms with everyone. He is discreet and diplomatic and has a very good understanding of human nature. He is also strong-willed and provided he has the necessary backing he can go far in life. He does, not, however, suffer adversity well and can become moody and depressed when things are not working out as he would like. He has a particularly good manner with children, is very intuitive and there are some Fire Rabbits who are even noted for their psychic ability.

Earth Rabbit: 1939, 1999

The Earth Rabbit is a quiet individual, but nevertheless very astute. He is realistic in his aims and prepared to work long and hard in order to achieve his objectives. He has good business sense and is invariably lucky in financial matters. He also has a most persuasive manner and usually experiences little difficulty in getting others to fall in with his plans. He is held in high esteem by his friends and colleagues and his views are often sought and highly valued.

PROSPECTS FOR THE RABBIT IN 2011

The Tiger year (14 February 2010–2 February 2011) is an active and fast-moving one and there will have been times when the Rabbit has despaired of its pace or the demands placed upon him. However, he is both wise and perceptive and by remaining aware and adaptable he can fare well in the latter months. Also, with his own year rapidly approaching, what he is able to do now can often be to his future benefit.

In his work the Rabbit could find he has to cope with extra pressures. However, while the closing months of the Tiger year can be demanding, by using his judgement and skills to advantage he can not only achieve some impressive results but also help his standing and prospects. It is worth the Rabbit making the extra commitment, for the last quarter of the year could see some interesting work possibilities emerge.

The Rabbit can also look forward to much activity in his home and social life at this time. Domestically, there will be a lot to do and think about, including a possible family get-together, visits to others and some practical undertakings, often of a maintenance nature. With his talent for organizing, the Rabbit will be very much at the centre of all that goes on, but he does need to draw on the assistance of others where necessary and not shoulder too much by himself. Socially, he can look forward to quite a few occasions, with November to January an often busy time.

In general, the Tiger year will ask a lot of the Rabbit but will prepare him for some of the opportunities and good fortune that his own year can bring.

The Year of the Rabbit begins on 3 February and will be a fine and auspicious one for the Rabbit. By nature he is generally cautious and does not embark on change lightly, but during his own year he will feel more certain and be ready to act and seize his opportunities. And with the favourable aspects that prevail, his own year holds considerable promise for him.

The Rabbit's work prospects are especially favourable and many Rabbits will now reap the rewards of their recent hard work. The Rabbit's prospects will be very much helped by his own personal qualities, including his ability to relate so effectively to others. In 2011 he will have much in his favour.

Many Rabbits will feel the time is now right for them to move forward, and such are the aspects that they should not only keep alert for promotion opportunities in their existing place of work but also make enquiries elsewhere. Very quickly they could find attractive opportunities they will be keen to pursue. The initiative to take action rests with the Rabbit himself, but once he makes the decision to move forward, a lot can open up for him. February to April and October could see some good possibilities, but throughout the year the Rabbit should remember this is *his* year and when he is focused on something, important doors can *and will* open for him.

This also applies to Rabbits who are keen to make more substantial career change. By seeking advice and considering different options, they could discover new types of work which offer an interesting personal challenge and have growth opportunities for the future. In some cases the type of work the Rabbit decides on will involve considerable adjustment to his routine and a steep learning curve, but his actions can help him feel more motivated and energized than he has been for some time.

Rabbits seeking work should also be open to possibility and not be too restrictive in what they are prepared to consider. Advice they obtain from agencies, friends and contacts could alert them to positions worth considering. Even though there may be some disappointments in their quest, by remaining persistent they will find their resolve will prevail and in many cases help them secure positions they can build on in the future. Work-wise, this is a progressive year.

The Rabbit's financial prospects are also encouraging and in addition to an increase in income some may be able to supplement their earnings through an interest or enterprising idea they have, or benefit from a gift. To make the most of this upturn the Rabbit should consider reducing any borrowings and, if possible, set something aside for the longer term. With good control, he can improve his position as well as enjoy some of his carefully considered purchases. With this being his own year, he can also enjoy some luck, and if he sees a competition, especially one involving skill or judgement, he would do well to enter.

He can also derive a lot of satisfaction from his interests and hobbies over the year and should allow himself the time to enjoy and develop these. Some Rabbits may decide to set themselves specific challenges, including learning or improving a skill or tackling a particular project. Whatever he does, by spending time in ways he enjoys, the Rabbit can derive considerable pleasure from how certain projects and ideas progress.

The Rabbit enjoys good relations with many people and over the year will find himself in demand. May, August, September and December could be particularly busy months socially. Rabbits currently enjoying romance could see this blossom and become more significant as the year progresses, while for the unattached Rabbit a fortuitous meeting could quickly become meaningful. Love, romance and the close relations the Rabbit enjoys with those around him can help make his own year all the more meaningful.

The Rabbit's home life will also be busy over the year and there may be good cause for a celebration. This could be a marriage, an addition to the family, an academic success or a promotion, but many a Rabbit's household will enjoy some good news during the year. Sometimes this will involve a coming together of family members, some of whom the Rabbit may not have seen for some time, and such occasions will also give many Rabbits a sense of pride.

With some of the events of the year, together with the busy schedules of many in the Rabbit's household, there does need to be good communication, however. In addition, if the Rabbit is troubled by pressures or uncertainties at any time, it is important that he speaks out. With others keen to help and support him, problems can often be quickly solved and concerns eased.

Overall, the Year of the Rabbit holds excellent prospects for the Rabbit himself, but it does call on him to act. This is his year and he needs to seize his opportunities. In his work, promotion or new horizons beckon, while domestically and socially he can look forward to some personal successes. By acting on his aims and aspirations, he can make this year one of the best if not *the* best he has enjoyed for a long time.

The Metal Rabbit

This is the Metal Rabbit's own year and can be a significant one. However, to get the most from this auspicious time, he will need to remain active and set about his hopes and plans in earnest. This is a year for action.

One of the most pleasing of the year's aspects is the Metal Rabbit's relations with others. Not only will he enjoy many shared activities but will also be grateful for the affection and support shown him. Loved ones will often be keen to mark this new decade of his life in style and there will be some surprises in store. There will also be opportunities for many Metal Rabbits to travel and whether taking a main holiday or going away for a short break, they will not only enjoy visiting some interesting places but also the chance to spend time with others. A main characteristic of the Metal Rabbit's own year will be the family and social opportunities it will bring.

In addition to any celebrations surrounding his sixtieth birthday, there will also be other events for the Metal

Rabbit to mark, perhaps an anniversary, the birth of a grandchild, the success of a loved one or another family or personal milestone. Whatever the cause, the year will certainly have a celebratory feel to it.

Throughout the year the Metal Rabbit will be helped by talking though his plans and discussing his hopes and any concerns. Involving others will not only make certain situations clearer but also lead to more happening. This includes any home improvements or purchases the Metal Rabbit may be considering as well as decisions concerning his work situation. Here, talking through his options will often help him determine in his own mind what it is best for him to do. During the year good communication and the support of others will be both helpful and significant.

Over the year the Metal Rabbit will see a noticeable upturn in his social life. In addition to meeting up with his friends, he could find certain interests bringing him into contact with others, and any Metal Rabbits who are alone and would welcome more company, could find their own year bringing quite a transformation. Also, throughout the year the Metal Rabbit should keep alert for events he might enjoy or interesting places he would like to visit. Whether these are exhibitions, open days, shows or other forms of entertainment, if he does his best to go, he can inject an element of fun into the year. May, August, September, December and early January 2012 could see the most social activity.

Quite a few Metal Rabbits will also give some thought to their own personal development over the year and set themselves a new challenge or goal. In particular, if there is a subject or skill the Metal Rabbit feels could be useful, he should follow it up. This is very much a time for action. Those Metal Rabbits who are keen to improve fitness levels or diet would do well to seek guidance, and if they follow up the recommendations given they will be pleased to have started something definite and beneficial.

The Metal Rabbit's financial prospects are also encouraging and some will benefit from a maturing policy, gift or bonus. However, to make the most of any improvement, the Metal Rabbit should set some money aside for specific purposes and, if possible, the longer term.

As this will be a busy year for him, he could be tempted to put correspondence aside to deal with later, especially if of a routine or bureaucratic nature. However, in some cases delay or insufficient attention could be to his disadvantage and throughout the year the Metal Rabbit should attend to correspondence, tax and financial matters carefully and within the required time limits.

At work this can be a year of interesting developments. Although many Metal Rabbits will be content to remain with the duties they know well, change is in the air and they may find themselves concentrating on new challenges and objectives. Although what is asked of the Metal Rabbit may be demanding, it will give him the chance to use particular strengths, have greater input and test ideas, and over the year he may well find certain aspects of his work particularly satisfying and enjoy some notable success.

For Metal Rabbits who are seeking work or keen to make a change, including those desiring a position involving fewer hours or less commuting, their own year can again bring some interesting opportunities. To benefit, these Metal Rabbits should widen the scope of what they are prepared to consider as well as keep alert for possibilities. Openings can arise in unexpected ways – maybe through an advert seen by chance, something overheard, a sudden idea or advice from a friend – and to benefit the Metal Rabbit does need to be receptive and act quickly. Opportunities could come his way at almost any time and the months from February to April and October are likely to see some particularly interesting developments.

Overall, the Metal Rabbit's own year holds great potential for him, but it is very much a case of acting on his ideas and seizing his opportunities. With a positive 'can do' attitude, he can accomplish a great deal. In addition, he will be encouraged by the support and affection of those close to him and, as he will quickly find, in his own special year he will have a great deal working in his favour as well as some moments of good fortune.

TIP FOR THE YEAR
Enjoy your relations with those around you. Encourage joint activities, move plans ahead and, if keen to increase your social circle, become involved in activities you can share with others. Also, keep alert for sudden opportunities. Your own year can be rewarding and bring several special and important developments. Do act on these.

The Water Rabbit

The Water Rabbit likes to proceed slowly but surely and while a lot will have happened in recent years there will have been times when he will not have felt in control. Events and pressures may have concerned him and certain plans may not have gone as well as he had hoped. However, this will be a much more promising year and will give him the chance to make headway and enjoy some deserving (and sometimes overdue) success.

In work matters the Water Rabbit could benefit from some particularly good opportunities. Often a result of recent activity, he will find himself being offered greater responsibilities or well placed for promotion with his present employer. Here his reputation, commitment and in-house knowledge will be real assets. For those keen to progress their career in other ways, again their background and qualities can stand them in excellent stead. By keeping alert and making a special effort with their applications and at interview, they may be offered a significant opportunity. A key feature of the Rabbit year is that the Water Rabbit will feel better able to move his career in the direction *he* wants, and his abilities and reputation will serve him well.

Over the year there will also be other factors in his favour. With his conscientious and personable nature, the Water Rabbit enjoys good working relations with many, and those he meets over the year will also be impressed and encouraging. This can again help his prospects. This is an excellent year for networking, building up contacts and raising his profile.

Water Rabbits who start the Rabbit year dissatisfied should try to draw a line under what has gone before and focus on the present and near future. This is *their* year and new opportunities will appear, giving many the chance to prove themselves in new ways. Water Rabbits who now secure work after having looked for some time may well find that a position they obtain will have the potential for future development and the skills they acquire can open up other possibilities as well. The start of the Rabbit year to April and October could see some particularly encouraging developments, but in general the Rabbit year supports Rabbits well, and with self-belief and resolve, the Water Rabbit can benefit from some excellent opportunities.

Another area that is favourably aspected is the Water Rabbit's personal interests. For those who are skilled in a particular area, this is an excellent year to make more of their talents and knowledge. Rabbits are often known for their creativity and many Water Rabbits could take particular delight in what they are able to do, and if they can promote any work or display their skills, they could enjoy an encouraging response. Water Rabbits who prefer outdoor activities or have other interests will also find that these can bring them much pleasure over the year as well as be excellent ways to keep their often full lifestyle in balance.

The progress the Water Rabbit enjoys at work can also lead to an improvement in income, but to benefit he will need to keep careful watch on his outgoings. Also, when considering more expensive purchases, he should take the time to compare costs, options and ranges. This will lead to more suitable choices as well as save unnecessary outlay. Water Rabbits, take note.

The Water Rabbit's home life will bring him much pleasure this year and many will enjoy some excellent family news, perhaps becoming grandparents or celebrating a graduation or other family success. Also, family members will often look to the Water Rabbit for advice or assistance and set much store by his judgement. During the year, the Water Rabbit will find himself very much at the heart of family life and this can be a busy and gratifying year for him.

His social life is also favourably aspected and he will have quite a few opportunities to go out. This will be another rewarding part of his year, with May, August, September, December and early January especially busy. For Water Rabbits who are alone, new friendships can be made and, for some, romance can beckon. A lot can go in the Water Rabbit's favour this year and by keeping active and being open to opportunity he can make this a year of pleasing personal developments.

Overall, the Year of the Rabbit will be an encouraging one for the Water Rabbit and he will feel bolder, more inspired and readier for action. And over the year his talents and resolve can reward him well. This is a year for progress and there will be some deserving successes to enjoy.

TIP FOR THE YEAR
Remain determined and use your abilities well. You know you have it within you to succeed and this year will offer you good opportunities. It is one in which you can make things happen. Good luck.

The Wood Rabbit

This is an encouraging year for the Wood Rabbit and will bring excellent opportunities to make progress. However, over the year he would do well to remember the Chinese proverb, 'Set long-term goals, but work on short-term tasks.' This is a year to think ahead but also make the most of the present.

In his work the Wood Rabbit can see some significant developments. For Wood Rabbits who are well established in a particular type of work this is a year when they will be encouraged to take their skills further. Sometimes this could involve considerable adjustment to their working pattern, but by taking their opportunities these Wood Rabbits will be able to move their career forward and also gain experience they can build on later. What is achieved this year can not only take the Wood Rabbit's career to a new level but also give him the chance to prove himself in new ways. Progress made now can often have far-reaching implications.

For Wood Rabbits who are feeling staid or unfulfilled in their present job, again the Rabbit year will bring opportunities for change. Rather than continue to drift or remain in an unsatisfactory situation, these Wood Rabbits should give serious thought to what it is they really want to do and where their talents and interests lie. They should also seek advice, including contacting professional organizations and agencies. By taking the initiative they could be advised of fresh possibilities to consider.

This also applies to those Wood Rabbits seeking work. By remaining active and indicating to prospective employers their commitment and willingness to learn, they may be offered a position that is not only a welcome contrast to what they have been doing previously but also something they can build on in the future. This is a year for keeping the long term in mind but concentrating on the present.

With this being a year for self-improvement, all Wood Rabbits should take advantage of any training that is available. In these fast-moving times it is important that they keep their skills up to date. For those intent on major career change, it could be worth obtaining additional qualifications. February to April and October could see some interesting opportunities, but throughout this is a year for the Wood Rabbit to remain active, keep alert for openings and use any chances that come his way for personal development.

The progress the Wood Rabbit makes at work can also lead to an increase in income and for many this will be a financially improved year. The Wood Rabbit should remain disciplined and make provision for his commitments and more substantial plans and purchases, but with good control and care, he can manage well this year.

He will see a lot of activity in his home life, especially as several family members will be involved in change. As a result there will be some important adjustments to be made and good co-operation and support will be vital. At times of pressure and change, the Wood Rabbit should be open and communicative, allowing others to help, understand and be involved. The events of the year can bring benefits, but the Wood Rabbit's household will need to support and assist one another, especially at busy times.

The Rabbit year will, however, also see some family highlights and whether marking personal achievements or enjoying certain activities, the Wood Rabbit will appreciate the times he spends with his loved ones. In addition, both younger and more senior relations will be particularly grateful for the assistance the Wood Rabbit is able to give.

The Wood Rabbit's social life can also bring him much pleasure. Not only will he enjoy meeting up with his friends but he will also be encouraged by their support and understanding. One long-standing friend could be particularly helpful this year. The Wood Rabbit will often delight in interests and activities he is able to share and there will be much for him to enjoy. Wood Rabbits who would welcome a more active social life or are keen to start a new activity will find that following up their ideas and going out more will reward them well. For the unattached Wood Rabbit, the Year of the Rabbit could mark the start of a special romance. This is a positive time and May, August, September and December could see much social activity.

Overall, the Year of the Rabbit holds considerable promise for the Wood Rabbit and will suit his ambitious yet careful nature. It is a year that offers scope and opportunity and if he takes his chances and looks to move forward, his achievements can not only be to his present advantage but also his future benefit. This is a year for bearing in mind longer-term goals but concentrating on what can be done in the present. And with good relations with others and many activities and occasions to enjoy, this can be a pleasing and personally rewarding year for the Wood Rabbit.

TIP FOR THE YEAR

Look to progress, but also to develop. This is an encouraging time, with what you achieve being an investment in yourself and your future. Use it wisely, for its benefits can be far-reaching. Also value and enjoy the support of those close to you.

The Fire Rabbit

The Fire Rabbit has a very intuitive nature and is able to gauge situations and people well. Over the year his abilities will prove of considerable use, helping him to make important progress as well as enjoy exciting developments in his personal life.

For any Fire Rabbit who may start the year dissatisfied with his present situation this is a year to draw a line under past disappointments and look to move on. The aspects in the Rabbit year are especially encouraging and this a time to focus on the present and move ahead. It is not one to be held back by what has gone before.

This is especially the case in the Fire Rabbit's work situation. For any Fire Rabbits who feel unfulfilled, are disappointed with recent progress or consider they have been treated badly, this is a time to seize the initiative and embark on change. To do nothing will only prolong their misery and discontent. Not only should these Fire Rabbits actively make enquiries but also contact organizations, companies and agencies for information and advice. With effort and determination, many could secure an ideal new position which will give them an interesting personal challenge. In some cases considerable adjustments to routine may be needed, with some Fire Rabbits moving or being involved in retraining, but over the year important possibilities can open up for many.

This also applies to Fire Rabbits who are seeking work. Although some could be feeling disheartened, they should remember this is *their* year and one for showing their true spirit. With determination and the willingness to adapt and learn, they could secure a new position, even if sometimes on a temporary basis, that could lead to other possibilities. February to April and mid-September to the end of October could see some important work developments, but chances can arise suddenly throughout the year and when they do, the Fire Rabbit should act swiftly and without delay.

For Fire Rabbits who are well established in a particular career this can be an encouraging year. During it they should keep alert for opportunities that will allow them to add to their knowledge and become better known. Whether networking, attending courses or joining professional organizations, by raising their profile they can do their reputation and prospects considerable good. Work-wise, the Rabbit year offers scope and possibility and the Fire Rabbit's actions and the experience he gains can be to his present and future advantage.

The progress the Fire Rabbit makes at work can also help financially, and many Fire Rabbits will enjoy a rise in income over the year. However, with an active personal life, many different interests and prospective purchases, the Fire Rabbit will still need to exercise a certain care and discipline. Without this there will be times when he spends far more than anticipated and, as a consequence, may have to cut back on certain plans. He can do a lot this year, but does need to keep a close watch on spending. Also, if entering into any major transaction he needs to check the obligations he is taking on and, where necessary, obtain appropriate advice. Although a fortunate year financially, this is not one in which to be lax.

The Fire Rabbit can derive a lot of pleasure from his interests over the year. For the more creative, the way they are able to use their skills and develop their ideas could be especially satisfying, with the encouragement and advice they are given spurring them on. Many will also enjoy the social opportunities certain interests bring. With this a year favouring personal development, some Fire Rabbits could also become immersed in a new activity and revel in the challenge this brings.

The Fire Rabbit is also likely to find himself in demand socially, with parties, events and sometimes celebrations to attend. For those who are keen to build up their social circle, perhaps having recently moved because of work, the Rabbit year can see quite a transformation. A chance meeting, often stemming from a personal interest, can lead to a significant new friendship and, for some, true love. Affairs of the heart are strongly aspected and the Rabbit year can be a very special one in the Fire Rabbit's personal life.

Domestically, this can also be an eventful year. With the Fire Rabbit likely to be making progress and experiencing change, it is important that he talks over the options he may be considering, as well as any concerns he may have, with those around him. Although he will often have his own thoughts, the suggestions and encouragement of loved ones (especially those who speak from experience) can be reassuring and helpful.

With the active nature of the year, many Fire Rabbits will also be involved in some upheaval. This could involve moving to other accommodation or making changes to their existing home. What they do can be both disruptive and time-consuming, but considerable benefits can follow on. With this very much a year for a joint approach, tackling projects with others can make them easier to complete as well as more satisfying for all concerned.

Whether domestically, socially, professionally or personally, this is a year of progress and personal development and it will give the Fire Rabbit an excellent chance to move ahead, enjoy some well-deserved success and gain new skills and experience. The Rabbit year holds great opportunity for him and is a time to enjoy.

TIP FOR THE YEAR
Believe in yourself. Develop your skills and keep alert for opportunities. Important progress can be made now and experience gained. Also, enjoy your personal life. You have much to offer and this is a special and auspicious time for you.

The Earth Rabbit
This will be a satisfying year for the Earth Rabbit, with many of his activities going well. To get full benefit from it he does need to be clear about what he hopes to do, but with plans in mind and the support of others, he can see a lot happen.

Earth Rabbits born in 1939 will be greatly helped over the year by family and close friends. In particular, when they have ideas they are keen to carry out, they should allow time to talk these over with those around them and consider options and, if applicable, costs. With a pooling of thoughts and ideas, some exciting plans can be set in motion.

Some of the Earth Rabbit's thinking will involve purchases he is considering. Whether this involves equipment that would make certain tasks easier, such as a new computer, or improving home comforts, he will often delight in what he buys and the difference it can make. If he is planning to have any practical work carried out in his home, the more fully this can be thought through, the less disruptive it is likely to be and better the eventual result.

The Rabbit year is one for forging ahead with ideas, but time does need to be allowed for reflection and planning.

The Earth Rabbit can look forward to some pleasing events in his family life and may well feel proud over a celebration that takes place. In addition, despite a considerable gap in years, younger relations will often be grateful for the time and support he is able to give.

The Earth Rabbit will also enjoy the active nature of the year. This can include travel and visits to relations as well as more local trips and excursions. Some Earth Rabbits will decide to make more use of nearby amenities and whether visiting places of interest, including exhibitions, museums and specially arranged events, or joining a local course or social group, they could find their immediate neighbourhood offering far more than they may have realized.

The Earth Rabbit should also seize any chances he has to further his interests. Whether sharing his knowledge, meeting other enthusiasts or absorbing himself in a project, he will find that some feedback or success he enjoys could give him a personal fillip over the year.

With his warm and sincere nature, the Earth Rabbit is highly regarded by many and will again value meeting up with friends and attending social events. His interests can also be good ways to spend time with others, and for the lonely and those who would welcome additional company, their local area can again offer possibilities worth pursuing. To learn more about these, it would be worth these Earth Rabbits making enquiries at their local library or community centre. Positive action will be well rewarded. The Earth Rabbit should remember this *is* the Year of the Rabbit and make the most of this special time.

When dealing with finance and paperwork, he will need to be his attentive and careful self. Although an encouraging year, it is still not one for risk, rush or inattention. If the Earth Rabbit has concerns over any matter, particularly forms or correspondence, he should seek advice. In some cases a helpline or information centre could provide the guidance he needs.

For Earth Rabbits born in 1999 this will also be a constructive year. With many having recently changed schools, or be about to do so in the Rabbit year, they will have the opportunity to settle down, become familiar with the resources and facilities available to them and make new friendships. Over the year many will grow considerably in confidence and start interests and subjects which will bring out certain strengths.

Another factor in the young Earth Rabbit's favour is his attitude. The Earth Rabbit has an inquisitive, enthusiastic and interested nature and this will help him learn and develop. Should there be specific activities he would like to try out over the year, he should let others know. It will be to his advantage to avail himself of the help and support that is there for him. This also applies to any personal or school concerns he has. Those around him will be keen to help, but to benefit the Earth Rabbit will need to be forthcoming.

Whether born in 1939 or 1999, the Earth Rabbit's willingness to act can make this a constructive year. With the support he has and the ideas and interests he is keen to develop, he is well placed to make this a year of accomplishment. A lot can go well for him this year and bring him both pleasure and personal satisfaction.

Act on your ideas. To do nothing will lead to nothing, but with a willingness to move your plans forward, the Year of the Rabbit can be special *and* significant. Use it well and enjoy the rewards that your actions and initiatives make possible.

FAMOUS RABBITS

Margaret Atwood, Drew Barrymore, David Beckham, Harry Belafonte, Pope Benedict XVI, Ingrid Bergman, St Bernadette, Jeff Bezos, Gordon Brown, Nicolas Cage, Michael Bublé, Lewis Carroll, Fidel Castro, John Cleese, Confucius, Marie Curie, Johnny Depp, Albert Einstein, George Eliot, W. C. Fields, James Fox, Sir David Frost, Cary Grant, Edvard Grieg, Oliver Hardy, Seamus Heaney, Tommy Hilfiger, Bob Hope, Whitney Houston, Helen Hunt, John Hurt, Anjelica Huston, Chrissie Hynde, Enrique Iglesias, Clive James, Henry James, Sir David Jason, Angelina Jolie, Michael Jordan, Michael Keaton, John Keats, Lisa Kudrow, Gina Lollobrigida, George Michael, Sir Roger Moore, Andrew Murray, Mike Myers, Brigitte Nielsen, Graham Norton, Michelle Obama, Jamie Oliver, George Orwell, Edith Piaf, Brad Pitt, Sidney Poitier, Romano Prodi, Ken Russell, Elisabeth Schwarzkopf, Neil Sedaka, Jane Seymour, Neil Simon, Frank Sinatra, Sting, Quentin Tarantino, J. R. R. Tolkien, KT Tunstall, Tina Turner, Luther Vandross, Queen Victoria, Muddy Waters, Orson Welles, Hayley Westenra, Walt Whitman, Robin Williams, Kate Winslet, Tiger Woods.

3 FEBRUARY 1916 ⁓ 22 JANUARY 1917   *Fire Dragon*

23 JANUARY 1928 ⁓ 9 FEBRUARY 1929   *Earth Dragon*

8 FEBRUARY 1940 ⁓ 26 JANUARY 1941   *Metal Dragon*

27 JANUARY 1952 ⁓ 13 FEBRUARY 1953   *Water Dragon*

13 FEBRUARY 1964 ⁓ 1 FEBRUARY 1965   *Wood Dragon*

31 JANUARY 1976 ⁓ 17 FEBRUARY 1977   *Fire Dragon*

17 FEBRUARY 1988 ⁓ 5 FEBRUARY 1989   *Earth Dragon*

5 FEBRUARY 2000 ⁓ 23 JANUARY 2001   *Metal Dragon*

THE
DRAGON

THE PERSONALITY OF THE DRAGON

I like giving things a go.
Sometimes I succeed,
sometimes I fail.
Sometimes the unexpected happens.
But it is the giving things a go
and the stepping forward
that make life so interesting.

The Dragon is born under the sign of luck. He is a proud and lively character and has a tremendous amount of self-confidence. He is also highly intelligent and very quick to take advantage of any opportunity. He is ambitious and determined and will do well in practically anything he attempts. He is also something of a perfectionist and will always try to maintain the high standards he sets himself.

The Dragon does not suffer fools gladly and will be quick to criticize anyone or anything that displeases him. He can be blunt and forthright in his views and is certainly not renowned for being either tactful or diplomatic. He does, however, often take people at their word and can occasionally be rather gullible. If he ever feels that his trust has been abused or his dignity wounded, he can sometimes become very bitter and it will take him a long time to forgive and forget.

The Dragon is usually very outgoing and is particularly adept at attracting attention and publicity. He enjoys being in the limelight and is often at his best when he is confronted by a difficult problem or tense situation. In some respects he is a showman and he rarely lacks an audience. His views are highly valued and he invariably has something interesting – and sometimes controversial – to say.

He also has considerable energy and is often prepared to work long and unsocial hours in order to achieve what he wants. He can, however, be rather impulsive and does not always consider the consequences of his actions. He also has a tendency to live for the moment and there is nothing that riles him more than to be kept waiting. The Dragon hates delay and can get impatient and irritable over even the smallest of hold-ups.

The Dragon has an enormous faith in his abilities, but he does run the risk of becoming over-confident and unless he is careful he can sometimes make grave errors of judgement. While this may prove disastrous at the time, he does have the tenacity and ability to bounce back and pick up the pieces again.

The Dragon has such an assertive personality, so much willpower and such a desire to succeed that he will often reach the top of his chosen profession. He has considerable leadership qualities and will do well in positions where he can put his own ideas and policies into practice. He is usually successful in politics, show business, as the manager of his own department or business, and in any job that brings him into contact with the media.

The Dragon relies a tremendous amount on his own judgement and can be scornful of other people's advice. He likes to feel self-sufficient and there are many Dragons who cherish their independence to such a degree that they prefer to remain single throughout their lives. However, the Dragon will often have numerous admirers and many will be attracted by his flamboyant personality and striking looks. If he does marry, he will usually marry young, and will find himself particularly well suited to those born under the signs of the Snake, Rat, Monkey and Rooster. He will also find that the Rabbit, Pig, Horse and Goat make ideal companions and will readily join in with many of his escapades. Two Dragons will also get on well together, as they will understand each other, but the Dragon may not find things so easy with the Ox and Dog, as both will be critical of his impulsive and somewhat extrovert manner. He will also find it difficult to form an alliance with the Tiger, for the Tiger, like the Dragon, tends to speak his mind, is very strong-willed and likes to take the lead.

The female Dragon knows what she wants in life and sets about everything she does in a determined and positive manner. No job is too small for her and she is often prepared to work extremely hard to secure her objectives. She is immensely practical and somewhat liberated. She hates being bound by routine and petty restrictions and likes to have sufficient freedom to go off and do what she wants to do. She will keep her house tidy, but is not one for spending hours on housework – there are far too many other things that she prefers to do. Like her male counterpart, she has a tendency to speak her mind.

The Dragon usually has many interests and enjoys sport and other outdoor activities. He also likes to travel and often prefers to visit places that are off the beaten track rather than head for popular tourist destinations. He has a very adventurous streak in him and providing his financial circumstances permit – and the Dragon is usually sensible with his money – he will travel considerable distances during his lifetime.

The Dragon is a very flamboyant character and while he can be demanding of others and in his early years rather precocious, he will have many friends and will nearly always be the centre of attention. He has charisma and so much confidence that he can often become a source of inspiration to others. In China he is the leader of the carnival and he is also blessed with an inordinate share of luck.

THE FIVE DIFFERENT TYPES OF DRAGON

In addition to the 12 signs of the Chinese zodiac there are five elements and these have a strengthening or moderating influence on the signs. The effects of the five elements on the Dragon are described below, together with the years in which they were exercising their influence. Therefore those Dragons born in 1940 and 2000 are Metal Dragons, those born in 1952 are Water Dragons, and so on.

Metal Dragon: 1940, 2000

This Dragon is very strong-willed and has a particularly forceful personality. He is energetic, ambitious and tries to be scrupulous in his dealings with others. He can also be blunt and to the point and usually has no hesitation in speaking his mind. If people disagree with him or are not prepared to co-operate, he is more than happy to go his own way. He usually has very high moral values and is held in great esteem by his friends and colleagues.

Water Dragon: 1952

This Dragon is friendly, easy-going and intelligent. He is quick-witted and rarely lets an opportunity slip by. However, he is not as impatient as some of the other types of Dragon and is prepared to wait for results rather than expect everything to happen at once. He has an understanding nature and is willing to share his ideas and co-operate with others. His main failing is a tendency to jump from one thing to another rather than concentrate on the job in hand. He has a good sense of humour and is an effective speaker.

Wood Dragon: 1964

The Wood Dragon is practical, imaginative and inquisitive. He loves delving into all manner of subjects and can quite often come up with some highly original ideas. He is a thinker and a doer and has the drive and commitment to put many of his ideas into practice. He is more diplomatic than some of the other types of Dragon and has a good sense of humour. He is very astute in business matters and can also be most generous.

Fire Dragon: 1916, 1976

This Dragon is ambitious, articulate and has a tremendous desire to succeed. He is a hard and conscientious worker and is often admired for his integrity and forthright nature. He is very strong-willed and has considerable leadership qualities. He can, however, rely a bit too much on his own judgement and fail to take into account the views and feelings of others. He can also be rather aloof and it would certainly be in his own interests to let others join in more with his various activities. He usually enjoys music, literature and the arts.

Earth Dragon: 1928, 1988

The Earth Dragon tends to be quieter and more reflective than some of the other types of Dragon. He has a wide variety of interests and is keenly aware of what is going on around him. He also has clear objectives and usually has no problems in obtaining support and backing for any of his ventures. He is very astute in financial matters and often able to accumulate considerable wealth. He is a good organizer, although he can at times be rather bureaucratic and fussy. He mixes well with others and has a large circle of friends.

PROSPECTS FOR THE DRAGON IN 2011

The Dragon likes to keep himself occupied and in the Tiger year (14 February 2010–2 February 2011) there will certainly be a lot for him to do. Tiger years favour activity and the closing months of this one will be a busy and interesting time for the Dragon.

In his work he will often have to deal with increased pressures. Sometimes this could be the result of staff shortages or seasonal demand, but the closing months will certainly be busy. However, by prioritizing, using his skills to advantage and working closely with his colleagues, he can accomplish a great deal as well as add to his reputation and experience. For Dragons who are seeking work or looking to make headway, August and November could see some good possibilities, but generally the closing months of the Tiger year will provide many with opportunities to move forward.

The Dragon will also see an increase in spending at this time. To help, he should aim to spread out some of his purchases as well as keep alert for favourable buying opportunities. Many Dragons will also have opportunities to travel towards the end of the year and the more this can be planned and saved for in advance, the more the Dragon will be able to do while away. Financially, this is a time for good control.

With the busy nature of the Tiger year, it is also important that the Dragon preserves quality time for spending with family and friends. In his home life, if he discusses plans in advance, he can have many activities, including travel, to look forward to. He will also appreciate meeting up with his friends and attending a variety of social events. However, when in company he does need to listen carefully to the views of others in order to avoid misunderstandings.

Overall, the Tiger year will be busy but in many ways constructive for him.

The Year of the Rabbit begins on 3 February and will be a steadier one for the Dragon. Lacking the pace of the Tiger year, it will give him the chance to concentrate on his priorities. Also, the following year is the Dragon's own year and the progress he makes now can often stand him in good stead for the auspicious times that lie ahead. This can be a valuable year for him and its consequences far-reaching.

For the many Dragons who have experienced recent change at work, the Rabbit year will give them the chance to settle and familiarize themselves with their duties. As a result, these Dragons will often feel more satisfied than they have for some while. Another positive aspect of the year will be the way many Dragons will become an integral part of a team. This will also help their reputation and prospects.

For Dragons seeking work or a change, the Rabbit year can be an excellent one in which to reappraise their situation. If they consider carefully the type of work they now want to pursue and seek advice, some interesting possibilities can start to emerge. Sometimes training or greater experience may be required, but this will give these Dragons something to work towards. In the meantime they should act quickly when they see an opening that interests them and may be able to secure a position that can provide them with useful experience and a platform they can build on. March, June, September and December could see some useful developments, but the main value of the Rabbit year will be the way the Dragon can further his own development and add to his knowledge. Some of his ideas this year can shape the direction of his career over the next few years.

With the steadier nature of the Rabbit year, the Dragon will also have more chance to appreciate his recreational pursuits. For any Dragon who has let interests lapse or would welcome new challenges, this is an excellent time to address this and reward themselves with some 'me time'. The Rabbit year is one of reappraisal and by setting time aside for personal development, the Dragon can find that important benefits can follow.

The Rabbit year can also bring some good travel opportunities. Any breaks and holidays the Dragon takes with his loved ones will be particularly appreciated.

His financial situation can also see an improvement this year. To make the most of this, the Dragon will need to manage his spending carefully and, where possible, make early provision for more sizable outlays. With good control, he can benefit from his prudence. Also, by keeping alert he could be lucky in some purchases he makes, possibly finding what he is looking for at a reduced price or in a most unusual place. His fine taste and eye for a good buy will be to his advantage this year.

With his active nature, the Dragon knows a great many people and over the year will have quite a few chances to go out and socialize. This can not only help keep his lifestyle in balance but also be a good way for him to relax, unwind and enjoy himself. April, May, August and December could be the busiest months socially.

For unattached Dragons, the Rabbit year can bring excellent opportunities to meet others, with many enjoying the start of a wonderful new romance. On a personal level, this can be a pleasing and positive year.

The Dragon's domestic life will also be a source of much contentment. Not only will he be encouraged by the support and affection shown him but also take pleasure in the activities that take place. This can be a constructive and meaningful year. However, while the aspects are encouraging, the Dragon does need to consult others and listen carefully to their views. Being such a dominant personality, he does like to hold sway and over the year it is important that he remains mindful of others and in some matters shows greater flexibility. Dragons, do take note. You may mean well, but inattention and inflexibility could cause difficulties which, with more consideration, could have been avoided. This warning apart, this will be a generally positive year for home and family matters.

Although the Rabbit year may lack the activity of some, it will give the Dragon a chance to add to the quality and balance of his lifestyle. It is a year for taking stock and being open to opportunity. In many ways it will be a pleasant and satisfying year and one in which the Dragon can do himself a lot of good.

The Metal Dragon

The Metal Dragon has a purposeful nature and when he sets himself an objective he pursues it with considerable might. And this year his tenacity will reward him well.

For Metal Dragons born in 1940 this is an excellent year for tackling ideas they may have been considering for some while. These could be connected with their accommodation or interests and personal development, but 2011 is very much a time for exploring options and taking action. Also, if the Metal Dragon involves those around him, other possibilities could arise. This is a year of scope *and* exciting possibility.

Many Metal Dragons will be keen to go ahead with plans they have for their accommodation. Some will move and the process itself can be slow but these Metal Dragons will feel happy with their decision and the benefits that follow on. Others will be keen to go ahead with some home improvements, including replacing outdated or inefficient equipment as well as treating themselves to some new comforts. Again some of their decisions will take longer than envisaged to carry out (the Rabbit year does not favour haste), but the Metal Dragon will be pleased with the results.

Another positive area concerns the Metal Dragon's interests and personal development. Over the years he will have built up considerable knowledge in certain areas and during the Rabbit year he will be able to put this to good use, perhaps by sharing his knowledge with others, going to special events or setting himself fulfilling projects. However, it is not only existing interests that can bring him pleasure this year. If there is a subject that has been intriguing him, he should aim to find out more. Some Metal Dragons may consider joining local classes, enrolling on courses or starting a new activity, and may even discover a talent they did not realize they had.

With the Rabbit year's emphasis on culture, another activity that will appeal to many Metal Dragons will be visiting places of interest in their area. These could include museums and galleries as well as special events and exhibitions. Some may also delight in local amenities, including gardens and recreational facilities. Here again, by following up his ideas and keeping himself informed about what is happening, the Metal Dragon will benefit. As the saying reminds us, 'There is no time like the present,' and with a spirit of enquiry, the Metal Dragon can gain a lot from this year.

With all the activities he has planned, he will need to manage his finances well. Particularly when going ahead with larger purchases or authorizing work that needs to be carried out, it would be worth him making comparisons and, where appropriate, obtaining several quotations. If he has any concerns, he should seek advice rather than make assumptions or deal with what could be complicated matters single-handedly. This is a year for vigilance and careful money management.

In his home life, by sharing decisions and combining ideas and effort, he will be pleased with what goes ahead. Metal Dragons who move will see some often exciting ideas emerging. Plans may not always proceed quickly, but gradually evolve over the course of the year.

The Metal Dragon will also follow the activities of family members with fond interest and may particularly enjoy visits to relations living some distance away. April, May, August, December and January could be especially busy months socially.

For Metal Dragons born in 2000, the Rabbit year can also be rewarding. Rabbit years favour learning and the exploration of personal talents and the young Metal Dragon should make the most of chances to try new activities and extend his knowledge. With willingness, he can derive much pleasure from what he does this year. Some Metal Dragons will start activities that will have growing importance in following years. The Rabbit year can start to reveal the talents of many a young Metal Dragon.

Whether born in 1940 or 2000, the Metal Dragon will find the Rabbit year a quietly satisfying one. It is a time to concentrate on his aims and to seize his opportunities. With an earnest approach, backed by the support and affection of others, he will find that much good can come from the year.

TIP FOR THE YEAR

Spend time enjoying your skills and personal interests. Your knowledge and talents can bring you much pleasure this year as well as open up other possibilities. Use your ideas and gifts well.

The Water Dragon

Compared to the activity of the preceding Tiger year and the excitement that awaits in 2012, the Year of the Water Dragon, the Rabbit year will be a quieter and steadier one for the Water Dragon. During it, he will have time to attend to matters which at busier times he may neglect. From a personal point of view, this can be an interesting and often fulfilling year.

In his work the Water Dragon will often be content to immerse himself in his activities and focus on his current objectives. Quite a few Water Dragons could also face some adjustments over the year as new methods of working are introduced or they are required to alter their schedule. However, by being flexible and drawing on their experience, many will be satisfied with the results they are able to achieve.

An important feature of the Rabbit year is that it is an excellent one for personal development and all Water

Dragons should aim to keep their skills up to date, take advantage of training and keep themselves informed about developments in their industry. Their experience, insights and willingness to learn can prove very helpful over the year. The Water Dragon also enjoys good working relations with many and may well take on a mentoring role or find others looking to him for guidance.

Most Water Dragons will remain with their present employer over the year, but those seeking work or looking to change would do well to widen the scope of what they are prepared to consider. With determination and flexibility, many could find interesting ways to draw on their considerable experience. Some might opt for temporary work and welcome the chance to do something different. March, June, September and December could see some interesting opportunities, and work-wise this is a year when the Water Dragon's skills and versatility can reward him well.

Another important aspect of the year will be the desire many Water Dragons will have to lead a more balanced lifestyle. Rather than conduct life at a heady pace, the Water Dragon will make a deliberate effort to set time aside for himself and his interests. As a result, he can make this a more satisfying time. If he has let certain interests lapse, this is an ideal year to renew them, set himself a fresh objective or take up something new. The Rabbit year also has a strong cultural flavour and the Water Dragon may be tempted to enrol on a course or improve a particular skill. Whatever he does, he will feel buoyed up by positive action. Any Water Dragon who may be feeling low or dissatisfied will find that starting a new interest or recreational activity can be of great personal help.

With Water as his element, the Water Dragon is a talented communicator, and if any of his interests brings him into contact with others or allows him to express himself in some way, he can derive especial pleasure from what he does.

He would also do well to give some consideration to his well-being this year, and if he feels he is lacking in exercise or that modifications to his diet could help, he should take advice on the most appropriate action to take. This is an excellent year for him to evaluate his lifestyle.

With his various commitments and plans for the year, including travel, he should also keep watch on his spending and set funds aside for specific requirements. This is a year for good financial management. Also, when dealing with financially related forms or entering into agreements, the Water Dragon does need to check the implications and question anything that may be unclear. This is not a year to be lax.

In his home life, the achievements of younger family members will be a source of especial delight and the Water Dragon's interest and support will be much appreciated. Another satisfying aspect of the year will be some of the tasks the Water Dragon decides to tackle, and he will be pleased to see his ideas take shape and plans materialize, even if sometimes slowly. His thoughtfulness and care can add to the pleasures of home life as well as strengthen the rapport he has with loved ones, and a key benefit of the Rabbit year is that it will give him more chance to spend time with others.

The Water Dragon can also look forward to some pleasing social occasions. He will enjoy going out to talk, relax and have fun and the Rabbit year is an excellent one for him to bring his lifestyle into balance. April, May, August and December could see a lot of social activity and for Water Dragons who would welcome new friendships, enquiring about interest groups and events in their area can bring an important new ingredient to their lifestyle and give them something enjoyable to look forward to.

In general, the Year of the Rabbit can be a satisfying one for the Water Dragon, particularly as it will allow him to enjoy the company of others and develop his interests and skills. A personally rewarding year.

TIP FOR THE YEAR
This is a year to bring balance to your lifestyle. Spend time with your loved ones and friends and pursuing and developing your interests. These aspects of your life are precious and can make this year all the more meaningful.

The Wood Dragon

One of the Wood Dragon's strengths is his practical nature. He has a good way of analyzing situations and choosing the right course of action. He is also realistic in what he sets out to do and over the Rabbit year his good sense and willingness to act will stand him in excellent stead. The Rabbit year can be a constructive and illuminating one for him and some of what he sets in motion during it can shape the next few years.

In his work the Wood Dragon will have a good chance to demonstrate his skills and qualities. He may not only find his work level increasing but also be faced with some challenging situations. Whether these are caused through delays, the slow workings of bureaucracy, technical problems or conflicting viewpoints, there will be occasions when the Wood Dragon's practical outlook and experience will prove invaluable. Some of the problems and issues that arise will test his ingenuity as well as give him the chance to learn about other aspects of his work. He can help this process by taking advantage of training opportunities, setting time aside for study and keeping up to date with developments in his industry. In this way he will be able to invest in himself as well as prepare himself for the opportunities that lie ahead. Many Wood Dragons will have the chance to make modest headway over the year and if they see an opening that appeals to them, they should put themselves forward. The more experience the Wood Dragon can gain, the stronger his future prospects.

For Wood Dragons seeking work or considering more major change, the Rabbit year can be a pivotal time. By thinking over what they want to do and investigating openings, many could succeed in taking on a new position and with it an interesting personal challenge. For some, this could involve an element of retraining, but with a willingness to learn, they will find this can bear important and sizeable fruit. As the Chinese proverb reminds us, 'Diligence leads to riches,' and the Wood Dragon's efforts this year can reward him well. March, June, September and December could see encouraging work developments.

The Wood Dragon can also look forward to an improvement in his financial situation, not only through an increase in earnings but in many cases also a hobby or interest supplementing his income. However, while any improvement will be welcome, to benefit the Wood Dragon will need to be disciplined in his handling of financial matters. This includes looking to reduce borrowings as well as making provision for large outlays. With care, he can improve his situation, but should he proceed on a more *ad hoc* basis, anything extra could quickly be spent and not always in the best way. Financially, this is a year for discipline.

The Wood Dragon can, however, gain a lot from taking advantage of opportunities to develop his interests. These not only help keep his lifestyle in balance but also give him a chance to relax, use his skills in other ways and sometimes enjoy social occasions. Some Wood Dragons could be tempted to take up something new, perhaps with a keep fit element. The recreational activities that the Wood Dragon pursues this year can certainly be both pleasurable and good for him.

He should also make sure his social life does not get sidelined due to other commitments. Keeping in contact with friends and going to social occasions can not only be fun but also allow him to share thoughts with those he may have known for a great many years. If he is considering an idea or is troubled by any matter, he should not forget that his many friends and acquaintances may have the expertise or contacts to help. His social life can benefit him in sometimes surprising ways. April, May, August, December and early January 2012 could see the most social activity.

Domestically, this promises to be a busy year, with many Wood Dragons giving time and support to both younger and more senior relations. Some family members could have important personal decisions to make and be especially grateful for the Wood Dragon's understanding and ability to see round situations or identify potential problems. Over the year many Wood Dragons will do much for their loved ones and be an important guide and influence.

With the Wood Dragon's often busy schedule and those around him often occupied with their own concerns as well, there will also need to be a certain flexibility in his household and a willingness to compromise over domestic arrangements. Here good discussion and planning can help. Also, should the Wood Dragon tackle any home or practical project over the year, he does need to allow sufficient time to complete it. He may be keen and willing, but in the Rabbit year things may not proceed as quickly or smoothly as he would wish. Although not an adverse year, 2011 can bring its interruptions, niggles and delays, which will need to be addressed and overcome.

One of the main benefits of the Rabbit year is its instructive nature. It will give the Wood Dragon the chance to develop his skills and what he is able to take from the current time will serve him well in following years. It is also important that he keeps his lifestyle in balance, enjoying his interests as well as supporting and spending time with friends and loved ones. This may not be a dynamic year, but it can be a satisfying and often pleasurable one.

TIP FOR THE YEAR
Regard this as an excellent year for furthering your knowledge and skills. Take advantage of training opportunities whenever you can. The progress you make this year can prepare you for some of the important possibilities that

will open up to you in the near future. Enjoy the year and use it profitably. Remember, 'Diligence leads to riches.'

The Fire Dragon

The Fire Dragon has a keen and enthusiastic nature and likes to involve himself in a great many things. He is not one for sitting on the sidelines. In the Rabbit year, he will need to show some patience and accept that his plans may not proceed as quickly as he would like. This will be a quiet year and lack the pace he favours, but it will still contain many pleasures and, importantly, some far-reaching benefits.

A significant feature of the Rabbit year is that it can be a time of reappraisal and taking stock. During the year it would reward the Fire Dragon to give some thought to his present position and consider possible directions for the next few years. These can relate to almost any aspect of his life – his interests, well-being, accommodation or career – but whatever his plans, he should discuss them with his loved ones and listen carefully to their thoughts and suggestions. As a result, some important possibilities will emerge which can give the Fire Dragon something positive to work towards. By considering improvements he can make and ways forward, he will feel he is doing something positive with possibly long-term value.

At work many Fire Dragons will be content to remain where they are and to continue using their skills and furthering their experience. During the course of the year the Fire Dragon may well have complex issues to handle or be forced to adjust to new ways of working. While this may be challenging, his focus and commitment will be recognized and to his advantage. He should also make the most of any training he is offered as well as use his chances to network. This can help both his present position and future prospects.

For Fire Dragons who are seeking work or would welcome more substantial change, the Rabbit year is an excellent one in which to take stock and consider various ways in which they could develop their skills. In their quest, they could find it helpful to talk to professional advisors or consider retraining. By giving serious thought to how they can best use their strengths, these Fire Dragons can benefit from some helpful suggestions and uncover some good opportunities. Sometimes what they are offered may not be all they were hoping for, but it can still give them an important base to build on and be a valuable entry into a company or industry. What the Fire Dragon achieves in the Rabbit year can be a prelude to the exciting developments that await in 2012.

In financial matters, he will need to be thorough. During the year he could take on new commitments and will need to make allowance for these in his budget as well as keep a close eye on his level of spending. Making advance provision for his plans and purchases and keeping alert for suitable buying opportunities will help. Financially, this is a year which requires good planning and careful management.

The Fire Dragon's home life will be busy and often special. Although the various members of his household will often be concerned with their own activities, if he takes an interest in what they are doing, this will not only be good for rapport and understanding but also make a real difference to what is achieved. Younger relations in particular could benefit from the advice and encouragement the Fire Dragon is able to give. With his keen nature, he could also suggest certain activities that everyone could enjoy, perhaps a family treat, a trip or a holiday. The consideration and time he gives to his home life can be beneficial for everyone concerned.

The Fire Dragon will also derive much pleasure from his personal interests and social life. By setting himself some aims or a new activity to do, he can make this a constructive and often beneficial time. In addition he should keep in regular contact with his friends, as they can be of considerable help to him, whether through offering advice, providing a listening ear or giving him the chance to relax and unwind. April, May, August and December could see the most social activity, with excellent chances to meet and get to know others.

Overall, the Year of the Rabbit can be a pleasant and personally rewarding one for the Fire Dragon. It may not be a year for fast results or major breakthroughs, but can be one of evaluation, appreciation and personal growth. And this will do the Fire Dragon good.

TIP FOR THE YEAR

Think about your current situation, the ways in which you would like to develop and what you would like to achieve in the near future. With some ideas and aims, you will find people and events often assisting you. What you start this year can greatly help your prospects, especially in the progressive Dragon year that follows.

The Earth Dragon

There is a Chinese proverb that contains good advice for the Earth Dragon this year. It is, 'Slow and steady wins the race.' The Earth Dragon can fare well this year, but it is a time for proceeding steadily and thoroughly. However, what the Earth Dragon can achieve now can be particularly instrumental in some of the successes he is to enjoy in the near future.

One of the key trends of Rabbit years is that they favour learning and personal growth, and during the year the Earth Dragon should take advantage of ways in which he can further his skills, experience and qualifications. Even if some of what he decides to tackle is in his own time and at his own expense, his ultimate gains can be substantial. This is a year for investing in himself *and* his future.

This theme of personal development extends both to work and personal interests. With the latter, if there is a skill the Earth Dragon feels could be useful or a subject that appeals to him, he should follow it up. Positive and determined action now can open up a lot for him in the future. Earth Dragons who favour more creative pursuits can enjoy some encouraging feedback and see some interesting possibilities emerging. The Rabbit year has considerable potential and Earth Dragons who are currently studying for qualifications will find that by remaining focused and disciplined, the gains they can make this year can have far-reaching value.

At work, for those Earth Dragons who are keen to build up their experience in a certain trade or industry, this is a year to show commitment and initiative. By concentrating on their duties and showing a willingness to learn, many will be able to broaden their role and be offered greater responsibilities and additional training. The good work the Earth Dragon does now can also help his subsequent career development and prepare him for future opportunities.

For Earth Dragons who are seeking work or not feeling fulfilled in their present position, the Rabbit year can open up some interesting possibilities. By looking at a wide range of options and seeking advice, they may well be successful in securing a new position, even if it is slightly different from what they originally intended. For some, this can mark their entry into what can be a long and rewarding profession. April, May, August and December could see some good opportunities, and even though the job-seeking process can at times be slow, with persistence and self-belief, the Earth Dragon will win through. And what he achieves this year can prepare him for the important developments that await in 2012.

The Earth Dragon's progress at work can also lead to an increase in income, but while this will be welcome, he will need to remain disciplined and watch his outgoings. Otherwise, when he is out, whether socially or shopping, he could end up spending far more than originally intended. Too many extravagances or unplanned purchases could mount up and result in economies having to be made later. Earth Dragons, take note. This is a year for careful budgeting.

One expense many Earth Dragons will have will be their social life, and this will be both active and enjoyable. Throughout the year the Earth Dragon will find himself in demand, with friends to meet, things to do and places to go. He could also find his social circle is set to increase as he gets to work with new colleagues or takes up new interests. For some, a chance meeting could develop into a serious romance, and affairs of the heart could add excitement and sparkle to the year. For socializing and meeting others, April to early June, August and December could be especially active months. Also, many Earth Dragons will enjoy their travels this year and these will often have a good social element.

With his various activities and the decisions he will need to make, the Earth Dragon would also do well to draw on the experience and advice of those close to him. Some senior relations could be especially helpful and provide assistance in ways he may not have anticipated. Although the Earth Dragon has an independent streak, he should be forthcoming and prepared to talk over his options and any dilemmas or concerns. He is held in very high regard by those who are dear to him and over the year their love and support will be amply demonstrated.

Overall, this can be a constructive and satisfying year for the Earth Dragon. There will be excellent chances for him to add to his experience and show others his skills and potential. What he can achieve now can considerably strengthen his prospects, especially in the favourably aspected Dragon year that follows. His interests and personal life will also be a source of pleasure and pride, with his activities and relations with others adding something special to his year.

TIP FOR THE YEAR

Be thorough and determined. 'Slow and steady wins the race' and the skills you can demonstrate this year can strengthen your reputation, add to your experience and prepare the way for future success. Also, value your relations with others. Your friends and loved ones can be of great help and mean a lot to you during the year.

FAMOUS DRAGONS

Maya Angelou, Jeffrey Archer, Joan Armatrading, Joan Baez, Count Basie, Maeve Binchy, Sandra Bullock, Alexandra Burke, Michael Cera, Courteney Cox, Bing Crosby, Russell Crowe, Roald Dahl, Salvador Dali, Charles Darwin, Neil Diamond, Bo Diddley, Matt Dillon, Christian Dior, Placido Domingo, Fats Domino, Kirk Douglas, Faye Dunaway, Lee Evans, Dan Fogler, Bruce Forsyth, Sigmund Freud, Graham Greene, Rupert Grint, Che Guevara, James Herriot, Paul Hogan, Joan of Arc, Boris Johnson, Tom Jones, Immanuel Kant, Martin Luther King, John Lennon, Abraham Lincoln, Elle MacPherson, Queen Margrethe II of Denmark, Hosni Mubarak, Florence Nightingale, Nick Nolte, Sharon Osbourne, Al Pacino, Gregory Peck, Pelé, Edgar Allan Poe, Vladimir Putin, Keanu Reeves, Sir Cliff Richard, George Bernard Shaw, Martin Sheen, Alicia Silverstone, Ringo Starr, Princess Stephanie of Monaco, Dave Stewart, Karlheinz Stockhausen, Shirley Temple, Maria von Trapp, Louis Walsh, Andy Warhol, Raquel Welch, the Earl of Wessex, Mae West.

23 JANUARY 1917 ⁓ 10 FEBRUARY 1918   *Fire Snake*

10 FEBRUARY 1929 ⁓ 29 JANUARY 1930   *Earth Snake*

27 JANUARY 1941 ⁓ 14 FEBRUARY 1942   *Metal Snake*

14 FEBRUARY 1953 ⁓ 2 FEBRUARY 1954   *Water Snake*

2 FEBRUARY 1965 ⁓ 20 JANUARY 1966   *Wood Snake*

18 FEBRUARY 1977 ⁓ 6 FEBRUARY 1978   *Fire Snake*

6 FEBRUARY 1989 ⁓ 26 JANUARY 1990   *Earth Snake*

24 JANUARY 2001 ⁓ 11 FEBRUARY 2002   *Metal Snake*

THE
SNAKE

THE PERSONALITY OF THE SNAKE

I think
And think some more.
About what is,
About what can be,
About what may be.
And when I am ready,
Then I act.

The Snake is born under the sign of wisdom. He is highly intelligent and his mind is forever active. He is always planning and always looking for ways in which he can use his considerable skills. He is a deep thinker and likes to meditate and reflect.

Many times during his life he will shed one of his famous Snake skins and take up new interests or start a completely different job. The Snake enjoys a challenge and he rarely makes mistakes. He is a skilful organizer, has considerable business acumen and is usually lucky in money matters. Most Snakes are financially secure in their later years, provided they do not gamble – the Snake has the distinction of being the worst gambler in the whole of the Chinese zodiac!

The Snake generally has a calm and placid nature and prefers the quieter things in life. He does not like to be in a frenzied atmosphere and hates being hurried into making a quick decision. He also does not like interference in his affairs and tends to rely on his own judgement rather than listen to advice.

At times the Snake can appear solitary. He is quiet, reserved and sometimes has difficulty in communicating with others. He has little time for idle gossip and will certainly not suffer fools gladly. He does, however, have a good sense of humour and this is particularly appreciated in times of crisis.

The Snake is certainly not afraid of hard work and is thorough in all that he does. He is very determined and can occasionally be ruthless in order to achieve his aims. His confidence, willpower and quick thinking usually ensure his success, but should he fail it will often take a long time for him to recover. He cannot bear failure and is a very bad loser.

The Snake can also be evasive and does not willingly let people into his confidence. This secrecy and distrust can sometimes work against him and it is a trait that all Snakes should try to overcome.

Another characteristic of the Snake is his tendency to rest after any sudden or prolonged bout of activity. He burns up so much nervous energy that he can, if he is not careful, be susceptible to high blood pressure and nervous disorders.

It has sometimes been said that the Snake is a late starter in life and this is mainly because it often takes him a while to find a job in which he is genuinely happy. However, he will usually do well in any position that involves research and writing and where he is given sufficient freedom to develop his own ideas and plans. He makes a good teacher, politician, personnel manager and social adviser.

The Snake chooses his friends carefully and while he keeps a tight control over his finances, he can be particularly generous to those he likes. He will think nothing of buying expensive gifts or treating his friends or loved ones to the best theatre seats in town. In return he demands loyalty.

The Snake is very possessive and can become extremely jealous and hurt if he finds his trust has been abused.

The Snake is also renowned for his good looks and is never short of admirers. The female Snake in particular is most alluring. She has style, grace and excellent (and usually expensive) taste in clothes. A keen socializer, she is likely to have a wide range of friends and the happy knack of impressing those who matter. She has numerous interests and her opinions are often highly valued. She is generally a calm person and while she involves herself in many activities, she likes to retain a certain amount of privacy in her undertakings.

Affairs of the heart are very important to the Snake and he will often have many romances before he finally settles down. He will find that he is particularly well suited to those born under the signs of the Ox, Dragon, Rabbit and Rooster. Provided he is allowed sufficient freedom to pursue his own interests, he can also build up a very satisfactory relationship with the Rat, Horse, Goat, Monkey and Dog, but he should try to steer clear of another Snake as they could very easily become jealous of each other. The Snake will also have difficulty in getting on with the honest and down-to-earth Pig, and will find the Tiger far too much of a disruptive influence on his quiet and peace-loving ways.

The Snake certainly appreciates the finer things in life. He enjoys good food and often takes a keen interest in the arts. He also enjoys reading and is invariably drawn to subjects such as philosophy, political thought, religion or the occult. He is fascinated by the unknown and his enquiring mind is always looking for answers. Some of the world's most original thinkers have been Snakes, and although he may not readily admit it, the Snake is often psychic and relies a lot on intuition.

The Snake is certainly not the most energetic member of the Chinese zodiac. He prefers to proceed at his own pace and to do what he wants. He is very much his own master and throughout his life he will try his hand at many things. He is something of a dabbler, but at some time – usually when he least expects it – his hard work and efforts will be recognized and he will invariably meet with the success and the financial security he so desires.

THE FIVE DIFFERENT TYPES OF SNAKE

In addition to the 12 signs of the Chinese zodiac there are five elements and these have a strengthening or moderating influence on the signs. The effects of the five elements on the Snake are described below, together with the years in which they were exercising their influence. Therefore those Snakes born in 1941 and 2001 are Metal Snakes, those born in 1953 are Water Snakes, and so on.

Metal Snake: 1941, 2001
This Snake is quiet, confident and fiercely independent. He often prefers to work on his own and will only let a privileged few into his confidence. He is quick to spot opportunities and will set about achieving his objectives with an

awesome determination. He is astute in financial matters and will often invest his money well. He also has a liking for the finer things in life and a good appreciation of the arts, literature, music and food. He usually has a small group of extremely good friends and can be generous to his loved ones.

Water Snake: 1953

This Snake has a wide variety of interests. He enjoys studying all manner of subjects and is capable of undertaking quite detailed research and becoming a specialist in his chosen area. He is highly intelligent, has a good memory and is particularly astute when dealing with business and financial matters. He tends to be quietly spoken and a little reserved, but he does have sufficient strength of character to make his views known and attain his ambitions. He is very loyal to his family and friends.

Wood Snake: 1965

The Wood Snake has a friendly temperament and a good understanding of human nature. He is able to communicate well and often has many friends and admirers. He is witty, intelligent and ambitious. He has numerous interests and prefers to live in a quiet, stable environment where he can work without too much interference. He enjoys the arts and usually derives much pleasure from collecting paintings and antiques. His advice is often highly valued, particularly on social and domestic matters.

Fire Snake: 1917, 1977

The Fire Snake tends to be more forceful, outgoing and energetic than some of the other types of Snake. He is ambitious, confident and never slow in voicing his opinions, and he can be very abrasive to those he does not like. He does, however, have many leadership qualities and can win the respect and support of many with his firm and resolute manner. He usually has a good sense of humour, a wide circle of friends and a very active social life. He is also a keen traveller.

Earth Snake 1929, 1989

The Earth Snake is charming, amusing and has a very amiable manner. He is conscientious and reliable in his work and approaches everything he does in a level-headed and sensible way. He can, however, tend to err on the cautious side and never likes to be hassled into making a decision. He is adept in dealing with financial matters and is a shrewd investor. He has many friends and is very supportive towards the members of his family.

PROSPECTS FOR THE SNAKE IN 2011

The Tiger year (14 February 2010–2 February 2011) is characterized by a great deal of activity and the Snake may have felt unsettled during it. Snakes like to proceed in measured ways and follow carefully laid plans rather than be caught up in fast-moving and sometimes frenzied situations.

The year's often hectic pace shows no sign of slowing in the closing months and the Snake will have a lot to deal with. To ease some of the pressure, he should concentrate on priorities and involve others in his various activities. This is no time for him to go it alone or isolate himself from others.

This particularly applies to his working situation. Far more will be achieved through joint effort than independent action and the Snake should aim to work closely with his colleagues. Although the closing months of the Tiger year can be demanding, some interesting possibilities can still arise.

Another feature of the Tiger year is that it favours the new, and one benefit for the Snake is the opportunities it will bring to try out new interests or recreational pursuits. If he sees something that appeals to him or has an idea that intrigues him, he should follow it up. Personal interests and travel opportunities can bring him particular pleasure in the final Tiger months.

The Snake will also see a lot happen in both his home and social life at this time. September and December could be two especially busy months, and to fit in all the Snake wants, good liaison and some flexibility will be necessary.

Overall, the Tiger year can be a challenging one for the Snake, but he will learn a lot during it and enjoy some particularly rewarding occasions in his home and social life and through the various activities he pursues.

The Year of the Rabbit starts on 3 February and will be a much improved one for the Snake. Not only will he feel more in control of his situation but also find greater fulfilment in many of his activities. He will also have the chance to make more of his specific talents. However, while the aspects may be favourable, this will still be a busy year and it is important that the Snake continues to prioritize his affairs and keeps his lifestyle well balanced.

His work prospects are particularly encouraging. Rabbit years favour creativity and expression and this one will give the Snake an excellent chance to profit from his strengths. Snakes whose work allows them to express themselves in some way or involves an element of creativity could find what they do well received and benefit from some fine opportunities. The Rabbit year will offer many Snakes the chance to do what they are good at and this will lead to some notable successes.

For those who start the year unfulfilled in their present position or seeking employment, the Rabbit year will offer the chance to re-establish themselves and take on a new and often suitable role. This is very much a year for moving ahead and following up ideas and opportunities. Openings could arise in the first weeks of the Rabbit year, or even just before it, and in April, May and September, but throughout the year, whenever the Snake sees an opportunity, he should act swiftly.

However, while the aspects are encouraging, to do well this year the Snake *will* need to put in the effort and give that little bit more. It will be worth it, for with commitment and good use of his talents, he can find the rewards of the year are substantial.

The progress the Snake makes in his work can also lead to an increase in income, and financially this can be an improved year. To benefit fully, the Snake could find it helpful to spend some time evaluating his financial position, including his outgoings, obligations and borrowings. In some cases a few changes could make a noticeable difference and allow him to put the money he is able to save to better use. This is a year for good financial management.

The Snake's home life will see much activity this year and there will need to be good co-operation and willingness to help one other, especially at busy times. The Snake and others in his household also need to make sure their work and other activities do not make too many incursions into their home life and that quality time together is preserved. With the pressures some Snakes will be under this year, this may be difficult, but it is essential that the Snake sets aside time for sharing with his loved ones. Fortunately many Snakes appreciate the importance of this, but in this active year it is something all need to be aware of.

With travel favourably aspected, the Snake should also consider taking a holiday or going on a short break with his loved ones. The chance to unwind and spend time together can do everyone good.

The Rabbit year also has an aesthetic quality and with the Snake's fine taste, he may well decide to make some enhancements to his home. He will very much enjoy making his choices and seeing his ideas take shape. However while the end result will be pleasing, time does need to be allowed to complete such projects. With everything else that is happening, they could take longer than anticipated.

In view of the pressures of the year the Snake also needs to make sure his social life does not fall off, as it can do him a lot of good. March, April, July, August and December could see the most social activity, with the Snake's work, travels and interests all giving him the chance to meet up with others. For the most part this can bring him much pleasure, but a warning does need to be sounded: an indiscretion or lapse could lead to complications and embarrassment. Snakes, take note. The Rabbit year can cause problems for the unwary.

In most respects the Rabbit year is one of considerable opportunity for the Snake. In particular he will have the chance to make more of his strengths and enjoy some well-deserved success. But this will come at a cost. The pressures will be considerable and the Snake will be kept busy. Over the year it is essential that he balances his lifestyle and preserves time for enjoying his interests, valuing his friends and loved ones and appreciating the rewards he so works hard for. This can be a successful year, but maintaining balance will be key.

The Metal Snake

This can be a satisfying year for the Metal Snake, with many of his activities going well. He can also look forward to some often meaningful times with loved ones and friends.

One of the areas which the Rabbit year particularly favours is personal development. Rabbit years are ideal for study, cultural pursuits and reflection, and over the year the Metal Snake should take the opportunity to further his knowledge and skills, possibly by setting time aside to read, going on courses or taking up the challenge of learning a new skill. By doing something constructive and purposeful, he can not only benefit from his new knowledge but also improve his general well-being.

Metal Snakes who start the year feeling bored or listless or who do not have an interest that particularly inspires them at the moment should make it an early priority to look at possibilities and enquire about locally run courses and other activities. They will be surprised at how a new challenge can revitalize them. Some good friendships can also be made through becoming involved in new interests. March, April, July, August and December could see the most social activity.

In considering new activities, some Metal Snakes may decide to take up keep fit classes in their area or disciplines such as *tai chi*, Pilates or yoga. By following up their ideas, they will benefit from what they do as well as welcome the camaraderie and support that develops with those they meet.

With travel favourably aspected, many Metal Snakes can also look forward to a special holiday over the year and some may choose to mark their seventieth year by travelling to a destination they have long wanted to see. By giving careful thought to any holidays and breaks, they will delight in what they are able to do. Here again this is a year for making and following through plans. Some Metal Snakes will also enjoy visiting places of interest and beauty spots in their area and the spontaneous nature of some of these visits will add to the fun.

This will also be a pleasing year domestically, with family and close friends often keen to celebrate the Metal Snake's seventieth birthday in style. The love and affection he is shown will genuinely touch him and emphasize the important part he plays in the lives of those close to him.

In addition, the Metal Snake will very much appreciate the chances he will have to spend time with others.

Whether this is enjoying mutual interests, tackling home or garden projects, taking advantage of local amenities or attending events, there will be great emphasis this year on doing things with others. Metal Snakes who are grandparents or great grandparents will also take much pleasure in following the progress of younger family members. Their experience and practical outlook could be particularly useful when some relations seek out their advice.

Although 2011 is well aspected, no year is ever free of problems and this will be no exception. If the Metal Snake is troubled by any matter, it is important that he speaks out. He does so much for others that he should allow them the chance to help him in return

Also, when dealing with any financially related paperwork, he should be thorough and careful and attend to matters within the time limits required. To pay scant attention could be to his disadvantage.

He also needs to be careful in any potentially awkward situations. A lapse, risk or indiscretion could cause difficulty. These words only apply to a few Metal Snakes, but do be warned.

For Metal Snakes born in 2001 the Rabbit year holds much promise. Its emphasis is on personal development and with a willing and keen attitude the young Metal Snake can derive much pleasure from what he does, whether in his education or through his personal interests. He will also enjoy the company and support of those around him. The one thing for him to remember is not to go against his better judgement and get carried away by high jinks or activities he has misgivings about. Rabbit years can present difficulties for the risk-taker. Metal

Snakes, be warned, but otherwise enjoy this promising year.

The Rabbit year offers all Metal Snakes, whether born in 1941 or 2001, an excellent chance to enjoy their skills and interests and the positive action they take will help to make this a personally pleasing and beneficial year. And the love and support of others will make the start of this new decade in their life all the more meaningful.

TIP FOR THE YEAR
Enjoy sharing activities with those around you. Their support and encouragement can help you to get far more out of the year. Also consider developing your knowledge and interests or taking up a new activity. This can have considerable benefit.

The Water Snake

The Water Snake is set to do well this year and will be able to make more of certain strengths and enjoy considerable personal success. This can be a rewarding and fulfilling year for him.

To make the most of the prevailing aspects, however, the Water Snake will need to take the initiative. He is very much in the driving seat in the Rabbit year and will be able to determine how he fares. With self-belief and the willingness to put himself forward, he will find his efforts paying off.

In his work he could have particular problems to deal with or be involved in new initiatives and will find his expertise and in-depth knowledge serving him well. This year he will have an excellent chance to prove himself and reap some well-deserved rewards. Many Water Snakes will be able to make important progress in their current place of work and in some cases secure the promotion they have been working towards for some time.

Others, however, will feel ready for change. For these Water Snakes, as well as those seeking work, the Rabbit year can be an important one. By giving careful thought to what they want to do and keeping alert, many will spot an opportunity that intrigues them and offers potential benefits. Sometimes this will be very different from positions they have previously held but will allow them to develop their skills in new ways. Rabbit years can reward Water Snakes well, but it is a case of seizing the initiative. February, April, May and September could see some interesting work developments.

Whether in work or seeking it, the Water Snake can also help his position by working closely with others. Those in work will find that being an active and co-operative team member will not only lead to a greater level of achievement but also help their reputation and standing, while those seeking work or desiring change would do well to contact agencies and others able to advise. This is not a time for the Water Snake to be too independent in attitude. If he is willing to put himself forward and show a certain flexibility, the Rabbit year offers him considerable possibility.

Another area which is favourably aspected is the Water Snake's personal interests. Again this is a year when he can develop his knowledge, skills and ideas. For Water Snakes who are creatively inclined, this can be a particularly satisfying time. Also, if a new activity should appeal to the Water Snake, he should follow it up. The Rabbit year can give him the chance to try out a variety of new pursuits.

For some Water Snakes, their interests can also have some financial benefit, and with the progress that many will make in their work will come an increase in income. However, the Water Snake will still need to manage his finances carefully. In view of his commitments, including assisting family members, and the other plans he may have, he should keep track of his spending and make allowance for more substantial outgoings. He could also benefit from reviewing his general position and attend to tax and other financial matters promptly. This is a year to be thorough, attentive and aware.

In his home life, he can look forward to some special developments. Not only will those close to him encourage his activities and plans, but younger relations could also have important news to celebrate. Domestically, this promises to be a full, interesting and sometimes surprising year.

With travel favourably aspected, the Water Snake will also enjoy any holidays or breaks he takes. There could be some additional travel opportunities towards the end of 2011 or early in 2012.

The Water Snake is well known for his thoughtful and considerate nature and during the year family and friends will often seek out his advice and will set much store by his judgement. Similarly, should he have concerns at any time, it is important that he gives others the chance to reciprocate. This is no year for being too independent or keeping anxieties hidden.

While the year is encouragingly aspected in so many ways, the Water Snake does need to manage his time well. With work pressures and all his other commitments, there will be occasions when he is preoccupied and time spent with others is sacrificed. He does need to watch that this does not work to his detriment. Another potential difficulty to be aware of is that he could become involved in an awkward or embarrassing situation. Rabbit years can sometimes be rife with scandal and rumour and the Water Snake does need to be remain on his guard and avoid lapses or indiscretions. Water Snakes, take note.

With the various activities the Water Snake pursues over the year, he will, however, often have an increasing number of social opportunities. To benefit, he should make the most of these. It is by being active, enjoying time with others and using his qualities to advantage that he can get the most from the year. March, April, July, August and December could be the busiest months socially.

Overall, the Year of the Rabbit has considerable potential for the Water Snake, but it rests with him to put himself forward and to use his skills and ideas wisely. For the active and enterprising, this can be a successful year and will often be made more special by the support and encouragement of others.

TIP FOR THE YEAR
This is a year to have self-belief and put yourself forward. Be bold and enterprising. With willingness and initiative, a lot can open up for you. Also, draw on the support and goodwill of those around you. You have much in your favour this year. Use it well.

The Wood Snake
This will be a year of considerable opportunity for the Wood Snake. However, while it can be successful, it will

also be busy and during it the Wood Snake will need to make sure he keeps his lifestyle in balance. Fortunately he is disciplined and thoughtful and usually maintains a good work–lifestyle balance, but it is something all Wood Snakes need to be aware of during the year.

Domestically, this can be a year of considerable activity. The Wood Snake and those close to him could be involved in changes concerning their work and routine. Sometimes working hours will be different, more commuting will be involved or time may be spent working away from home. Adjustments will need to be made, but with support, understanding and co-operation, new routines will soon take shape and initial pressures be eased.

With this being such a busy year, it is important that the Wood Snake is open and communicative and discusses any ideas he may be considering or concerns he may have. However, mixed in with all the activity will be some special and meaningful occasions. It will also be beneficial for the Wood Snake to set time aside for joint undertakings and enjoy an occasional treat or trip out. In this busy year it is important that quality time with loved ones does not suffer.

This also applies to the Wood Snake's social life. Despite the many demands on his time, he should keep in regular contact with his friends as well as go to events that appeal to him. Not only can his social life be a good way for him to relax and unwind but also give him the chance to meet others and benefit from their advice. March, April, July and December could see the greatest social activity. However, as with other Snakes this year, the Wood Snake needs to make sure that he does not place himself in any awkward or potentially embarrassing situation. Rabbit years can cause problems for the unwary. Wood Snakes, be warned.

It is also important that the Wood Snake preserves time for his recreational pursuits. He could be tempted to drive himself hard and let more pleasurable aspects of life take a back seat, but his recreational activities can do him a lot of good, as they allow him to unwind, relax or just do something different. With the Rabbit year favouring culture, the Wood Snake may also take a greater interest in events and performances held in his area.

In work matters the Rabbit year holds great potential for him. With his expertise and the competence he has shown in recent undertakings, he will be excellently placed to build on his current position. If opportunities are lacking in his current place of work or he feels unfulfilled, he should actively make enquiries and keep alert for other possibilities. For the determined Wood Snake, good progress is possible this year. February, April, May and September could see some interesting developments, but action and initiative can reward the Wood Snake at any time.

The prospects are also encouraging for those Wood Snakes seeking work. While some may have become disillusioned with their situation, by keeping faith with what they know they can do and remaining alert, many could secure a useful opportunity and, once back on the employment ladder, have a base from which to progress.

Work-wise, the Rabbit year will ask a lot of the Wood Snake, especially when taking on and adjusting to a new role, but he will be keen to rise to the challenge and acquit himself well.

The advances many Wood Snakes will make in their career will also bring an increase in income, but to benefit the Wood Snake will need to manage his finances well. Without discipline, any increase could quickly be spent, and where possible the Wood Snake should aim to set funds aside for his commitments and plans rather than proceed on too much of an *ad hoc* basis. Many Wood Snakes will also be involved in some additional family expenses over the year and the more these can be budgeted for in advance, the better.

Overall, the Wood Snake can fare well in the Rabbit year, but it will be a busy 12 months. It can be a time of achievement and progress, but it is essential that the Wood Snake preserves time to share with his loved ones and enjoy the rewards his efforts will bring.

TIP FOR THE YEAR
Value those around you. Their love and support will be of great importance to you this year. Also, despite the often considerable demands on your time, do not neglect your well-being. Give yourself the chance to rest and unwind as well as enjoy recreational pursuits. In this successful year, *do* keep your lifestyle in balance.

The Fire Snake

There is a Chinese proverb which the Fire Snake would do well to bear in mind this year. It is, 'Read and reap the rewards.' By being prepared to further his knowledge and skills, he can make this a constructive and successful year.

At work the Rabbit year can bring some good possibilities. As a result of his recent work the Fire Snake will often be well placed to put in for greater responsibilities. This is very much a year for moving forward in his career. If openings are limited where he is or he feels frustrated in his present role, he should make a determined effort to look elsewhere. With persistence and willingness, many Fire Snakes will be able to make important strides this year and take their work to a new level.

To help this process, it will often be a case of 'read and reap the rewards'. When making an application, if the Fire Snake finds out more about the company and duties involved, his initiative will be noticed and strengthen his application. Similarly, if progress requires him to go on training or refresher courses or study for another qualification, by being prepared to make the effort he can help his present *and* future situation. Even if some studying or courses have to be conducted in his own time, what he does now will be an investment in himself and his future.

This also applies to Fire Snakes who are seeking work. By actively following up vacancies, preparing their applications with care and taking advantage of the support available to them, again including training or other guidance, many will be successful in securing a position that can give them experience in a new area. February, April to early June and September could see some important work developments, but the Rabbit year in general offers the Fire Snake considerable scope, particularly in developing his skills.

With many Fire Snakes taking on new work responsibilities and the pressures this will entail, it is important the Fire Snake does not neglect his well-being. In particular, he should make sure he takes regular and appropriate exercise, especially if his work is sedentary, and that he eats a balanced and nutritious diet. To keep himself in good form he does need to look after himself.

He should also make sure his personal interests do not suffer due to other activities. He needs time to relax and unwind and his recreational pursuits are a source of pleasure as well as often an outlet for some of his talents. With the Rabbit year's emphasis on personal development some Fire Snakes may set themselves a project or personal goal for the year, but whatever the Fire Snake does, by spending time in ways he enjoys, he can get much benefit from his interests over the year.

The progress he makes in his work can also bring an increase in his income, but with the Fire Snake's existing commitments and family and accommodation plans, he will need to manage his finances carefully. Transactions and purchases should not be rushed and the terms of any new agreements carefully checked. This is a year for control and discipline.

The Fire Snake often has a circle of very close friends and during the year will appreciate chances to meet up with them or, if this is not always possible, to be in contact by e-mail or phone. Their friendship and support will mean a great deal to him, especially at times of pressure. Many Fire Snakes will also have the chance to reciprocate by offering advice in turn. In this busy year, the Fire Snake's close friends can prove particularly important to him.

He should also not let the pressures and activities of the year prevent him from going out, as he needs chances to unwind and enjoy himself. Any Fire Snake who is alone or has had some recent personal difficulty can find that a new friendship or romance can add considerable excitement to the year. March, April, July, August and December could see the most social activity. One note of caution does, though, need to be sounded: a lapse or indiscretion could cause great problems. Fire Snakes, do be careful.

The Fire Snake's home life will also see considerable activity during the year. In view of the various commitments of family members, there will need to be good liaison and co-operation. With willingness and understanding, however, pressures can be eased and unexpected benefits can sometimes follow on from all the activity. Whether carrying out improvements on his home, enjoying shared interests or taking an interest in others' activities, the Fire Snake will value the bond he has with those around him and over the year he could give important support to both younger and more senior relations.

Overall, the Rabbit year holds good prospects for the Fire Snake. It is a year to make the most of his strengths. By building on these, the Fire Snake can make good progress. With willingness and determination, he will find that a lot is possible. However, he will be kept busy over the year and it is important that he keeps his lifestyle in balance and gives time to his loved ones, his interests and himself.

TIP FOR THE YEAR
Look to further your skills and interests. This can reward you well, whether in opening up possibilities, bringing you personal satisfaction or giving rise to other benefits. Time and effort invested in yourself now can reap some fine and often long-term rewards.

The Earth Snake

The Earth Snake will have been involved in a lot of change in recent years. Some of this will have gone well for him, but there could also have been disappointments and frustrations. In the Rabbit year his fortunes are set to improve.

Relations with others will be particularly important. For some Earth Snakes, their love for another can add excitement and sparkle to their year, with some significant personal news, decisions or developments in store. For the unattached, Cupid's arrow could strike at any time, with many finding romance and enjoying the love of someone special. Sometimes a romance can start in the unlikeliest of ways but seem as if it is meant to be.

In addition to the important part affairs of the heart will play, the Earth Snake will enjoy the many social opportunities the year can bring. Whether meeting up with friends or getting to know new people through his interests, work or changes in circumstances, he will find his social circle set to increase. Even though some Earth Snakes can be reserved, all Earth Snakes should make the most of their invitations this year. Not only can they enjoy themselves but also benefit from the camaraderie, support and advice others can offer. March, April, July, August and December will be busy months socially as well as being good times for meeting others.

However, while the Earth Snake's social life and relations with others can bring him much happiness, he does still need to be vigilant and avoid placing himself in any awkward or potentially difficult situation. An indiscretion has the potential for being very damaging. Earth Snakes, *do* take careful note.

With some of the decisions the Earth Snake has to take this year, he would also find it of value to talk to close family members rather than keep his thoughts and any uncertainties to himself. If he is forthcoming, others will be better able to understand and help. The Earth Snake himself will often have the chance to reciprocate some of the support he is given by assisting a family member with a certain matter or undertaking. In the Rabbit year his relations with his family can be meaningful and often helpful, but he does need to be willing to listen and contribute.

There will be chances for many Earth Snakes to travel over the year and this will be something the Earth Snake will enjoy planning and look forward to. In addition to any holiday he takes, he will also enjoy any weekends or short breaks away and appreciate some of the varied things he gets to do.

One of the main features of the Rabbit year is that it is a time favouring culture and learning, and the Earth Snake will be excellently placed to benefit. With his enquiring nature and personal ambitions, if he takes advantage of any ways he can add to his knowledge and skills, he can substantially improve his situation and prospects. Those Earth Snakes currently studying for qualifications can make important headway this year and what they learn will have long-term value.

For Earth Snakes in work there will often be scope to increase their role and learn about other aspects of their industry. With willingness and commitment the Earth Snake can not only add to his skills and work experience but also impress more senior colleagues. A key benefit of the Rabbit year is that it will give the Earth Snake an excellent chance to develop and become more established.

For those Earth Snakes seeking work or to change their present role, again the Rabbit year can provide some important openings. Although the economic climate may not always allow them to do exactly what they want, by widening the scope of what they are prepared to consider and showing themselves ready to learn, many will secure what can be a significant opportunity. February, April to early June, and September could see some important developments.

The encouraging nature of the year also applies to the Earth Snake's interests, and by setting time aside for activities he enjoys, he can take much pleasure from them. Creative pursuits could develop in an often exciting manner and if the Earth Snake is able to involve others in what he does or get additional guidance this can add to the pleasure and meaning of his pursuits.

In matters of finance, he will need to keep a watchful eye on his spending. With an often lively social life, the various activities he is keen to pursue, travel plans and other commitments, his outgoings can mount up and need to be managed well. Also, should he have uncertainties over a financial matter at any time during the year, he should seek advice and clarify the terms and implications.

Overall, the Year of the Rabbit can be a busy and personally exciting one for the Earth Snake. Not only will there be excellent opportunities for him to gain important new experience (and sometimes qualifications), but his personal life can bring him a great deal of pleasure. Over the year he should take the initiative and make the most of himself as well as enjoy and further his considerable talents.

Develop your skills and knowledge. This can benefit you now and prepare you for future opportunities. Also, value and enjoy the company and support of those around you. Your relations with others can be especially important. Treasure them.

FAMOUS SNAKES

Muhammad Ali, Ann-Margret, Lord Baden-Powell, Kim Basinger, Ben Bernanke, Björk, Tony Blair, Michael Bloomberg, Michael Bolton, Brahms, Pierce Brosnan, Casanova, Chubby Checker, Jackie Collins, Tom Conti, Cecil B. de Mille, Bob Dylan, Sir Edward Elgar, Sir Alex Ferguson, Sir Alexander Fleming, Mahatma Gandhi, Greta Garbo, Art Garfunkel, J. Paul Getty, Dizzy Gillespie, W. E. Gladstone, Goethe, Princess Grace of Monaco, Stephen Hawking, Audrey Hepburn, Jack Higgins, Liz Hurley, James Joyce, Stacy Keach, Ronan Keating, J. F. Kennedy, Carole King, Courtney Love, Mao Tse-tung, Chris Martin, Henri Matisse, Robert Mitchum, Piers Morgan, Alfred Nobel, Mike Oldfield, Jacqueline Onassis, Sarah Jessica Parker, Pablo Picasso, Mary Pickford, Daniel Radcliffe, Franklin D. Roosevelt, Mickey Rourke, J. K. Rowling, Jean-Paul Sartre, Franz Schubert, Shakira, Charlie Sheen, Brooke Shields, Paul Simon, Delia Smith, Ben Stiller, Taylor Swift, Madame Tussaud, Shania Twain, Dionne Warwick, Charlie Watts, Ruby Wax, Kanye West, Oprah Winfrey, Virginia Woolf.

11 FEBRUARY 1918 ∼ 31 JANUARY 1919   *Earth Horse*

30 JANUARY 1930 ∼ 16 FEBRUARY 1931   *Metal Horse*

15 FEBRUARY 1942 ∼ 4 FEBRUARY 1943   *Water Horse*

3 FEBRUARY 1954 ∼ 23 JANUARY 1955   *Wood Horse*

21 JANUARY 1966 ∼ 8 FEBRUARY 1967   *Fire Horse*

7 FEBRUARY 1978 ∼ 27 JANUARY 1979   *Earth Horse*

27 JANUARY 1990 ∼ 14 FEBRUARY 1991   *Metal Horse*

12 FEBRUARY 2002 ∼ 31 JANUARY 2003   *Water Horse*

THE
HORSE

THE PERSONALITY OF THE HORSE

There are many worn paths,
but the most rewarding
is the one you decide on and forge yourself.

The Horse is born under the signs of elegance and ardour. He has a most engaging and charming manner and is usually very popular. He loves meeting people and likes attending parties and other large social gatherings.

The Horse is a lively character and enjoys being the centre of attention. He has many leadership qualities and is much admired for his honest and straightforward manner. He is an eloquent and persuasive speaker and has a great love of discussion and debate. He also has a particularly agile mind and can assimilate facts remarkably quickly.

He does, however, have a fiery temper and although his outbursts are usually short-lived, he can often say things that he will later regret. He is also not particularly good at keeping secrets.

The Horse has many interests and involves himself in a wide variety of activities. He can, however, get involved in so much that he can often waste his energies on projects that he never has time to complete. He also has a tendency to change his interests rather frequently and will often get caught up in the latest craze or 'in thing' until something more exciting turns up.

The Horse also likes to have a certain amount of freedom and independence. He hates being bound by petty rules and regulations and as far as possible likes to feel that he is answerable to no one but himself. But despite this spirit of freedom, he still likes to have the support and encouragement of others in his various enterprises.

Due to his many talents and likeable nature, the Horse will often go far in life. He enjoys challenges and is a methodical and tireless worker. However, should things go against him and he fail in any of his enterprises, it will take a long time for him to recover and pick up the pieces again. Success to the Horse means everything. To fail is a disaster and a humiliation.

The Horse likes to have variety in life and will try his hand at many different things before he settles down to one particular job. Even then, he will probably remain alert to see whether there are any better opportunities for him to take up. He has a restless nature and can easily get bored. He does, however, excel in any position that allows him sufficient freedom to act on his own initiative or brings him into contact with a lot of people.

Although the Horse is not particularly bothered about accumulating great wealth, he handles his finances with care and will rarely experience any serious financial problems.

The Horse also enjoys travel and loves visiting new and faraway places. At some stage during his life he may be tempted to live abroad for a short period of time and due to his adaptable nature will find that he will fit in well wherever he goes.

The Horse pays a great deal of attention to his appearance and usually likes to wear smart, colourful and rather distinctive clothes. He is very attractive to others and will often have many romances before he settles down. He is loyal and protective to his partner, but despite his family commitments he still likes to retain a certain measure of independence and have the freedom to carry on with his own interests and hobbies. He will find that he is especially well suited to those born under the signs of the Tiger, Goat, Rooster and Dog. He can also get on well with the Rabbit, Dragon, Snake, Pig and another Horse, but he will find the Ox too serious and intolerant for his liking. He will also have difficulty in getting on with the Monkey and the Rat – the Monkey is very inquisitive and the Rat seeks security, and both will resent the Horse's rather independent ways.

The female Horse is usually most attractive and has a friendly, outgoing personality. She is highly intelligent, has many interests and is alert to everything that is going on around her. She particularly enjoys outdoor pursuits and often likes to take part in sport and keep-fit activities. She also enjoys travel, literature and the arts, and is a very good conversationalist.

Although the Horse can be stubborn and rather self-centred, he does have a considerate nature and is often willing to help others. He has a good sense of humour and will usually make a favourable impression wherever he goes. Provided he can curb his slightly restless nature and keep tight control over his temper, he will go through life making friends, taking part in a multitude of different activities and generally achieving many of his objectives. His life will rarely be dull.

THE FIVE DIFFERENT TYPES OF HORSE

In addition to the 12 signs of the Chinese zodiac there are five elements and these have a strengthening or moderating influence on the signs. The effects of the five elements on the Horse are described below, together with the years in which they were exercising their influence. Therefore those Horses born in 1930 and 1990 are Metal Horses, those born in 1942 and 2002 are Water Horses, and so on.

Metal Horse: 1930, 1990
This Horse is bold, confident and forthright. He is ambitious and a great innovator. He loves challenges and takes great delight in sorting out complicated problems. He likes to have a certain amount of independence and resents any outside interference in his affairs. He has charm and a certain charisma, but he can also be very stubborn and rather impulsive. He usually has many friends and enjoys an active social life.

Water Horse: 1942, 2002
The Water Horse has a friendly nature and a good sense of humour and is able to talk intelligently on a wide range of topics. He is astute in business matters and quick to take advantage of any opportunities that arise. He does, however, have a tendency to get easily distracted and can

change his interests – and indeed his mind – rather frequently, and this can often work to his detriment. He is nevertheless very talented and can often go far in life. He pays a great deal of attention to his appearance and is usually smart and well turned out. He loves to travel and also enjoys sport and other outdoor activities.

Wood Horse: 1954

The Wood Horse has a most agreeable and amiable nature. He communicates well with others and is able to talk intelligently on many different subjects. He is a hard and conscientious worker and is held in high esteem by his friends and colleagues. His opinions are often sought and, given his imaginative nature, he can often come up with some very original and practical ideas. He is usually widely read and likes to lead a busy social life. He can also be most generous and often holds high moral views.

Fire Horse: 1966

The element of Fire combined with the temperament of the Horse creates one of the most powerful forces in the Chinese zodiac. The Fire Horse is destined to lead an exciting and eventful life and to make his mark in his chosen profession. He has a forceful personality and his intelligence and resolute manner bring him the support and admiration of many. He loves action and excitement and his life will rarely be quiet. He can, however, be rather blunt and forthright in his views and does not take kindly to interference in his own affairs or to obeying orders. He is a flamboyant character, has a good sense of humour and will lead a very active social life.

Earth Horse: 1918, 1978

This Horse is considerate and caring. He is more cautious than some of the other types of Horse, but is wise, perceptive and extremely capable. Although he can be rather indecisive at times, he has considerable business acumen and is very astute in financial matters. He has a quiet, friendly nature and is well thought of by his family and friends.

PROSPECTS FOR THE HORSE IN 2011

The Tiger year (14 February 2010–2 February 2011) has a certain vitality to it and during it the Horse will have found himself in demand. Over the year many Horses will have seen an increase in social activity as well as been able to make headway in their work and other projects.

In what remains of the Tiger year the Horse will continue to have a lot to do. His social life will remain busy and during the closing months of the year he could get to meet and impress quite a few people, and for the unattached, romantic prospects are promising.

Domestically, there will also be an increase in activity, with often a lot being decided quickly and happening in a short space of time. These can be full and lively months, although the Horse will need to be accommodating over certain arrangements.

With so much happening, this will be an expensive time and the Horse should keep close watch on his spending levels and, if possible, spread out costly or seasonal purchases.

He will have a good chance to benefit from his strengths at this time and by keeping alert for opportunity and following through ideas, whether in his work or personal interests, he will find his initiative and know-how can reward him well. Those Horses currently looking for work should act quickly when they see appropriate vacancies, as an early application will stand many in good stead.

In general, the Tiger year can be a very active one for the Horse and he will often do well.

The Year of the Rabbit begins on 3 February and will be a generally encouraging one for the Horse. With his ability to focus on the things he wants and willingness to put himself forward (the Horse is renowned for his drive and industrious nature), he can fare well, although throughout the year he will still need to keep his wits about him. While the aspects may be on his side, this is not a time for being too independent in his actions or taking undue risks. Horses, take note. The signs are promising, but haste and ill-thought out actions could undermine your prospects.

In his work the Horse could benefit from some interesting and unexpected developments. Often as a result of recent activities, there will be chances for him to move his career forward. Sometimes this could be due to restructuring, new initiatives or promotion possibilities being created as staff leave. Over the year the Horse will often be well-placed to benefit, with his reputation and in-house knowledge helping his prospects. Throughout the year it is also important that he is prepared to adjust to new procedures, adapt his skills and undertake any training required. It will be beneficial for him to watch his sometimes independent tendencies and make the best of his situation *as it is* rather than fretting about how he would like it to be. March, May, September and October could see encouraging work developments, but by keeping alert and informed, the Horse could spot possibilities at almost any time of the year.

The aspects are also encouraging for Horses who are keen to further their experience by moving elsewhere or who are seeking work. Again the Horse will need to be flexible, alert and persistent, but with determination and effort, he may well secure the opportunity he has been seeking. And when it comes, it will be well deserved.

Another important feature of the Rabbit year is that it will give the Horse the chance to gain new skills and experience. Whether this comes through new responsibilities he is given or other opportunities, by making the most of the chance to learn, the Horse will not only find himself accomplishing more but also prepare himself for new possibilities, including some that will arise in the closing months of the Rabbit year.

The Horse's progress at work can also lead to a modest rise in income, but he will need to manage his finances with care. When considering more expensive purchases he would do well to take the time to consider various possibilities, and should he be borrowing, check the terms and obligations carefully. He should also be disciplined when he is out and about. Too many impulse purchases can mount up, and in his often active social life he could be tempted to spend far more than intended. Financially, this can be a reasonable year, but it requires good control over the purse-strings.

The Horse has always been able to fill his time wisely and in the Rabbit year there will be no shortage of things he will want to do. He will derive much pleasure from his interests, especially those that take him out of doors or allow him to use his skills. In addition quite a few Horses could take on an interest-related role this year. Those who are members of a society or group could be asked to do more and some could decide to serve their community in some way, perhaps helping a charity or other cause. Many a Horse has a caring and public-spirited nature and during the Rabbit year will become more active and involved in community activities.

Many Horses will also give some thought to their well-being over the year, with some deciding to start a new fitness regime or make dietary improvements.

The Horse can also look forward to a rewarding social life, with May, June, August, September and December particularly busy months. There will be plenty of opportunities to get to know new people, although for the unattached, the path of true love may not always run smooth. Sometimes romance may flounder or different outlooks lead to a drifting apart. Rather than build up high expectations in the early stages of a new romance, it would be better for the Horse to show patience and let things develop naturally. Some Horses can find happiness this year and others despair. Those in an existing relationship will find that by being willing to support each other and share activities, they can often strengthen their bond, but new romances are likely to be more problematical.

The Horse's home life can, however, be a source of much happiness to him. Some Horses could see an addition to their family this year or have reason to celebrate a particular achievement. Although the Horse will often be involved in his own activities and commitments, if he makes sure time is preserved for sharing with his loved ones, this will be helpful for understanding and rapport as well as give everyone involved a sense of satisfaction.

Generally, the Year of the Rabbit will be a pleasant and constructive one for the Horse. In his work he will often have the chance to add to his experience and take on greater responsibilities, and what he achieves now can prepare him for further success in following years. He will also find his personal interests and recreational activities bringing him satisfaction, while on a personal level he will be much in demand. Both his home and social life will be active and by joining with others, he can make a lot happen. Overall this is a year of fine personal development and it rests with the Horse to remain active and build on his many strengths.

The Metal Horse

This will be an eventful year for the Metal Horse and while not all his plans may develop as anticipated, over the year some important opportunities can open up for him. This is a year to be alert, flexible *and* show commitment.

For Metal Horses currently in education this will be a significant year. Not only will they be giving much time and attention to their studies but also consideration to their future. Some could already have identified specific career areas, while those who are undecided will find that tutors and advisers could be particularly helpful in making suggestions. Some significant decisions can be made during the Rabbit year.

Although a lot of pressure will be placed on the Metal Horses currently studying, by remaining disciplined and using their time well they can derive much personal and future benefit from what they do.

In addition, the Rabbit year can open up other possibilities. There could be clubs, groups and recreational facilities available to the Metal Horse which are not only fun but sometimes also an outlet for other talents. Those whose interests are creative can find this an inspiring time, with their talents often being recognized and encouraged. The Rabbit year holds great promise for the Metal Horse and during it he should make the most of the opportunities available.

For those Metal Horses in work the Rabbit year can bring excellent opportunities to develop their skills and working knowledge and move on to greater responsibilities. The Rabbit year offers considerable scope to the Horse and it is very much a case of showing commitment and being prepared to put himself forward. Many Metal Horses in work could find themselves being encouraged by more senior figures and advised of possibilities or career paths to consider. During the year the Metal Horse will impress quite a few and benefit accordingly.

For Metal Horses seeking work it will be very much a case of remaining persistent and flexible. With fierce competition for certain jobs, the Metal Horse will need to stress his experience, strengths and desire to learn. Securing a position may not be easy, but once the Metal Horse has a foothold on the employment ladder and demonstrates his potential, other possibilities can follow on. March, May and September to early November could see some important work developments, but at any time the Metal Horse could be surprised by how quickly and favourably one of his applications works out.

Over the year, however, he could face some large expenses. These could be connected with travel, purchasing equipment needed for interests or work, or accommodation, socializing and transport. With careful budgeting the Metal Horse will be generally pleased with all he is able to do, but this is a year for keeping strict control over the purse-strings.

The Rabbit year will also see an increase in social activity, with the Metal Horse finding himself in great demand, with parties to go to and opportunities to spend time with friends. The Rabbit year can be an often lively and enjoyable one, although affairs of the heart may not always proceed smoothly. At the start of any new romance it would be best for the Metal Horse to be patient and see how it develops rather than build up high expectations in the early stages. If it is to endure, at least that way each will have had the chance to get to know the other at leisure and without undue pressure. May, June, August, September and December could be the busiest months socially.

The Horse has an adventurous nature and quite a few will be tempted to travel over the year. The more this can be planned and budgeted in advance, the more the Metal Horse will be able to do while away.

As with other Horses, the Metal Horse cherishes his independence and is not always the most forthcoming when talking about concerns or decisions he may be considering. However, in the Rabbit year he should make every effort to overcome his reticence. By discussing his options with family and close friends, he will not only benefit from the support and advice offered but also help rapport and understanding. In his home life, if he is able to help with certain household activities and, in some cases, assist someone who is experiencing difficulty, his thoughtfulness will be particularly appreciated. For many Metal Horses their home life this year can also have some special moments, including celebrations held to mark their twenty-first birthday.

Overall, the Rabbit year holds great promise for the Metal Horse and will give him the chance to make more of his strengths and further his knowledge. With commitment and self-belief, he can not only benefit from current opportunities but also prepare himself for future success. He will also take great pleasure in pursuing his interests and social life and even though the path of true love may not always run smooth, in the main this will be an encouraging and personally rewarding year.

TIP FOR THE YEAR

Give some thought to your future. Suggestions that are made now and opportunities that arise can have considerable long-term value. Also, develop the special talents you have, particularly those connected with your personal interests. These can give you much pleasure as well as offer some personal benefit.

The Water Horse

The Water Horse will appreciate the more settled nature of the Rabbit year. Rather than feeling fraught or pressured by a great deal of activity, he can enjoy a greater sense of contentment.

His home life can be particularly meaningful and by being open and communicative, he could set some interesting plans in motion. Whether these involve adding new comforts or making home improvements, the Water Horse and those close to him will enjoy making their choices and the benefits that follow on. Water Horses who have gardens will also take pleasure in being outdoors and in what they grow.

The Water Horse will also enjoy sharing various activities, whether joint interests or trips out. If there are places in his locality he has been meaning to visit or activities he has considered trying out, this is a year to follow up his ideas. Positive action, preferably with others, can reward him well.

He will also take a fond interest in the activities of family members and will often give time to helping those with young children. In addition he may well be thrilled by some family developments. With Water as his element, he is a talented communicator and over the year family members will often appreciate his thoughts, views and conversational talents. While much will go well, should any misgivings or concerns arise, if the Water Horse addresses these and, if appropriate, seeks advice, helpful solutions can often be found and problems eased. Here again openness and sharing can be to the benefit of all.

There will also be some good chances for the Water Horse to travel this year. In addition to visiting local attractions and places of interest, he could be tempted by some attractive offers and will often enjoy what he gets to do. The Rabbit year can be a particularly satisfying one for him, especially as ideas take shape and opportunities open up.

With his enquiring nature the Water Horse takes an interest in a great many things and during the year may well decide to learn about a new subject or develop a particular skill. If so, he could quickly become absorbed by what he does. Those Water Horses who feel it would be beneficial to take more exercise or improve their diet will find that by seeking advice they can benefit from the positive changes they make.

A lot that the Water Horse does over the year will also have a good social element, including his travels and the interests he pursues. Those Water Horses who are members of a local group could find themselves invited to do more, while other Water Horses may help a charity or campaign for a cause. For any Water Horse who is feeling lonely, perhaps having moved to a new community or seen other changes in their circumstances, this is very much a year to become more involved in locally run activities and pursue interests which will bring him into contact with others. Positive action will reward these Water Horses well, but the initiative does rest with them. May, June, August, September and December could be particularly busy months socially.

The Water Horse can also enjoy some positive financial developments this year, perhaps being eligible for additional benefits or allowances, receiving a gift, or benefiting from the fruition of a policy. With the plans and hopes he has for the year, anything extra will be welcome. However, he does need to take his time when considering purchases and attend to financial paperwork with care. He should also seek advice on anything that is unclear. With care, good advice and a bit of luck, though, financially this can be an improved year.

Overall, the Rabbit year holds good prospects for the Water Horse. With his keen and enquiring nature, he will enjoy a lot of what he sets out to do. His domestic and social life can be a source of considerable pleasure, and his interests, whether existing or new, can be satisfying as well as often bring him other benefits. This is very much a year for seizing his opportunities and appreciating what is available to him.

TIP FOR THE YEAR
Enjoy the moment. Actively follow up your ideas, plans and hopes. With a willing attitude and the support of others, you can make this a satisfying and personally pleasing year. Use it well.

The Wood Horse

The Wood Horse will have experienced a lot in recent years. There will have been personal successes and times which have meant a great deal, but also setbacks, pressures and disappointments. As the Rabbit year starts, a great many Wood Horses can draw a sigh of relief. This will be a more settled year and one that will bring some good opportunities. It is also a time for focusing on the present and near future rather than being held back by disappointment or regret.

As the year begins, the Wood Horse could find it helpful to give some thought to what he wants to do during it. With something definite to work towards, he will not only be able to use his time and energies more effectively but also be more likely to benefit from luck and serendipity. Purposeful action can and *will* reward him this year.

One area which can be especially rewarding is his own personal development. This is very much a year for building on his knowledge and strengths. Whether setting time aside for study, enrolling on a course or deciding to take up a new interest, by doing something definite the Wood Horse will feel he is not only benefiting personally from his actions but also moving himself forward in some way.

In thinking over his plans, he may also consider home and garden projects, personal aims he could set himself (perhaps relating to diet, exercise and general lifestyle balance) or what he may be hoping to achieve work-wise. Whatever he decides to do, by setting himself some objectives, he will be able to get far more out of the year.

In his work the Rabbit year can bring some interesting developments. For the many Wood Horses who are well established in a particular career, the Rabbit year will offer the chance to build on their expertise, perhaps through being given new objectives. Here the Wood Horse's background and skills will be a great asset. While he may be proficient in a certain area, he should also keep himself informed of developments affecting his work as well as be willing to learn new techniques or adapt to changes. With commitment and a certain flexibility, he can make steady progress throughout the year.

For Wood Horses who are seeking work, either at the start of the Rabbit year or during it, events could take a sometimes curious course. By keeping alert and widening the scope of what they are prepared to consider, many of these Wood Horses could benefit from an unexpected opportunity, perhaps securing a position they did not anticipate being offered or being alerted to one by chance.

What they are presented with may involve quite a bit of learning and adjustment, but the Wood Horse will be determined to make the most of the chance to prove himself in new ways. The Rabbit year will require effort and commitment, but the opportunities it brings can be significant. By remaining alert and persistent, the Wood Horse could uncover possibilities at almost any time during the year, but March, May and September to early November could see some particularly interesting work developments.

The progress the Wood Horse makes at work can also help him financially and many Wood Horses will increase or be able to supplement their earnings over the year. However, to benefit, the Wood Horse will need to keep a close watch on his spending and ideally set funds aside for specific requirements. With control and discipline, he can improve his position, but good management is required. He should also deal with financial paperwork carefully and promptly. A delay or oversight could be to his disadvantage. Wood Horses, take note. In financial matters, discipline is very much the order of the year.

The Rabbit year can be a personally satisfying one for the Wood Horse and the time he spends on his interests can bring him considerable pleasure. This is an excellent year for developing ideas and skills, and some Wood Horses could also benefit from joining a local group of enthusiasts or going to events or exhibitions. The Rabbit year will bring many possibilities.

There will also be some good travel opportunities for the Wood Horse during the year, some arising at short notice. By taking advantage of these, he will often enjoy his time away. Here again, some early planning in the first few months of the year could be helpful.

Another factor in the Wood Horse's favour this year will be the support he receives from others. Not only can friends and relations sometimes alert him to possibilities or make useful suggestions, but he will also welcome the lively conversations and good times that will be had. May, June, September, December and early January could see the most social activity.

This will also be a busy and rewarding year in the Wood Horse's home life. Again, a lot can be gained by planning activities in advance, and whether these concern practical projects, travel plans or general hopes for the year, if thoughts and ideas are talked through, more will be agreed upon and ultimately happen. As the Chinese proverb states, 'Well begun is half done,' and making plans early on in 2011 could be especially helpful.

Throughout the year the Wood Horse will also do much to help and advise others, although there will be occasions when he will speak candidly (the Wood Horse has never been one to skirt round issues). Despite this, his judgement will be recognized and appreciated. In addition, some assistance he is able to give certain relations will be of more value than he may realize. Domestically, this will be a full and often personally gratifying year.

Overall, the Year of the Rabbit holds encouraging prospects for the Wood Horse, but to make the most of the prevailing aspects he does need to decide on his aims and priorities and act accordingly. With good planning and use of his time and energy, he can achieve a great deal.

Decide on what you want to get out of the year and make plans. With something to work towards, you can achieve far more this year and your positive actions can also make this a personally rewarding time.

The Fire Horse

The dynamic nature of the Fire element combined with energy of the Horse makes the Fire Horse an active and influential figure. Never one to do things by half, he is bold, enterprising and keen to make the most of himself. This year he can fare well, although he will need to temper the excesses of his sometimes exuberant nature. This is no year for rush, haste or impulsive action, but for steady and persistent effort.

At work there may be some interesting developments. Although many Fire Horses will be content in their present position, the Rabbit year can bring significant change. As colleagues move on or internal reorganization takes place, the Fire Horse could find his duties changing and be offered the chance to take on greater responsibilities. Some of what happens may not be what the Fire Horse was anticipating, but by being willing to adapt and learn, he can not only gain valuable new experience but also be able to prove himself in new ways.

Throughout the year he should aim to work closely with colleagues as well as be willing to put forward ideas and suggestions. By being actively involved, he can not only make his work more fulfilling and improve his results, but also emphasize his strengths. Initiative will reward many a

Fire Horse this year. All Fire Horses should also make the most of their chances to network. This can be to both their present and future advantage.

One of the main benefits of the Rabbit year will be the chance it will give the Fire Horse to add to his skills and strengths. This will often come as a result of new duties he takes on, but he can also benefit by considering learning new skills or reading up on subjects that appeal to him. Some Fire Horses may be tempted to enrol on a course or consider working towards another qualification, and this can often bring personal satisfaction as well as potential gain.

For Fire Horses who are feeling staid in their present role and consider their prospects limited, as well as those seeking work, the Rabbit year can again take an interesting course. By talking to friends and contacts, registering with employment agencies and seeking advice, many of these Fire Horses could identify other ways in which they could use their experience. With an open mind and the willingness to take on new challenges, they could secure a position which will have scope for future development. Work-wise, the Rabbit year is an encouraging one, with March, May, September, October and January 2012 presenting some particularly good opportunities.

Although many Fire Horses lead an active lifestyle, it could also be worth the Fire Horse giving some consideration to his general level of exercise and diet over the year. If he feels either could be improved, he should seek medical advice on the best way to proceed. A few changes may make a noticeable difference, especially to energy levels.

With his wide variety of interests and activities, the Fire Horse will come into contact with many people this year and may make some firm friendships. May, June, August, September and December could be particularly busy months. For the unattached, new romance will need to be nurtured carefully. Rush or high expectations in the early stages can lead to disappointment. Fire Horses, do take note and let any new romance develop in its own time and without pressure or haste.

The Fire Horse will also see considerable activity in his home life and for those who are parents, there could be anxious moments as younger relations prepare for important exams or take decisions affecting their future. Although the Fire Horse respects their independence, any encouragement and assistance he can give will make an important difference. When pressures or problems arise, a willingness to talk these through can help everyone concerned. Amid all the activity of the year, the Fire Horse should also make sure that time is set aside for enjoying shared interests and activities. Some spontaneous occasions could be particularly appreciated.

In money matters the Fire Horse will need to remain vigilant. Although his progress at work can lead to an increase in income, his commitments and many activities will mean his outgoings are relatively high and will need to be monitored carefully. This is a year for good management. Also, the Fire Horse should be wary of entering into agreements without checking the full implications or succumbing to too many impulse buys. Haste can result in unnecessary expense and sometimes inferior purchases. Fire Horses, do take note.

Although the Rabbit year may lack the activity of some, it can be a constructive one for the Fire Horse. Developing his knowledge, skills and interests will be personally gratifying and helpful both now and in the near future. He will also benefit from being forthcoming and liaising with others. Overall, a positive year with some far-reaching benefits.

TIP FOR THE YEAR

Use opportunities to build on your skills and knowledge and take on new challenges. By adapting and moving yourself forward you can get a lot out of the year as well as open up other possibilities for the future.

The Earth Horse

The Earth Horse has a keen and enterprising nature and in the Rabbit year his earnest approach can serve him particularly well. This may not be a time for major breakthroughs, but it can be a constructive and personally valuable one.

A key feature of the Rabbit year is that it is a time when many Earth Horses will give some thought to their current situation and ways of improving it. With their future aspirations, some may consider the time is right to obtain a further qualification, while others may be keen to take a particular interest or recreational pursuit further. Whatever the Earth Horse would like to do, he should look at ways in which he can move forward, whether by study, practice or setting himself a new objective. Earth Horses who have creative interests could see them develop in an encouraging manner. This is very much a year for the Earth Horse to make more of his talents.

Any Earth Horse who has let his personal interests lapse in recent years due to other demands on his time should aim to rectify this early on in the Rabbit year. He could either pick up a former interest or start something new, but with purposeful use of some of his free time, he can gain much personal value from his activities.

If the Earth Horse's current lifestyle does not afford him much regular exercise, it could also be worth him considering a new fitness discipline, or perhaps activities such as cycling, swimming or extra walking. By obtaining appropriate advice on the best way to proceed, he can find the measures he takes can benefit him as well as sometimes be fun.

A factor in the Earth Horse's favour this year will be the support and encouragement he receives from family, friends and colleagues. In some cases new interests could lead to new friendships or have a pleasing and unexpected social element. For the unattached, romantic possibilities can arise suddenly, although any romance does need to develop in its own time, without pressure or undue expectations. For many Earth Horses it may be best to enjoy the present and see what happens. May, June, August, September and December could see the most social activity.

In his work situation the Rabbit year can see some important developments. Changes may be introduced which affect the Earth Horse's working patterns, and although he may have some misgivings, by keeping informed about what is being introduced, he will be better prepared. Also, what happens during the year can give him the chance to further his skills. Some of the Rabbit year may be personally demanding, but it can be productive and have long-term value as far as his career is concerned.

For Earth Horses who are seeking work or keen to make a change, again the Rabbit year will often bring the opportunity to use their skills in new ways. By looking at various possibilities and talking to agencies and contacts, they could find interesting suggestions being made and possibilities opening up. Some of these Earth Horses may decide to get a new qualification, while others may consider retraining or switching to a different industry or type of work altogether, but the emphasis this year is on development and many will benefit from what they are able to learn. They should also use any chances they have to build up contacts as well as take an informed interest in their new company and, where appropriate, industry. What opens up for many Earth Horses this year can have long-term significance, and a good start will help their subsequent development. March, May, September, October and January 2012 could see some important work developments.

The advances many Earth Horses make at work this year can also lead to an increase in income, although they will need to be disciplined in their spending and make early and adequate provision for plans and major expenses. The better the Earth Horse can control his outgoings, the more he will ultimately get to enjoy.

He can also look forward to a busy and rewarding home life. During the year many an Earth Horse's household will enjoy some pleasing developments. The Earth Horse himself will often play a key role in domestic affairs, although he should make sure everyone does their fair share around the house and he does not shoulder too much single-handedly. Similarly, if he has any concerns, he should be forthcoming, as with the help of others, tensions can often be defused and problems solved. In this busy year, co-operation and good communication will be key.

Overall, the Year of the Rabbit offers considerable scope for the Earth Horse and by embracing it and seizing his opportunities, he stands to gain a great deal. It is a year in which to broaden his skills and give some thought to his lifestyle – an interesting and fulfilling time.

tip for the year
Seize the moment. Develop your skills and strengths and move forward. This is a year of considerable scope and what you do now can have long-term benefits.

FAMOUS HORSES

Roman Abramovich, Neil Armstrong, Rowan Atkinson, Ingmar Bergman, Leonard Bernstein, Joe Biden, James Blunt, Helena Bonham Carter, David Cameron, James Cameron, Jackie Chan, Ray Charles, Chopin, Sir Sean Connery, Billy Connolly, Kevin Costner, Cindy Crawford, James Dean, Clint Eastwood, Chris Evans, Harrison Ford, Aretha Franklin, Bob Geldof, Samuel Goldwyn, Billy Graham, Gene Hackman, Rolf Harris, Rita Hayworth, Jimi Hendrix, Janet Jackson, Calvin Klein, Lenin, Annie Lennox, Pixie Lott, Sir Paul McCartney, Nelson Mandela, Angela Merkel, Michael Moore, Ben Murphy, Sir Isaac Newton, Louis Pasteur, Katie Price (Jordan), Dennis Quaid, Gordon Ramsay, Lou Reed, Rembrandt, Helena Rubenstein, David Schwimmer, Martin Scorsese, Barbra Streisand, Kiefer Sutherland, Patrick Swayze, John Travolta, Kathleen Turner, Vivaldi, Robert Wagner, Denzel Washington, Emma Watson, Billy Wilder, Andy Williams, Brian Wilson, Jacob Zuma.

1 FEBRUARY 1919 ⁓ 19 FEBRUARY 1920   *Earth Goat*

17 FEBRUARY 1931 ⁓ 5 FEBRUARY 1932   *Metal Goat*

5 FEBRUARY 1943 ⁓ 24 JANUARY 1944   *Water Goat*

24 JANUARY 1955 ⁓ 11 FEBRUARY 1956   *Wood Goat*

9 FEBRUARY 1967 ⁓ 29 JANUARY 1968   *Fire Goat*

28 JANUARY 1979 ⁓ 15 FEBRUARY 1980   *Earth Goat*

15 FEBRUARY 1991 ⁓ 3 FEBRUARY 1992   *Metal Goat*

1 FEBRUARY 2003 ⁓ 21 JANUARY 2004   *Water Goat*

THE
GOAT

THE PERSONALITY OF THE GOAT

Amid the complexities of life,
it is the ability to appreciate that is so special.

The Goat is born under the sign of art. He is imaginative, creative and has a good appreciation of the finer things in life. He has an easy-going nature and prefers to live in a relaxed and pressure-free environment. He hates any sort of discord or unpleasantness and does not like to be bound by a strict routine or rigid timetable. He is not one to be hurried against his will, but despite his seemingly relaxed approach to life, he is something of a perfectionist and when he starts work on a project he is certain to give his best.

The Goat usually prefers to work in a team rather than on his own. He likes to have the support and encouragement of others and if left to deal with matters on his own he can get very worried and tend to view things rather pessimistically. Wherever possible he will leave major decision-making to others while he concentrates on his own pursuits. If, however, he feels particularly strongly about a certain matter or has to defend his position in any way, he will act with great fortitude and precision.

The Goat has a very persuasive nature and often uses his considerable charm to get his own way. He can, however, be rather hesitant about letting his true feelings be known and if he were prepared to be more forthright he would do much better as a result.

The Goat tends to have a quiet, somewhat reserved nature, but when he is in company he likes he can often become the centre of attention. He can be highly amusing, a marvellous host at parties and a superb entertainer. Whenever the spotlight falls on him, his adrenaline starts to flow and he can be assured of giving a sparkling performance, particularly if he is allowed to use his creative skills in any way.

Of all the signs in the Chinese zodiac, the Goat is probably the most gifted artistically. Whether it is in the theatre, literature, music or art, he is certain to make a lasting impression. He is a born creator and is rarely happier than when occupied in some artistic pursuit. But even in this he does well to work with others rather than on his own. He needs inspiration and a guiding influence, but when he has found his true *métier*, he can often receive widespread acclaim and recognition.

In addition to his liking for the arts, the Goat is usually quite religious and often has a deep interest in nature, animals and the countryside. He is also fairly athletic and there are many Goats who have excelled in some form of sporting activity or who have a great interest in sport.

Although the Goat is not particularly materialistic or concerned about finance, he will find that he will usually be lucky in financial matters and will rarely be short of the necessary funds to tide himself over. He is, however, rather self-indulgent and tends to spend his money as soon as he receives it rather than make provision for the future.

The Goat usually leaves home when he is young but he will always maintain strong links with his parents and the other members of his family. He is also rather nostalgic and is well known for keeping mementoes of his childhood and souvenirs of places that he has visited. His home will not be particularly tidy, but he knows where everything is and it will be scrupulously clean.

Affairs of the heart are particularly important to the Goat and he will often have many romances before he finally settles down. Although he is fairly adaptable, he prefers to live in a secure and stable environment and he will find that he is best suited to those born under the signs of the Tiger, Horse, Monkey, Pig and Rabbit. He can also establish a good relationship with the Dragon, Snake, Rooster and another Goat, but he may find the Ox and Dog a little too serious for his liking. Neither will he care particularly for the Rat's rather thrifty ways.

The female Goat devotes all her time and energy to the needs of her family. She has excellent taste in home furnishings and often uses her considerable artistic skills to make clothes for herself and her children. She takes great care over her appearance and can be most attractive to others. Although she is not the most organized of people, her engaging manner and delightful sense of humour create a favourable impression wherever she goes. She is also a good cook and usually derives much pleasure from gardening and outdoor pursuits.

The Goat can win friends easily and people generally feel relaxed in his company. He has a kind and understanding nature and although he can occasionally be stubborn, he can, with the right support and encouragement, live a very satisfying life. And the more he can use his creative skills, the happier he will be.

THE FIVE DIFFERENT TYPES OF GOAT

In addition to the 12 signs of the Chinese zodiac there are five elements and these have a strengthening or moderating influence on the signs. The effects of the five elements on the Goat are described below, together with the years in which they were exercising their influence. Therefore those Goats born in 1931 and 1991 are Metal Goats, those born in 1943 and 2003 are Water Goats, and so on.

Metal Goat: 1931, 1991

This Goat is thorough and conscientious in all that he does and is capable of doing very well in his chosen profession. Despite his confident manner, he can be a great worrier and he would find it helpful to discuss his concerns with others rather than keep them to himself. He is loyal to his family and employers and will have a small group of particularly close friends. He has good taste and is usually highly skilled in some of aspect of the arts. He is often a collector of antiques and his home will be very tastefully furnished.

Water Goat: 1943, 2003

The Water Goat is very popular and makes friends with remarkable ease. He is good at spotting opportunities but does not always have the necessary confidence to follow them through. He likes to have security both in his home life and work and does not take kindly to change. He is articulate, has a good sense of humour and is usually very good with children.

Wood Goat: 1955

This Goat is generous, kind-hearted and always eager to please. He usually has a large circle of friends and involves himself in a wide variety of activities. He has a very trusting nature but he can sometimes give in to the demands of others a little too easily and it would be in his interests if he were to stand his ground more often. He is usually lucky in financial matters and, like the Water Goat, is very good with children.

Fire Goat: 1967

This Goat usually knows what he wants in life and often uses his considerable charm and persuasive personality to achieve his aims. He can sometimes let his imagination run away with him and has a tendency to ignore matters that are not to his liking. He is rather extravagant in his spending and would do well to exercise a little more care when dealing with financial matters. He has a lively personality, many friends, and loves attending parties and social occasions.

Earth Goat: 1919, 1979

This Goat has a considerate and caring nature. He is particularly loyal to his family and friends and invariably creates a favourable impression wherever he goes. He is reliable and conscientious in his work but sometimes finds it difficult to save and never likes to deprive himself of any little luxury he might fancy. He has numerous interests and is often very well read. He usually derives much pleasure from following the activities of the various members of his family.

PROSPECTS FOR THE GOAT IN 2011

The Tiger year (14 February 2010–February 2011) is fast paced and for many a Goat can be an unsettling time. With increased pressures and sudden changes, parts of the year can be demanding and in the remaining months there will be little let up in the activity.

In his work the Goat will need to remain on his mettle and concentrate on the tasks and often considerable challenges before him. Progress will not be easy and his situation could be compounded by delays, problems or the unhelpful attitude of those around him. But while this can often be a pressurized time, the qualities the Goat can demonstrate and the experience he gains can prepare him for the opportunities soon to emerge. September and November could see some interesting developments, including for those Goats seeking work, and pleasingly the Goat's prospects will enjoy a noticeable improvement in the next Chinese year.

With the closing months of the year being a generally more expensive time, he should, however, keep watch over his spending and be wary of risk or buying too much on impulse.

His domestic and social life are both set to become busier at this time, but while the Goat will very much enjoy the activities that take place, including the chance to spend time with some people he does not often see, he will need to remain flexible. The Tiger year is no respecter of rigid timetables and plans could be subject to sudden change. However, sometimes spontaneity can bring extra meaning and the Goat will often enjoy himself as well as play a full part in what goes on.

The Year of the Tiger is never the easiest of years for the Goat, but as it draws to a close his prospects will brighten considerably.

The Year of the Rabbit starts on 3 February and ushers in a much more positive time for the Goat. After the pressures and vexations of the previous Ox and Tiger years, there will now be more opportunity for him to make progress at work as well as enjoy pleasing developments in his personal life. The Rabbit year is an encouraging one and a time to concentrate on the present and make the most of opportunities.

Throughout the year the Goat will benefit from the support and goodwill of others and whenever he is considering possibilities or has decisions to make, it would be worth discussing his options with those who are able to advise. Sometimes just the process of talking will help the Goat to clarify in his own mind what it is best for him to do.

He can also benefit through meeting new people and over the year will have the chance to widen his social circle and make some good friends. In some cases those he meets will be in a similar situation to his own and there will be a natural rapport and understanding.

For Goats who would welcome company or new friends, this is very much a year for going out more and perhaps joining social groups or taking part in activities in their area. By taking positive action these Goats will soon get to meet others and may bring a sparkle to their life that has been missing in recent years. For the unattached, this can be a wonderful year for finding romance, while for those newly in love, this can be a blissful and heady time, with many settling down together or marrying. For relations with others, the Rabbit year can be exciting and meaningful, and the Goat can enjoy considerable personal happiness. February, April, July and September could see the most social activity, but such are the aspects that opportunities to meet others could occur at almost any time.

The Goat's home life is also likely to see much activity over the year and many a Goat household will be faced with alterations to domestic routines and arrangements. Here co-operation and some flexibility will be needed. However, Goats are likely feel inspired this year and be keen to make changes to their home, and the projects the Goat sets himself will bring a great deal of pleasure to all concerned, although the actual process could take longer and involve more effort than anticipated.

In addition to the benefits any home improvements may bring, the Goat will appreciate sharing activities and interests with his loved ones over the year. Once again his input can be the driving force behind a lot that happens, with some of his suggestions leading to some fine family occasions. His home life may not only be rewarding this year but there could be the additional excitement of a new family member or a celebration, anniversary or special birthday to mark.

The Goat's work prospects are also promising and for those Goats who feel unfulfilled or are seeking work, the Rabbit year can bring some excellent opportunities. However, in his quest for a new position, the Goat should not act alone. Through seeking advice, he could be alerted to possibilities, vacancies or options he may not have been aware of. Also, when applying for a position, if he finds out about the company and duties involved, he can make his application more relevant and likely to be noticed. Securing a position will take persistence, but the Goat's keen nature, talents and potential will shine through and he may well be successful in gaining a position that will often be in welcome contrast to what he has previously been doing. March, May, October and November could see some good opportunities.

For Goats who are established in a particular career, again the Rabbit year offers the chance to make progress, although to benefit these Goats will need to actively promote themselves. If not, opportunities could slip by. Unfortunately it is a temptation for some Goats to coast along and remain in their comfort zone, but this is not the way for them to fulfil their potential. In the progressive Rabbit year, they should put themselves forward.

The Goat's progress at work can also lead to an increase in income and financially this can be an improved year. As a result, the Goat will often decide to go ahead with certain home purchases and plans and by keeping alert could be particularly fortunate in finding items that meet his requirements perfectly. His eye for quality, taste and value will be in excellent form this year. However, at all times he should heed his instincts and if any financial matter causes concern or doubt, check the details and implications.

Although the aspects are generally favourable for the Goat this year, he should not neglect his well-being. To keep himself in good form he does need to pay attention to his diet and take appropriate exercise, and if he has a succession of particularly busy days followed by late nights, he does need to allow time to catch up on sleep. To drive himself too hard or not take adequate care could leave him prone to minor ailments. In addition, if he is involved in strenuous or hazardous activities, he needs to follow the correct procedures. Where his well-being is concerned, this is a year for care.

In most respects the Rabbit year is a positive and encouraging one for the Goat. It is, though, a time for action. In 2011 the Goat needs to believe in himself and take the initiative. He can benefit from the support of others and will enjoy the social opportunities that arise and, in many cases, the love of another, but he does need to act. This is a promising and personally rewarding year for him.

The Metal Goat

The element of Metal gives the Goat added determination. The Metal Goat knows he has it in him to accomplish a great deal and will be keen to get this new decade in his life off to a promising start. And his abilities will serve him well. This is a positive year with some good times and personal success ahead.

The Metal Goat can look forward to a full and often lively social life. With his circle of friends, there will be parties and events to enjoy and interests and news to share. Some Metal Goats may also travel with friends, and socially this promises to be an active and pleasurable year. Those who move to a new area because of their work or education will find this gives them the opportunity to build up a new social circle and, in the process, make what will become long-standing friends. The year is also favourable for romance, with many who are unattached feeling the effects of Cupid's arrow. A chance encounter could develop in a meaningful way and affairs of the heart add excitement to the year. Such are the aspects that some Metal Goats could settle down with a partner or start a family. February to April, July and September will see the greatest amount of social activity and personally this can be a special year.

Although the Metal Goat will often be immersed in his own activities, throughout the year it is important that he speaks openly about his activities, hopes and plans, and draws on the advice and support of those around him. Whether parents or other close relations, they not only have his best interests at heart but valuable experience behind them and in some matters could give suggestions or mention implications the Metal Goat may not have considered. Also, during the year he could himself have occasion to offer help and so demonstrate his thoughtful and caring side.

Where his personal interests are concerned, this is very much a year to develop ideas and skills. Whether the Metal Goat prefers more physical and outdoor activities or creative and expressive pursuits, by using his time well, he can gain a great deal of personal satisfaction from what he does.

For any Metal Goat who has thoughts of taking an interest or skill further, perhaps even to a professional level, it would be worth seeking the guidance of an expert. This can be a significant year for the Metal Goat, but opportunities do need to be grasped and suggestions acted upon.

This also applies to those Metal Goats who are studying for qualifications. Although the Rabbit year will bring its distractions (especially socializing), by being disciplined and focused on his studying, the Metal Goat can look forward to making major strides. As a result of what he learns, he may find himself revising his ideas about what he wants to do. The Rabbit year can open up ideal possibilities and, as some Metal Goats will find, existing plans and intentions do not need to be set in stone, particularly as more appropriate ways ahead are uncovered or new opportunities emerge.

Metal Goats in education should also take advantage of the facilities available to them at their place of learning, whether clubs, extra tuition, advice centres or equipment. With their future aspirations, what they can do now can prepare them for the possibilities that lie ahead.

With a busy social life, the possibility of travel and the range of other activities he carries out, there will be many temptations for the Metal Goat to spend money this year and he should be disciplined with his finances and make sure he sets sufficient funds aside for specific requirements. This is a year for good budgeting.

For Metal Goats in work or seeking work, this is also a year of important developments. Although some may feel their work is routine and not always fulfilling, change is on the way. By keeping alert for opportunities, many will be given the chance to take on greater responsibilities. Commitment and initiative will be recognized and well rewarded this year. Should opportunities be lacking where they are, these Metal Goats should actively look elsewhere. They will often find their existing position and experience a valuable platform to build on. The Metal Goat's efforts and self-belief can make his twentieth year an important one with long-term benefits.

Metal Goats who are seeking work should be persistent as well as draw on the advice and help available to them. By putting in the effort, especially in making their applications relevant, they will find that doors *will* open for them. March, May and mid-September to November could see some important work developments, with the Rabbit year giving many Metal Goats the opportunity to make headway and show their potential.

The Year of the Rabbit not only marks the start of a new decade in the Metal Goat's life but can have far-reaching value. This is a time for putting in the effort and making the most of opportunities. With willingness and perseverance, the Metal Goat can do his prospects a lot of good. Personally, the Rabbit year can be special for him, with a busy social life, new friendships and perhaps romance. He will have a lot in his favour and this is a year in which to take action *and* enjoy himself.

TIP FOR THE YEAR
With so much happening, do keep your lifestyle in balance. Enjoy your personal interests and social opportunities, but

do not let them distract you from work or studying. In this favourable year focus and self discipline will reward you and help you to make more of your considerable potential.

The Water Goat

This will be a pleasing and settled year for the Water Goat and, after the pressures of more recent years, be one he will very much appreciate. Many of his plans and activities will proceed in an encouraging way and the Rabbit year can bring some interesting opportunities.

One of the Water Goat's main strengths is his creativity. Not only does the Water element help make him an effective communicator but he also possesses great imagination and over the year he will often take the opportunity to explore some of his ideas. For the many Water Goats who enjoy creative pursuits, including art, writing, music or craftwork, these can not only absorb them this year, but in some cases also generate considerable praise. Rabbit years favour creativity and this will suit many a Water Goat well.

The Water Goat will also find this an inspiring time and, in addition to enjoying his creative interests, will often be keen to look into different activities and subjects. Sometimes these will be an extension of what he already does, but new pursuits can also hold much appeal. Whenever the Water Goat has an idea or sees something that intrigues him, he should follow it up. With the Rabbit year favouring culture, some Water Goats could take particular delight in visiting places of historic interest as well as going to exhibitions and events. Again, acting on his ideas can bring the Water Goat much personal pleasure.

Some of his activities will also be good ways to meet others and his social life can enjoy a noticeable upturn this year. Water Goats who are alone, especially those who have experienced personal difficulties in recent years, will find that by going out more and joining others in various activities, their actions, together with their fine ability to communicate and connect, can lead to some important new friendships. The Water Goat's relations with others are superbly aspected this year. For a few, the Rabbit year can also bring romance. February, April, July and September could see the most social activity.

The Water Goat can also look forward to a full and interesting home life. As always, he will follow the activities of his loved ones with great fondness, though he may also worry over certain problems they may have. The Water Goat has great empathy, and while this is valuable in so many situations, it can sometimes be a burden. However, he should take heart, knowing that his concern, time and support are of genuine value to those he cares for. Over the year, younger relations in particular will be very grateful to him.

However, while the aspects are encouraging, as with any year, problems can still arise. At such times the Water Goat would do well to resolve them quickly rather than ignore them or let them linger on unresolved. For all his fine qualities, the Water Goat's capriciousness does not always help matters and over the year he will need to be careful not to annoy others with his indecisiveness or frequent changes of mind.

Financially, he can enjoy some luck during the year and may well receive a gift or something extra from another source. In addition he could be particularly fortunate in some purchases. His observant nature will serve him well in spotting special offers and other bargains. Some Water Goats may also be able to put a profitable hobby or idea they have to good use. However, the Water Goat should not be lax in dealing with important paperwork, including insurance renewals, or keeping receipts and guarantees safe. This may be a good year financially, but it is not one for carelessness or inattention.

Overall, the Water Goat will find the Rabbit year a satisfying one. It is a time for him to use his ideas and talents, with creative pursuits particularly well aspected. The affection and goodwill he enjoys will also help him a great deal, as well as make the year all the more pleasurable.

TIP FOR THE YEAR
Set your plans in motion. With action, support and your various skills, you will find that a lot can work out favourably for you.

The Wood Goat
The Rabbit year can mark a shift in fortunes for the Wood Goat. After the pressures and uncertainty of recent years, this can be a more encouraging and hopeful time. And although some Wood Goats may start the year feeling despondent, this is very much a time for concentrating on the present *and* acting in a determined fashion. With resolve, support and some of the opportunities soon to arise, this can be an interesting year.

In work matters the Rabbit year will see some important developments. For the many Wood Goats who are well established in their career, the Rabbit year can offer the chance to become involved in more specialist duties or new undertakings. Although this could involve considerable adjustment, it could also offer new incentives and be a welcome change from their present role. This is very much a year for keeping alert for opportunities and acting on those that appeal.

For Wood Goats who feel there is a limited scope where they currently are, as well as those seeking work, the Rabbit year can again be a time of interesting developments. By making enquiries and exploring possibilities, these Wood Goats could discover other ways in which they could use their skills. For some, the Rabbit year can take their work in a new direction. Making headway will require effort, persistence and self-belief, but the Rabbit year will give many Wood Goats the opportunity they have been wanting for some time.

Also, whether the Wood Goat remains with his present employer or is seeking a new position, over the year he should make the most of his communication skills. Not only is he creative but he can be very effective in putting himself and his ideas across.

March, May, October and November could see some encouraging work developments and, as many Wood Goats will find, when possibilities open up, events can move surprisingly quickly.

The progress the Wood Goat makes in his work can also help him financially. Many Wood Goats will also benefit from some additional funds or bonuses. Although anything extra will be welcome, the Wood Goat will need to remain disciplined and manage his finances well. This is a year when good control can make a considerable difference.

Over the year the Wood Goat could be tempted by some travel opportunities and, where possible, he should follow these up. A change of scene can do him considerable good.

Another beneficial aspect of the year will be his personal interests. By exploring his ideas, furthering his knowledge and setting himself some rewarding projects, the Wood Goat can gain a lot from what he does and the opportunities, whether social or otherwise, that follow on.

With his amiable nature the Wood Goat enjoys excellent relations with many people and over the year will see an upturn in his social life, with many activities and special occasions to look forward to. For some, new friendships can add something extra to this already promising year, with the first quarter of the year and July and September seeing the most social activity.

The Wood Goat's domestic life will be busy, with some personal and family successes to enjoy. However, with so much activity there will need to be good liaison and co-operation, and flexibility over some arrangements would be helpful. This is no year for the Wood Goat to risk undermining rapport through moments of intransigence or capriciousness. Wood Goats, take note. With thoughtfulness and good communication, however, this will be a full and rewarding year domestically.

Overall, the Rabbit year is an encouraging one for the Wood Goat, but it does require him to be firm in his intentions and go after what he wants. To profit from the opportunities that will come his way he needs to be bold and sometimes come out of his comfort zone. He should also have faith in his ideas and promote them. With willingness and effort, this can be a pleasant and rewarding time for him.

TIP FOR THE YEAR

Be active. A lot can open up for you this year, and with determination, you can make good progress. Also, enjoy your interests and value your relations with others. Both are valuable and precious aspects of your life.

The Fire Goat

Many Fire Goats will have felt hindered in recent years. Not only will they have had to cope with what may have seemed never-ending pressure, but there could also have been some disappointments. However, the Rabbit year can mark a change in fortune, with some hopes being realized and events turning the Fire Goat's way. This is a year of opportunity and some often significant developments.

One of the most important aspects of the Rabbit year will be the opportunity the Fire Goat will have to make more of his particular strengths. Finally he will have the chance to grow, develop and show some of his true potential. Personally, too, this is a time for moving forward and making the headway that may have eluded him in recent times.

In his work the Fire Goat could benefit from some particularly good opportunities. Whether hoping to secure promotion as colleagues leave or applying for positions which will give him more scope and responsibility, he should keep alert and look to advance. With determination and the willingness to adapt and learn, many Fire Goats can make important progress this year and take their work to a new level.

In his quest to better himself, the Fire Goat will often find colleagues and contacts helpful, either in giving advice, alerting him to possibilities or providing references and recommendations. One of the Fire Goat's talents is his ability to get on well with people and now is the time for his recent good work to be recognized and rewarded. In addition, his resourcefulness will be an important asset. Not only may he see possibilities which others have overlooked, but some of his ideas and input will impress others and help his prospects. The Rabbit year will give him an excellent chance to use his strengths to good and often telling effect.

This also applies to those Fire Goats seeking work. Although the process can be wearying and often disheartening, this is very much a time for the Fire Goat to have faith and persist. His resourcefulness and strengths can shine through and he may well benefit from an opportunity that arises almost by chance or from deciding to take his career in a different direction. Important doors can open for many a Fire Goat this year, and with determination and self-belief, these Fire Goats can make advances which can have future potential. March, May, October and November could see some significant work developments but such are the aspects that when the Fire Goat sees an opportunity or has an idea he considers worth exploring, he should waste no time. Work-wise, the Rabbit year holds great promise.

The progress the Fire Goat makes at work can also help his income, and financially this can be a much improved year. Some Fire Goats may also be able to supplement their income by putting an interest to profitable use or using a skill in some way. Again the Fire Goat's enterprise and resourcefulness can help. However, he will still need to manage his finances carefully. Without control, spending levels could creep up and during the year the Fire Goat should take the time to plan more substantial purchases and avoid rush or buying on impulse. Where possible, he should also set funds aside for travel. Going to an interesting destination (which need not be too far away) can do him good.

Although the Fire Goat usually keeps himself active, it is also important that he pays attention to his well-being over the year. To be neglectful of diet or exercise could leave him prone to minor ailments or lacking in energy. Fire Goats, do take note.

Also, while the Fire Goat will often be kept busy with his various commitments, he should make sure his interests and recreational pursuits do not get sidelined. These can be beneficial and many Fire Goats will take especial pleasure in more creative activities as well as those that take them out of doors.

With his excellent people skills, the Fire Goat has a wide range of friends and acquaintances, and his social life is favourably aspected this year. He will often enjoy going out and value the friendship and support of others. February, April, July and September could see the most social activity. For the lonely, or those who have recently moved to a new area or have neglected their social life of late, this part of their life can take on new meaning this year, with chances to meet others, join social groups and in some cases find new love. Personally, the Rabbit year holds pleasing prospects for the Fire Goat.

In his home life this will also be a full and eventful year. For Fire Goats who are parents there could be some important decisions, with some children changing school or making choices affecting their education. The advice and encouragement the Fire Goat is able to give will be important and appreciated. In addition to helping younger family members, many Fire Goats could assist more senior relations, and here again their help will be valued. Over the year the Fire Goat will find himself in demand, juggling a great many things and doing a lot for his loved ones. But although this will be a busy time, his home life and the rapport he has with others will mean a great deal to him.

In general, the Rabbit year offers much scope and promise for the Fire Goat, and by making the most of his ideas, opportunities and strengths he can not only make good headway but also enjoy a more satisfying and pleasurable time. This is a year for venturing forward and reaping some well-deserved rewards.

TIP FOR THE YEAR
Believe in yourself and know that you can accomplish a great deal this year. With resolve, backed by your skills and resourcefulness, you can make things happen. Also value your relations with those who are dear to you. You will play an important part in their lives this year and they in yours. Overall, a positive and constructive year.

The Earth Goat
This will be an exciting year for the Earth Goat, with important developments in several areas of his life.

Rabbit years favour relations with others and for many Earth Goats this can be a happy and significant year. Some will become parents or see an addition to their family, while those with young children will often delight in their progress. By giving time to those he loves, the Earth Goat can look forward to many wonderful shared moments.

He will also enjoy the plans he carries out with those around him and the way ideas and hopes take shape. For many Earth Goats, these will relate to improvements to their accommodation. Where décor and furnishings are concerned, the Earth Goat's eye for quality and style will be a real asset. Some Earth Goats may move to accommodation which better suits their requirements and will delight in setting up their new home and stamping it with their personality. Domestically, this can be a busy but potentially exciting year.

The Earth Goat can also look forward to a lively social life. His interests, work and existing social circle can all lead to him meeting others and making new friends and acquaintances. For the unattached, romantic prospects are strong, with many Earth Goats meeting their future partner this year. Where relations with others are concerned, this can be a special year. February, April, July and September could see the most social activity, although at most times of the year the Earth Goat will have something to look forward to.

For any Earth Goat who has had personal difficulties in recent years and is currently alone, this is a time to draw a line under what has gone before and concentrate on the present. By going out, becoming involved in new interests and being prepared to move on in life, these Earth Goats will find that new doors can open for them and new friendships be made. The Rabbit year is supportive of the Earth Goat and during it he should make the most of himself and his opportunities.

Being born under the sign of art, many Earth Goats have a strongly imaginative nature. In the Rabbit year they should use and promote their talents, and those whose work is in any way expressive could enjoy some pleasing success. Any projects the Earth Goat sets himself or skills he chooses to learn can not only be satisfying but also often beneficial in other ways.

The Earth Goat should also give some consideration to his well-being this year. With a busy lifestyle, long days and, if a parent, disturbed nights, he could find he is more susceptible to colds and minor ailments than usual and not always at his best. To avoid this, he should make sure he has a healthy diet and sufficient exercise and allows himself time to catch up on rest when necessary. Also, if carrying out any hazardous activity, he needs to take precautions and follow guidelines.

In his work the Rabbit year can open up some interesting possibilities. Although many Earth Goats will now be well established in a particular line of work, new opportunities could arise. In his existing place of work the Earth Goat could be encouraged to take on new responsibilities and gain experience in another area. This could bring considerable change and readjustment, but at the same time give the Earth Goat new goals and incentive.

There will also be some Earth Goats who feel the time is now right to make a change and are tempted by opportunities elsewhere. Here again the positions these Earth Goats take on could be different from what they have done before and could ask a lot of them. However, they will also often allow them to make more of their skills and specialist knowledge and this will be something they will appreciate.

The Rabbit year is an encouraging one and many Earth Goats will make important progress during it. Late February, March, May, October and November could see some interesting work developments.

For Earth Goats who are seeking work, the Rabbit year is a time of opportunity and new starts. By considering a wide range of possibilities and being open to advice, quite a few Earth Goats will secure a new position that is considerably different from those they have previously held. Importantly, this can not only give these Earth Goats experience in a new area but also introduce them to a type of work which can open up future possibilities for them. For the willing and determined, this can be a significant year as far as their future direction is concerned.

The progress made at work can also help the Earth Goat's income, although with his accommodation plans and personal expenses (especially if he becomes a parent or has a young family), he will need to remain disciplined and manage his budget well. Large purchases need to be carefully thought through and the terms and obligations checked. This is a year to be thorough and to make early provision for outgoings wherever possible.

Overall, the Year of the Rabbit will be a full and personally exciting one for the Earth Goat. It will give him the opportunity to make good headway and develop his skills and can also see some great personal and family times, with news and successes to share and exciting plans to realize. In so many ways, this is a year to move forward *and* enjoy.

Be positive, bold and believing. There is much you can achieve this year. Look for opportunities to develop your skills and put yourself forward. With initiative and determination, you will find a lot can open up for you. Also, enjoy your relations with others. Personally, this can be a rich and wonderful time.

FAMOUS GOATS

Pamela Anderson, Jane Austen, Daniel Bedingfield, Jenson Button, Lord Byron, Coco Chanel, Mary Higgins Clark, Nat 'King' Cole, Jamie Cullum, Robert de Niro, Catherine Deneuve, Charles Dickens, Ken Dodd, Sir Arthur Conan Doyle, Umberto Eco, Douglas Fairbanks, Will Ferrell, Dame Margot Fonteyn, Jamie Foxx, Noel Gallagher, Bill Gates, Mel Gibson, Whoopi Goldberg, Mikhail Gorbachev, John Grisham, Oscar Hammerstein, George Harrison, Billy Idol, Julio Iglesias, Sir Mick Jagger, Norah Jones, Nicole Kidman, Sir Ben Kingsley, Matt le Blanc, John le Carré, Doris Lessing, Franz Liszt, James McAvoy, Sir John Major, Michelangelo, Joni Mitchell, Rupert Murdoch, Randy Newman, Des O'Connor, Sinead O'Connor, Michael Palin, Eva Peron, Pink, Marcel Proust, Keith Richards, Julia Roberts, Nicolas Sarkozy, Philip Seymour Hoffman, William Shatner, Gary Sinise, Jerry Springer, Lana Turner, Mark Twain, Rudolph Valentino, Vangelis, Barbara Walters, John Wayne, Fay Weldon, Bruce Willis.

20 FEBRUARY 1920 ～ 7 FEBRUARY 1921 *Metal Monkey*

6 FEBRUARY 1932 ～ 25 JANUARY 1933 *Water Monkey*

25 JANUARY 1944 ～ 12 FEBRUARY 1945 *Wood Monkey*

12 FEBRUARY 1956 ～ 30 JANUARY 1957 *Fire Monkey*

30 JANUARY 1968 ～ 16 FEBRUARY 1969 *Earth Monkey*

16 FEBRUARY 1980 ～ 4 FEBRUARY 1981 *Metal Monkey*

4 FEBRUARY 1992 ～ 22 JANUARY 1993 *Water Monkey*

22 JANUARY 2004 ～ 8 FEBRUARY 2005 *Wood Monkey*

THE
MONKEY

THE PERSONALITY OF THE MONKEY

The more open to possibility,
the more possibilities open.

The Monkey is born under the sign of fantasy. He is imaginative, inquisitive and loves to keep an eye on everything that is going on around him. He is never backward in offering advice or trying to sort out the problems of others. He likes to be helpful and his advice is invariably sensible and reliable.

The Monkey is intelligent, well read and always eager to learn. He has an extremely good memory and there are many Monkeys who have made particularly good linguists. The Monkey is also a convincing talker and enjoys taking part in discussions and debates. His friendly, self-assured manner can be very persuasive and he usually has little trouble in winning people round to his way of thinking. It is for this reason that he often excels in politics and public speaking. He is also particularly adept in PR work, teaching and any job that involves selling.

The Monkey can, however, be crafty, cunning and occasionally dishonest, and he will seize any opportunity to make a quick profit or outsmart his opponents. He has so much charm and guile that people often don't realize what he is up to until it is too late. But despite his resourceful nature, he does run the risk of outsmarting even himself. He has so much confidence in his abilities that he rarely listens to advice or is prepared to accept help from anyone. He likes to help others but prefers to rely on his own judgement when dealing with his own affairs.

Another characteristic of the Monkey is that he is extremely good at solving problems and has a happy knack of extricating himself (and others) from the most hopeless of positions. He is the master of self-preservation.

With so many diverse talents the Monkey is usually able to make considerable sums of money, but he does like to enjoy life and will think nothing of spending his money on some exotic holiday or luxury he has had his eye on. He can, however, become very envious if someone else has what he wants.

The Monkey is an original thinker and despite his love of company, he cherishes his independence. He has to have the freedom to act as he wants and any Monkey who feels hemmed in or bound by too many restrictions will soon become unhappy. Likewise, if anything becomes too boring or monotonous, the Monkey will soon lose interest and turn his attention to something else. He lacks persistence and this can often hamper his progress. He is also easily distracted, a tendency that he should try to overcome. By concentrating on one thing at a time, he will almost certainly achieve more in the long run.

The Monkey is a good organizer and even though he may behave slightly erratically at times, he will invariably have a plan at the back of his mind. On the odd occasion when his plans do not work out, he is usually quite happy to shrug his shoulders and put it down to experience. He will rarely make the same mistake twice and throughout his life he will try his hand at many different things.

The Monkey likes to impress and is rarely without followers or admirers. Many are attracted by his good looks, his sense of humour, or simply because he instils so much confidence.

Monkeys usually marry young and for it to be a success their partner must allow them time to pursue their many interests and indulge their love of travel. The Monkey has to have variety in his life and is especially well suited to those born under the sociable and outgoing signs of the Rat, Dragon, Pig and Goat. The Ox, Rabbit, Snake and Dog will also be enchanted by his resourceful and outgoing nature, but he is likely to exasperate the Rooster and Horse, and the Tiger will have little patience with his tricks. A relationship between two Monkeys will work well – they will understand each other and be able to assist each other in their various enterprises.

The female Monkey is intelligent, extremely observant and a shrewd judge of character. Her opinions are often highly valued and, having such a persuasive nature, she invariably gets her own way. She has many interests and involves herself in a wide variety of activities. She pays great attention to her appearance, is an elegant dresser and likes to take particular care over her hair. She can be a doting parent and will have many good and loyal friends.

Provided the Monkey can curb his desire to take part in everything that is going on around him and concentrate on one thing at a time, he can usually achieve what he wants in life. Should he suffer any disappointment, he is bound to bounce back. He is a survivor and his life is usually both colourful and eventful.

THE FIVE DIFFERENT TYPES OF MONKEY

In addition to the 12 signs of the Chinese zodiac there are five elements and these have a strengthening or moderating influence on the signs. The effects of the five elements on the Monkey are described below, together with the years in which they were exercising their influence. Therefore those Monkeys born in 1920 and 1980 are Metal Monkeys, those born in 1932 and 1992 are Water Monkeys, and so on.

Metal Monkey: 1920, 1980

The Metal Monkey is very strong-willed. He sets about everything he does with dogged determination and often prefers to work independently rather than with others. He is ambitious, wise and confident, and is certainly not afraid of hard work. He is very astute in financial matters and usually chooses his investments well. Despite his somewhat independent nature, he enjoys attending parties and social occasions and is particularly warm and caring towards his loved ones.

Water Monkey: 1932, 1992

The Water Monkey is versatile, determined and perceptive. He also has more discipline than some of the other Monkeys and is prepared to work towards a particular goal rather than be distracted by something else. He is not always open about his true intentions and when questioned can be particularly evasive. He can be sensitive to criticism but also very persuasive and usually has little trouble in getting others to fall in with his plans. He has a very good understanding of human nature and relates well to others.

Wood Monkey: 1944, 2004

This Monkey is efficient, methodical and extremely conscientious. He is also highly imaginative and is always trying to capitalize on new ideas or learn new skills. Occasionally his enthusiasm can get the better of him and he can get very agitated when things do not quite work out as he had hoped. He does, however, have a very adventurous streak and is not afraid of taking risks. He also loves travel. He is usually held in great esteem by his friends and colleagues.

Fire Monkey: 1956

The Fire Monkey is intelligent, full of vitality and has no trouble in commanding the respect of others. He is imaginative and has wide interests, although sometimes these can distract him from more useful and profitable work. He is very competitive and always likes to be involved in everything that is going on. He can be stubborn if he does not get his own way and he sometimes tries to indoctrinate those who are less strong-willed than himself. He is a lively character, attractive to others and most loyal to his partner.

Earth Monkey: 1968

The Earth Monkey tends to be studious and well read, and can become quite distinguished in his chosen line of work. He is less outgoing than some of the other types of Monkey and prefers quieter and more solid pursuits. He has high principles, a very caring nature and can be most generous to those less fortunate than himself. He is usually successful in handling financial matters and can become very wealthy in old age. He has a calming influence on those around him and is respected and well liked. He is, however, especially careful about whom he lets into his confidence.

PROSPECTS FOR THE MONKEY IN 2011

Tiger years are active and although the Monkey likes to keep himself busy, during this one (14 February 2010–2 February 2011) he will need to be careful. Plans need to be thought through and this is no time for risk.

In what remains of the Tiger year the Monkey should proceed cautiously. Although he tends to be self-reliant, he should aim to consult others and be adaptable in approach. To be stubborn or too self-willed could undermine what he is hoping to do.

In his work he should keep himself informed of all that is going on around him, work closely with colleagues and be an active member of any team. With willingness and co-operation he can do his reputation and prospects a lot of good. For quite a few Monkeys, September to November could see interesting work developments.

With some of the pressures the Monkey may be under, it is also important he takes good care of his well-being. This includes allowing himself rest after busy periods and paying attention to his diet and level of exercise. If he is able, taking a break or holiday in the closing months of the year can do him a lot of good.

He should also keep his lifestyle in balance, including making the most of the social opportunities the year end can bring. Setting quality time aside for loved ones and taking a full part in family activities can lead to some particularly fine occasions. With awareness, co-operation and a desire to make the most of the moment, the Monkey can get a lot out of this time.

The Year of the Tiger does require the Monkey to be on his mettle but, resourceful and adaptable as he is, he will be able to fit a lot into the closing months and build on his achievements in the encouraging Rabbit year that follows.

The Year of the Rabbit begins on 3 February and will be a favourable one for the Monkey. During it he will be able to make far more of his personal talents and find many of his plans progressing well. This is a year of opportunity, with the Monkey often benefiting from the chances that come his way. For any Monkeys who have been concerned by developments during the Tiger year, this is a much more promising time and one when they should look to move on rather than feel hindered by what has gone before.

The Monkey's work prospects are especially favourable. Over the year his experience, ideas and contacts can serve him well and this, backed by his canny sense, can lead to some notable triumphs.

To benefit from the prevailing aspects, the Monkey will need to be active and take the initiative. One of his strengths is his innovative nature and whenever he has ideas he feels could benefit his situation, he should give these serious thought and look at ways in which they could be developed. Also, if his work is in any way creative, he should make the most of his talents. For many Monkeys this can be an inspiring time and their ideas and input favourably received.

With the knowledge the Monkey has built up, he may well be ideally placed for some of the opportunities that become available over the year. As more senior colleagues move on, some excellent promotion possibilities could arise or other changes could take place that will allow the Monkey to develop his talents in a new way. Work-wise, the Rabbit year can present some excellent chances and by putting himself forward the Monkey stands to benefit.

Many Monkeys will have the chance to progress with their current employer but for those seeking work or keen to move elsewhere, the Rabbit year can again open up important possibilities. By considering the type of work they would now like to do, these Monkeys could have some ideas which could indicate a way forward. Securing a new position may not be easy (it rarely is), but with a willingness to take on new challenges, the Monkey may be rewarded with a new and more fulfilling role. This is a progressive and encouraging time when the Monkey's approach, ideas and personable nature can lead to a lot opening up for him. March, April, October and November could see some important developments, but throughout the Rabbit year the

Monkey would do well to remember the proverb, 'Nothing ventured, nothing gained.' Fortune really will favour the bold, creative and enterprising Monkey this year.

In addition to the encouraging prospects concerning his work situation, the Monkey's interests are favourably aspected. For those Monkeys who enjoy creative and expressive pursuits, this is again an excellent year for enjoying their talents. Projects they set themselves can be especially satisfying and often lead on to other possibilities.

Another area which many Monkeys will give attention to will be their home. They will often feel inspired to make changes and will take pleasure in considering various possibilities and appreciating the improvements that follow. Some may decide to move altogether. This is very much a year for action and the Monkey will relish the chance to put his ideas into practice.

During the year he will also be supported by others, and by sharing his decisions and hopes, he will not only benefit from the encouragement given but also the advice and assistance offered. Although he will have his own definite views, by consulting others and being mindful of their feelings, he can make his relations with those around him all the better – and all more beneficial to him. He will also take pleasure in the activities of those around him and the year will certainly bring some good news and special occasions to enjoy. Also, so many Monkeys likely to be involved in change this year, whether related to accommodation or work, the more this can be talked through, the better for all. Domestically, this can be a fine and eventful year.

With all the activity of the year, the Monkey is likely to be more selective in his socializing than usual. However, while he will often be busy, he should still keep in regular contact with his friends and, if tempted by invitations or events, do his best to go. April to June, September and December could see the most social activity. Monkeys who are alone and would welcome new friendships, romance or a more fulfilling social life will find that pursuing their interests can turn out to be an excellent way to meet others. For a lucky few, romance can make this already promising year even more special.

The progress the Monkey makes at work can also help his income, but with some of the purchases he is keen to make, whether personally or for his home, he should take his time and keep alert for special offers or wait for favourable buying opportunities. He could be especially fortunate with some of his purchases, with his talent for spotting items in the most unusual of places leading to some ideal buys.

Overall, the Rabbit year can be a fine and encouraging one for the Monkey. It will give him the chance to benefit from his strengths and move his situation forward. His ideas and resourceful approach can also lead to more opening up for him. He will also value the support of those around him and delight in sharing ideas and activities. This is a positive year for him and by putting himself forward and seizing his opportunities, he can make this a successful and pleasing time.

The Metal Monkey

The Metal Monkey is set to do well this year. With his ability to gauge situations, relate to others and apply the skills he has built up over the years, he will not only be able to profit from some excellent opportunities but also experience a greater sense of fulfilment. This is a year for moving forward and enjoying considerable personal success.

Throughout the year the Metal Monkey will be assisted greatly by those around him, sometimes in ways he may not always be aware of. Whenever he has important decisions to make, he should talk to those whose judgement he values. Although he does like to keep his own counsel, this is very much a year when he needs to be forthcoming and seek advice and support.

In his home life he can look forward to some especially meaningful times and the time he gives to others can not only help his domestic life to be more special but also lead to more happening. There will be some fine occasions to enjoy and many a Metal Monkey household could see an addition to the family this year.

The Metal Monkey will also value some of the good and long-standing friendships he has. Again, friends will be supportive and can help with decisions or activities the Metal Monkey is keen to carry out. Shared interests can bring a great deal of pleasure, and for any Metal Monkey who moves to a new area, their interests can be an excellent way to meet others and build up a new social circle. Late March to June and September could see the most social activity.

For Metal Monkeys who are currently alone the Rabbit year can bring considerable change. This not only includes the possibility of some changing their accommodation (accommodation matters do figure strongly in Rabbit years) but some will fall in love, settle down with a partner or marry. A lot is set to happen in 2011, with the Metal Monkey's relationships with others making this a special and frequently exciting time.

Another favourably aspected area is the Metal Monkey's own personal development. Although he will have many demands on his time, he should aim to set regular time aside to further his interests and skills. This could be through attending a course, setting himself a challenge or trying out a new activity, but by doing something purposeful the Metal Monkey can often get much personal value from his interests over the year.

For the creatively inclined, this can be an inspiring time and if any Metal Monkey has aspirations to take a particular interest or skill further, this is very much a year when he should take what he does to a new level, including bringing his work to the attention of others. The Rabbit year very much favours creative endeavour.

This can also be an important year work-wise, and for any Metal Monkeys whose work is creative, it can be a particularly productive time. Over the year the Metal Monkey should make the most of his strengths and knowledge, including promoting his ideas as well as putting himself forward for promotion should the opportunity arise. With willingness, experience and his fine reputation, he can make excellent headway.

For Metal Monkeys who are seeking work or who feel there are limited prospects where they are, this is again a year of excellent possibility. By keeping alert, making enquiries and following up ideas, many will secure the chance they have been seeking. It may require effort and persistence, but their ability to seek out possibilities can prove especially useful and what opens up this year can shape their career and prospects for the next few years.

Another positive aspect of the year is the chance the Metal Monkey will have to develop particular skills, and as a result he may well feel more fulfilled in what he does. March, April, October and November could see some interesting work developments.

With the Metal Monkey's relations with others so favourably aspected this year, he should also make the most of his opportunities to network and meet others. His manner, ideas and skills will impress many. Again, the more active he is, the better he will fare.

His progress at work can also help him financially, but with accommodation matters highlighted and increased family and personal expenses, he will need to keep careful control over his spending. When considering particular purchases, he could also make savings by keeping alert for special offers rather than proceeding too hurriedly. Financially, this is a year for discipline.

Although this will generally be a positive time, no year is ever free from problems and 2011 will be no exception. When difficulties arise, the Metal Monkey does need to talk them through rather than keep them to himself. Also, events can work in curious ways. Sometimes certain applications will not go the Metal Monkey's way or his ideas will be rejected, but this will allow him to reconsider his approach or find something better. This is a year to remain active and retain self-belief.

Overall, the Year of the Rabbit is one of considerable possibility, and by using his strengths and ideas to advantage, the Metal Monkey can make good progress and achieve some deserving success. His personal life can be a source of much happiness and his interests and relations with others will also mean a great deal to him.

TIP FOR THE YEAR
Use your strengths and opportunities. This is a year for progress and one rewarding initiative and creativity. You have much in your favour, but you do need to act determinedly. Also enjoy your relations with others. Their love and support can inspire you.

The Water Monkey

This will be an exciting year for the Water Monkey and will give him the chance to explore possibilities as well as enjoy some great personal times. What he does now can influence the course of the next few years, sometimes more, and by making the most of this time, he will be investing in his future.

For Water Monkeys in education this can be an especially rewarding year. Many will particularly welcome the opportunity to specialize in areas which really interest them and with their willingness to learn and apply themselves, these Water Monkeys can make great strides. For those on creative courses, this can be an inspiring time and they will be encouraged to make more of their ideas and talents.

Although the majority of Water Monkeys will be absorbed in their education, there will, however, be some who are uncertain and disillusioned. They may feel they have chosen the wrong course or not be happy with their place of study. Rather than remain miserable and be unable to give their best, these Water Monkeys should re-evaluate their situation and speak to those with the experience and knowledge to help. Sometimes they could be advised of more suitable courses or alerted to other possibilities. With expert guidance, sometimes early mistakes can be corrected and be to the Water Monkey's long-term advantage.

Also, a particular feature of the Rabbit year will be the opportunities that can suddenly open up for the Water Monkey. He could have the chance to try new interests, join social groups or learn new subjects and skills. By embracing such opportunities he can extend his knowledge and have fun as well as widen his social circle. This is a year of exciting possibilities and the Water Monkey should use it well.

For Water Monkeys in work or seeking work this can be a year of interesting developments. Those in work will often be encouraged to put in for greater responsibilities, often in their present place of work. More senior personnel could be particularly helpful in giving advice on ways they could develop and future possibilities they could consider. This is a year for progress and many Water Monkeys will take on a greater and often more satisfying role during the course of it.

For Water Monkeys who are currently seeking a position, this can be a challenging but ultimately rewarding time. Seeking work will not be easy and competition may be fierce, but by rising to the challenge and showing resolve, the Water Monkey will find important doors opening for him. Sometimes he could help his quest by doing extra research on the company and work involved and so making his application more informed. With persistence and self-belief, many Water Monkeys will secure what can turn out to be an excellent platform on which to build.

March, April, October and November could see some encouraging work developments.

The Water Monkey will have many expenses this year and while he will enjoy his often active social life and the varied interests he pursues, he will need to keep a close watch on his outgoings. With many Water Monkeys likely to be keen to travel this year, any savings they can make towards this will often allow them to do more while away. Financially, this is a year for sensible control.

Having such a wide range of interests, the Water Monkey will find his social life will often be active and full. April to June, September and December are likely to be the busiest months socially.

For many Water Monkeys, affairs of the heart can also bring excitement to the year. However, rather than rush into any commitment or build up high expectations in the early stages of a romance, it may be best to let it evolve in its own time.

Also, while many Water Monkeys are outgoing and revel in company, there are exceptions, and any Water Monkey who feels alone or lacking in confidence will find that pursuing his interests (often one totally new) can bring him into contact with others and give him the chance to form some valuable new friendships. The Rabbit year *is* a supportive one and come the year end, many Water Monkeys will look back on what has happened over the last 12 months and marvel at all they have done and the transformation they have seen in their personal situation.

The Water Monkey also values his family and may have a special bond with a much older relation. Over the year, by being willing to share his thoughts with family members and keep them informed about what he is doing, he can not only benefit from their encouragement but also the assistance some are able to give. Over the year the Water Monkey's positive relations with those around him will help him in a great many ways.

Overall, the Year of the Rabbit is a year of progress and by putting himself forward and making the most of the chances available, the Water Monkey can benefit both now and in the future. This is a year to move forward and enjoy.

TIP FOR THE YEAR
Make the most of your ideas and talents. Use them, develop them, enjoy them. Also, draw on the support of others. With good guidance, you will be able to do far more. As a keen and enthusiastic Water Monkey, your future is full of possibility and what you do now can prepare you for the exciting times ahead.

The Wood Monkey

One of the hallmarks of the Monkey personality is his inquisitive and enquiring mind and over the year the Wood Monkey can look forward to immersing himself in a wide variety of activities and plans. Rarely will he be at a loss for things to do or ideas to follow up and a lot will go well.

As the Rabbit year starts the Wood Monkey could find it particularly helpful to give some thought to what he would like to do over the year. With ideas in mind he will find he is not only able to use his time and energy more effectively but also benefit from some of the opportunities that come his way. It is as if the moment thoughts and plans are set in motion, fate steps in and lends a helping hand.

The Rabbit year particularly favours personal development and if there is a skill the Wood Monkey has longed to develop or a subject that has been intriguing him, he should follow it up, perhaps through reading, private study or enrolling on a course. The Rabbit year has an expansive quality about it and many a Wood Monkey will be eager to improve himself in some way. Also, as he will find, once he takes action, other possibilities can open up, including putting new knowledge and skills to satisfying use or, if on a local course, meeting others.

Another area which many Wood Monkeys will consider this year will be their well-being. While some will be keen to take more exercise or improve their diet, they do need to seek medical guidance on the most appropriate way to proceed. Advice – and action – can make an important difference to how they feel.

The Wood Monkey will also be keen to travel during the year and several good opportunities could arise, including invitations to stay with family and friends and tempting travel offers. The Wood Monkey will often delight in some of the interesting places he gets to see during the year.

Culture also features strongly in the Rabbit year and some Wood Monkeys will take the opportunity to go to museums and exhibitions or spend time on family history or some other area of research that interests them. Again, by following up ideas and using time well, they will find their activities can bring them considerable satisfaction.

In view of all the Wood Monkey is likely to want to do this year, he will have many outgoings. As a result, he would do well to keep track of his spending as well as set regular sums aside for more major plans and purchases.

The more control he has, the more he can ultimately benefit. He also needs to attend to financial paperwork carefully and seek advice should he have any uncertainties. In financial matters, he will need to be vigilant and thorough.

With his sociable nature, the Wood Monkey always sets great store by his relations with others and this year he will find himself in considerable demand. Any Wood Monkeys who are lonely will find that local courses and social groups can be an excellent way to meet others, with April to June, September and December being active and often special months.

The Wood Monkey's domestic life will also be busy this year. His ideas and creativity will be to the fore and he is likely to be eager to carry out improvements to his home or even move. The Rabbit year will see many a Wood Monkey's household abuzz with activity, but he should be wary of risk or undue haste. By allowing time for options to be properly considered and costed, he will find his final decisions will be more appropriate.

In a lot of what the Wood Monkey does he will also value the input and encouragement of those close to him, but over the year he will need to be mindful of their views. In some instances, there may need to be compromise and a certain flexibility would be helpful.

Amid all the activity, the Wood Monkey will keenly follow the news of family members as well as celebrate the achievements of younger relations. In addition, those close to him will often be grateful for his advice on certain matters.

Overall, the Year of the Rabbit can be a pleasing and active one for the Wood Monkey. Creative activities can be especially satisfying. A lot can go well for the Wood

Monkey this year and he will benefit from the support of others as well as enjoy a certain amount of good fortune.

TIP FOR THE YEAR
Follow up your ideas. With positive and purposeful action, you can accomplish a great deal. This is an encouraging year and one of considerable possibility.

The Fire Monkey

This will be an important year for the Fire Monkey and may well see him giving some thought to his current lifestyle. What follows on from his deliberations can turn out to be far-reaching.

Many Fire Monkeys will have grappled with considerable pressures during the last few years, faced uncertainties and not always felt satisfied with what they have been able to achieve. One of the benefits of the Rabbit year is that it will give the Fire Monkey more scope to do what *he* wants as well as to go ahead with certain ideas. For many this will be a year of appraisal that will lead to some long-term personal gains.

One of the areas which is strongly favoured this year is personal growth and if there are subjects that interest the Fire Monkey, skills he would like to develop or activities he is keen to try, he should take action. Also, should he feel he has been weighed down by pressures in recent years and allowed his lifestyle to get out of balance, this is a year to correct this. By considering what he would like to do and setting aside time for recreational pursuits, he will often feel more content in himself and rediscover a sparkle and joy which may have been lacking in recent years. In 2011 some extra 'me time' can do many a Fire Monkey a lot of good.

With the Monkey being born under the sign of fantasy, many Fire Monkeys are creatively inclined and over the year quite a few will enjoy the chance to develop some of their ideas. Many will also delight in outdoor pursuits and again the Rabbit year will offer them more scope to do what they want.

With this a year of reappraisal, some Fire Monkeys will also decide to give some thought to their well-being, including making some modifications to their exercise levels and diet. With medical advice, their actions can benefit them as well as reinforce the personally constructive nature of the year.

The Fire Monkey can also look forward to some pleasing developments in his home life. Not only will he try to spend more quality time with his loved ones but will also enjoy sharing activities as well as helping others. Here his ability to empathize as well as sense what others may not yet be aware of can be of great value. His perceptiveness will be in great form this year. In addition, in many a Fire Monkey household there will be an important family event to look forward to and the Fire Monkey's organizational ability will be very much appreciated. Home life will often be special and rewarding this year.

Another promising aspect is travel and if possible the Fire Monkey should try to take a break or holiday with his loved ones. This can do everyone good.

The Fire Monkey should also give some attention to his social life and if this has suffered recently due to other activities, he should resolve to go out more. Particularly for those Fire Monkeys who have experienced loneliness in recent years, this is an ideal time for making more of what is available in the local area. For many their activities can lead to a brightening in their situation and, for the unattached, the possible dawning of meaningful romance. April to June, September, December and early January could see the most social activity.

This can also be an important year work-wise, with few Fire Monkeys remaining unaffected by the Rabbit year's subtle yet progressive aspects. Those who are well established in their career could be offered new responsibilities or the chance to develop certain skills. This could take some Fire Monkeys by surprise but give them a new and interesting challenge.

Many Fire Monkeys will remain in their present place of work, but for those who are seeking change or looking for a position, the Rabbit year can be one of important possibility. By giving careful thought to what it is they now want to do, these Fire Monkeys could identify possibilities to pursue. Securing a position will not be easy, but with determination and a willingness to adapt, including possibly retraining, many will be successful. March, April, October and November could see some important developments, but overall the Rabbit year is one of positive change.

Many Fire Monkeys will see a modest increase in their earnings this year, but with their plans and commitments, they will need to keep a close watch on spending levels. This is a year for careful control and should the Fire Monkey be involved in any large transaction, he should take his time and consider the implications and the options available.

Overall, the Rabbit year can be a positive one for the Fire Monkey, but a lot rests with him. With careful thought,

especially regarding his interests and personal development, he can often improve his lifestyle as well as enjoy
himself. His relations with others can be helpful, with
activities to share and some often pleasing personal or
family news to look forward to.

TIP FOR THE YEAR
Give some thought to what you want to do this year. Enjoy
and develop your interests, set yourself some new challenges
and appreciate what you have around you. This is a year of
considerable scope and personal opportunity. Use it well.

The Earth Monkey

There is a Chinese proverb which reminds us, 'Diligence
leads to riches,' and over the year the Earth Monkey's careful and considered approach can lead to some important
accomplishments. Also, with this being a favourable year
for self-improvement, his earnest nature can do a lot to
help both his present situation and future prospects. In
many ways this will be a constructive and progressive year.

The Earth Monkey has a creative streak and often not
only has good ideas but also the ability to see ways round
problems and to use his talents in imaginative ways. And
this can be an inspiring time for him. When he has ideas or
sees possibilities that interest him, he should follow them
up. With a willing approach, backed by his enthusiastic 'can
do' nature, he can make things happen.

At work the Rabbit year can open up some excellent
possibilities and bring important change. Particularly for any
Earth Monkeys who are feeling staid or dissatisfied in their

present role, opportunities can suddenly arise which can not only be a welcome change from what they have been doing but also give them greater scope and incentive. This may be in their present place of work or elsewhere, but in either case their reputation, previous experience and desire to move on will impress others and be to their advantage.

This also applies to Earth Monkeys seeking work. Although they may feel disillusioned or despondent about their prospects, by remaining persistent, seeking advice and drawing on their resourcefulness, they will uncover opportunities which will be well worth pursuing. The Earth Monkey's talents and qualities will once again serve him well this year and many will obtain a new position which can take their career in a different direction. Also, if the Earth Monkey is offered retraining or other courses to further his skills, he should take full advantage of this. Diligence can lead to some important opportunities.

For Earth Monkeys who are well established in their career the Rabbit year can also bring opportunities to progress. Whether these involve taking on different responsibilities or securing promotion, there will be scope for many Earth Monkeys to move their career forward and to develop their skills. March, April and October to early December could see some interesting developments.

This is also an excellent year for the Earth Monkey to give thought to his current lifestyle and follow up ideas he may have been nurturing for a while. These could include taking up new interests or recreational pursuits, starting a keep fit discipline or setting himself a certain objective or project. By following up his ideas, he can make this a satisfying time.

The Earth Monkey will also appreciate his often close

circle of friends. Not only will he welcome the chance to talk over ideas or get their views on certain matters, but interests that can be shared can be especially pleasing. For Earth Monkeys who may have neglected their social life in recent years, this is an excellent time for getting their lifestyle back into balance, and by going out, becoming more involved in their community and/or meeting fellow enthusiasts at societies or events, they can bring a positive new dimension to their life. April to June, September and December could be the most active months socially.

Domestically, this will be a full and active year. Accommodation matters will feature prominently on the agendas of many Monkeys and the Earth Monkey will often be keen to make improvements to his home and possibly garden. However, while he may have certain ideas, these do need to be discussed with others and carefully costed. Where practical undertakings are concerned, the more time spent preparing, the better the results.

In addition to practical undertakings, there will also be a lot happening in many an Earth Monkey household. Younger relations could be heavily involved in study or making decisions about their future, and here the Earth Monkey's encouragement and support can be of considerable value. Also, with his talent for coming up with ideas, he could propose activities or outings that will be appreciated by all concerned. Domestically, this can be a busy year.

In money matters, progress at work will help, but with the Earth Monkey's existing commitments and the plans he has for the year, he will need to remain disciplined. Financially, this is a year for diligence and care.

Overall, the Rabbit year offers great possibilities for the

Earth Monkey and while he may have taken knocks in recent years, his determination and the opportunities that come his way can reinvigorate him as well as allow him to expand on his experience. This is a year to move forward, develop skills and interests and make the most of opportunities. With determination and willingness, the Earth Monkey can make this a positive and personally pleasing year.

TIP FOR THE YEAR

You have a great talent for thinking creatively and being alert to possibility. Over the year, follow up your ideas and opportunities and look to further your skills and develop yourself personally and professionally. This is a year of great scope. Use it well, for your actions can lead to some important accomplishments.

FAMOUS MONKEYS

Gillian Anderson, Jennifer Aniston, Christina Aguilera, Patricia Arquette, Baroness Ashton, José Manuel Barroso, Patricia Cornwell, Daniel Craig, Joan Crawford, Leonardo da Vinci, Timothy Dalton, Bette Davis, Danny De Vito, Celine Dion, Michael Douglas, Mia Farrow, Carrie Fisher, Jake Gyllenhaal, Jerry Hall, Tom Hanks, Hugh Jackman, Katherine Jenkins, Julius Caesar, Alicia Keys, Gladys Knight, Bob Marley, Kylie Minogue, V. S. Naipaul, Peter O'Toole, Lisa Marie Presley, Debbie Reynolds, Little Richard, Mickey Rooney, Diana Ross, Tom Selleck, Rod Stewart, Jacques Tati, Elizabeth Taylor, Dame Kiri Te Kanawa, Justin Timberlake, Venus Williams.

———◆———

22 JANUARY 1909 ⁓ 9 FEBRUARY 1910   *Earth Rooster*

8 FEBRUARY 1921 ⁓ 27 JANUARY 1922   *Metal Rooster*

26 JANUARY 1933 ⁓ 13 FEBRUARY 1934 *Water Rooster*

13 FEBRUARY 1945 ⁓ 1 FEBRUARY 1946 *Wood Rooster*

31 JANUARY 1957 ⁓ 17 FEBRUARY 1958   *Fire Rooster*

17 FEBRUARY 1969 ⁓ 5 FEBRUARY 1970 *Earth Rooster*

5 FEBRUARY 1981 ⁓ 24 JANUARY 1982   *Metal Rooster*

23 JANUARY 1993 ⁓ 9 FEBRUARY 1994   *Water Rooster*

9 FEBRUARY 2005 ⁓ 28 JANUARY 2006   *Wood Rooster*

———◆———

THE
ROOSTER

THE PERSONALITY OF THE ROOSTER

With a clear destination
and firm will,
I raise my sails
to the winds of fortune.

The Rooster is born under the sign of candour. He has a flamboyant and colourful personality and is meticulous in all that he does. He is an excellent organizer and wherever possible likes to plan his various activities well in advance.

The Rooster is usually highly intelligent and very well read. He has a good sense of humour and is an effective and persuasive speaker. He loves discussion and enjoys taking part in any sort of debate. He has no hesitation in speaking his mind and is forthright in his views. He does, however, lack tact and can easily damage his reputation or cause offence by some thoughtless remark or action. He has a very volatile nature and should always try to avoid acting on the spur of the moment.

He is usually very dignified in his manner and conducts himself with an air of confidence and authority. He is adept at handling financial matters and organizes his financial affairs with considerable skill. He chooses his investments well and is capable of achieving great wealth. Most Roosters use their money wisely, but there are a few who are the reverse and are notorious spendthrifts. Fortunately, the Rooster has great earning capacity and is rarely without sufficient funds to tide himself over.

Another characteristic of the Rooster is that he invariably carries a notebook or scraps of paper around with him.

He is constantly writing himself reminders or noting down important facts lest he forgets – the Rooster cannot abide inefficiency and conducts all his activities in an orderly, precise and methodical manner.

The Rooster is usually very ambitious, but can be unrealistic in some of what he hopes to achieve. He occasionally lets his imagination run away with him and while he does not like any interference from others, it would be in his own interests to listen to their views a little more often. He also does not like criticism, and if he feels anybody is doubting his judgement or prying too closely into his affairs, he is certain to let his feelings be known. He can also be rather self-centred and stubborn over relatively trivial matters, but to compensate for this he is reliable, honest and trustworthy, and this is appreciated by all who come into contact with him.

Roosters born between the hours of five and seven, both at dawn and sundown, tend to be the most extrovert of their sign, but all Roosters like to lead an active social life and enjoy attending parties and big functions. The Rooster usually has a wide circle of friends and is able to build up influential contacts with remarkable ease. He often belongs to several clubs and societies and involves himself in a variety of different activities. He is particularly interested in the environment, humanitarian affairs and anything affecting the welfare of others. He has a very caring nature and will do much to help those less fortunate than himself.

He also gets much pleasure from gardening, and while he may not spend as much time in the garden as he would like, his garden is invariably well kept and productive.

The Rooster is generally very distinguished in his appearance and if his job permits he will wear an official uniform with great pride and dignity. He is not averse to publicity and takes great delight in being the centre of attention. He often does well at PR work or any job which brings him into contact with the media. He also makes a very good teacher.

The female Rooster leads a varied and interesting life. She involves herself in many different activities and there are some who wonder how she can achieve so much. She often holds very strong views and, like her male counterpart, has no hesitation in speaking her mind or telling others how she thinks things should be done. She is supremely efficient and well organized and her home is usually very neat and tidy. She has good taste in clothes and usually wears smart but very practical outfits.

The Rooster usually has a large family and takes a particularly active interest in the education of his children. He is very loyal to his partner and will find that he is especially well suited to those born under the signs of the Snake, Horse, Ox and Dragon. Provided they do not interfere too much in his various activities, the Rat, Tiger, Goat and Pig can also establish a good relationship with him, but two Roosters together are likely to squabble and irritate each other. The rather sensitive Rabbit will find the Rooster a bit too blunt for his liking, and the Rooster will quickly become exasperated by the ever-inquisitive and artful Monkey. He will also find it difficult to get on with the anxious Dog.

If the Rooster can overcome his volatile nature and exercise tact, he will go far in life. He is capable and talented and will make a lasting – and usually favourable – impression almost everywhere he goes.

THE FIVE DIFFERENT TYPES OF ROOSTER

In addition to the 12 signs of the Chinese zodiac there are five elements and these have a strengthening or moderating influence on the signs. The effects of the five elements on the Rooster are described below, together with the years in which they were exercising their influence. Therefore those Roosters born in 1921 and 1981 are Metal Roosters, those born in 1933 and 1993 are Water Roosters, and so on.

Metal Rooster: 1921, 1981

The Metal Rooster is a hard and conscientious worker. He knows exactly what he wants in life and sets about everything in a positive and determined manner. He can at times appear abrasive and he would almost certainly do better if he were willing to reach a compromise with others rather than hold so rigidly to his beliefs. He is very articulate and most astute when dealing with financial matters. He is loyal to his friends and often devotes much energy to working for the common good.

Water Rooster: 1933, 1993

This Rooster has a very persuasive manner and can easily gain the co-operation of others. He is intelligent, well read and enjoys taking part in discussions and debates. He has a seemingly inexhaustible amount of energy and is prepared to work long hours in order to secure what he wants. He can, however, waste a lot of valuable time worrying over minor and inconsequential details. He is approachable, has a good sense of humour and is highly regarded by others.

Wood Rooster: 1945, 2005

The Wood Rooster is honest, reliable and often sets himself high standards. He is ambitious, but he is also more prepared to work in a team than some of the other types of Rooster. He usually succeeds in life but does have a tendency to get caught up in bureaucratic matters and attempt too many things at the same time. He has wide interests, likes to travel and is very caring and considerate towards his family and friends.

Fire Rooster: 1957

This Rooster is extremely strong-willed. He has many leadership qualities, is an excellent organizer and is most efficient in his work. Through sheer force of character he often secures his objectives, but he does have a tendency to be very forthright and not always consider the feelings of others. If he can learn to be more tactful he can often succeed beyond his wildest dreams.

Earth Rooster: 1909, 1969

This Rooster has a deep and penetrating mind. He is efficient, perceptive and particularly astute in business and financial matters. He is also persistent and once he has set himself an objective, he will rarely allow himself to be deflected from achieving his aim. He works hard and is held in great esteem by his friends and colleagues. He usually enjoys the arts and takes a keen interest in the activities of the various members of his family.

PROSPECTS FOR THE ROOSTER IN 2011

The Rooster is a keen planner and is careful and meticulous. The Tiger year (14 February 2010–2 February 2011) is fast paced and not always a respecter of carefully laid plans or set procedures. Many a Rooster will have felt uneasy and disturbed by events in it and in the remaining months will need his wits about him.

However, while the Tiger year may not be the best for the Rooster, it will not be without its benefits. Sometimes events will force him into change which he might not otherwise have made. Although this can be uncomfortable, the Rooster will not only learn a great deal from what happens – including about himself – but also find new possibilities opening up. Particularly in the closing months, if he is willing to adapt to situations as they arise, he stands to benefit.

At work, increased demand or new changes could provide the chance to take on additional responsibilities, while those Roosters seeking work will find that by being flexible and widening the scope of what they are prepared to consider, many could secure an interesting new position at this time. As the Rooster will find, the Tiger year can be instructive.

The closing months could also bring additional expenses and the Rooster should keep track of his spending. If he is able to spread out certain purchases or wait for favourable buying opportunities, including end of year sales, this could help.

He will also find his social life busier in the closing quarter of the year and although he will often enjoy himself, he should watch his sometimes candid nature. A lack of tact could cause hurt or undermine rapport. Roosters, take note, and remember that the Tiger year does require care and thoughtfulness.

The Rooster will also play a full part in his home life towards the end of the Tiger year and enjoy some family get-togethers. By participating fully in domestic affairs he can make this an active and pleasing time. For some Roosters there could also be travel possibilities in the closing weeks of the year.

After the pressures and heady pace of the Tiger year, the Rooster can look forward to a quieter and more settled period. The Rabbit year starts on 3 February and will be a reasonable one for the Rooster. However, while progress is possible, he should keep his expectations realistic as well as be patient. Results can take some while to filter through and not everyone may share the Rooster's zeal or timetable!

At work many Roosters will decide to concentrate on the present rather than look too far ahead. If they have been involved in recent change, they will welcome the opportunity to become more established in their work and proficient in their duties. All Roosters should aim to work closely with their colleagues and be an active member of any team. This is a year which favours co-operation rather than an independent stance. In addition, the Rooster can do himself a lot of good by networking and getting himself better known. If relevant, joining a professional organization could be to his advantage. Any training the Rooster is offered or additional skills he can learn will also help. Even if this is something he has to do by himself, by adding to his knowledge he will not only find this personally and professionally rewarding but also valuable for his future development. A lot that the Rooster does this year can help pave the way for some of the more substantial opportunities that await in the following and more auspicious Dragon year.

Although work-wise the Rabbit year may seem slow moving, opportunities can arise quickly and whenever the Rooster sees openings that appeal to him, he should put himself forward without delay. This may not be a year for major breakthrough, but the experience gained can be an important factor in the Rooster's later success.

For Roosters seeking work, this will be a year for patience, persistence and sudden developments. Although some may despair, by keeping alert and exploring different possibilities, they could be given the chance they have been seeking. Sometimes this can seem all the more special as it follows on from a rejection. April, May, October and November could see some important work developments, but generally the experience the Rooster can gain this year can prove very instrumental in the future.

One area in which the Rooster will need to be especially careful is finance. Although Roosters are generally meticulous about keeping control over their outgoings, some are spendthrifts and in the Rabbit year the Rooster will need to remain disciplined and avoid too many unplanned purchases. Without care these can mount up and lead to economies having to be made later. The Rooster should also be wary of risks or speculative undertakings. This is a year to be careful and prudent.

The Rooster will also need to take care in his relations with others. Although his sense of responsibility and candid nature are valuable qualities, over the year he does need to take careful note of the views of others. To be too forceful, blunt or unaware could cause problems. Fortunately the Rooster is also perceptive, but the more aware he is this year and the more he listens to others, the better.

Socially, this may be a quieter year than some, but this should not prevent the Rooster from taking up invitations connected with his work (networking can do him a lot of good in 2011) or going to events that appeal to him. His personal interests can also bring him into contact with others and enable him to make some helpful contacts. March, May, September and December could see the greatest amount of social activity.

This can also be a satisfying year as far as the Rooster's home life is concerned, particularly if he ensures there is good communication between everyone in his household. Advice he is given by a loved one could be of special value, perhaps alerting him to a new possibility or a fresh way to develop an idea. In the Rabbit year it will reward the Rooster to listen carefully to his loved ones, for they speak very much with his interests at heart. In return there will be an excellent chance for him assist others. Over the year he will be particularly supportive, and whether helping a close relation with a problem or bolstering someone's confidence, his thoughtfulness will mean more than he may realize. He will also enjoy many of the domestic activities that take place, and quality time with his loved ones can do everyone good.

An important element of the Rabbit year is its emphasis on self-development. As the Rooster is a keen reader and has an inquisitive mind, he would do well to set time aside to follow up subjects that interest him. Extending his knowledge can not only be a satisfying use of his time but also give rise to future possibilities.

Generally, in the Rabbit year the Rooster will need to be careful, prudent and patient. Progress may be slow and in all he does the Rooster should be thoughtful and aware. This is no year for risk or impulsiveness. However, while the Rooster's exuberance may be tempered, the Rabbit year can have important significance for him. Next year will be one of great opportunity and what the Rooster can achieve now can prepare him for the excellent opportunities soon to emerge. Overall, a reasonable year with considerable and far-reaching benefits.

The Metal Rooster

This will be a valuable year for the Metal Rooster and while his actual progress may be modest, what he accomplishes can have significant future value. In many ways this can be regarded as a year of preparation for some of the very good opportunities that will emerge in coming years. Its importance should *not* be underestimated.

Also, as the Metal Rooster enters a new decade of his life, he will feel now is the time to move his situation forward and the plans he sets in motion can prove important in the longer term. The Metal Rooster knows he has the ability to achieve a great deal and over the year his resolve and determination will spur him on.

In his work, although this may not be a year for major advance (next year is more auspicious), many Metal Roosters will find their responsibilities changing and will have the chance to widen their skills and show what they can do. Here the Metal Rooster's commitment, along with his ability to work closely with colleagues, can help both his standing and his overall situation.

Most Metal Roosters will remain with their present employer over the year, but for those who are disillusioned with their work situation or seeking a position, this can be a significant time. By registering with employment agencies, talking to advisors and making their own enquiries, many could be alerted to possibilities to consider. Sometimes what opens up for these Metal Roosters will be a considerable change from what they have been doing but will give them a chance to develop and grow. For quite a few, 2011 can mark the start of a new phase in their career. April, May, October and November could see some interesting work developments.

The Rabbit year can be an expensive one and the Metal Rooster will need to remain disciplined in his spending and not succumb to too many impulse buys. With many Metal Roosters being tempted by travel this year or keen to hold some personal or family celebrations (including to mark their thirtieth birthday), they should budget carefully and save towards these and other plans. Also if entering into an agreement concerning accommodation or a transaction with long-term implications, the Metal Rooster should check the terms and, where necessary, seek professional guidance. In matters of finance this is a year for thoroughness, vigilance and planning ahead.

Although the Metal Rooster may decide to cut back on social activity this year, it is important he keeps in regular contact with his friends and does not deny himself the chance to go to events that appeal to him. His social life not only helps to keep his lifestyle in balance but also allows him to relax and unwind. In addition family and long-standing friends could have some surprises in store to mark this new decade in his life and their affection will mean a great deal to him. March, May, September and December could see the most social activity.

This will also be an eventful year as far as home life is concerned. Not only will the Metal Rooster give much support to those close to him but often be busy with household projects and other commitments. During some of the year he may feel his time and energy being spread in many directions, but by being well organized and prioritizing, he will often surprise himself with all he is able to do.

Also, although the Metal Rooster is conscientious and tackles a lot by himself, it is important that he fully involves his loved ones, letting them help at busy times or advise him over any concerns. In the Rabbit year he should not shoulder too much single-handedly.

A valuable feature of the year will be the opportunities the Metal Rooster will have to further his interests and skills. He will often feel ready to take on a fresh challenge and can get much pleasure and potential benefit from his actions. With enterprise, backed by his keen nature, he can certainly get this new decade in his life off to a promising start.

Overall, the Rooster year is an important and constructive one for the Metal Rooster and by taking advantage of the opportunities to develop his skills, he can prepare the way for future progress. Throughout the year he should liaise closely with others and will not only benefit from the support and encouragement he is given but often be buoyed up by the love and affection of those who are special to him.

TIP FOR THE YEAR
Focus on what you want and what you have to do. With concentrated effort, what you start now can have value both in the present *and*, importantly, future. Also, value your relations with others. Consult them, listen to them and enjoy their company.

The Water Rooster

The Rabbit year holds considerable opportunity for the Water Rooster and by making good use of it he can accomplish a great deal as well as sow some important seeds for the future. One of the main features of the Rabbit year is that it encourages personal growth and learning and the Water Rooster will be well placed to benefit from its influences.

Quite a few Water Roosters will be finishing courses, taking exams and be moving on to a new stage in their education during the year. Not only will these Water

Roosters feel ready for this but they will also welcome the chance to develop themselves in new ways.

However, while the Water Rooster can enjoy some well-deserved success this year, it will need to be worked for. In some cases new subject areas will be demanding, but by knuckling down to what he has to do and keeping the end results in mind, the Water Rooster will not only find his efforts paying off but the headway he makes giving him greater confidence. Not only can this be a successful year academically, but a valuable one personally, with the Water Rooster learning a lot about himself and starting to forge his own way in life.

With so much to do and some decisions to make concerning his future, it is also important that he talks to others and obtains proper guidance. If he is wondering about certain career options and the qualifications needed, he should contact those with the experience to advise. Similarly, if he has any concerns about his studies or any other matter, he should speak to those who are able to help. By being open, he can receive the support to ease his concerns. He should not feel he is alone this year.

Although a lot of time may be taken up with studying, the Water Rooster can derive considerable pleasure from developing other interests. Whether involved in the creative or performing arts (which are favourably aspected in the Rabbit year) or enjoying sport or other pursuits, what he does can be satisfying and often beneficial in other ways. And here again the Water Rooster should take advantage of any additional help and instruction available.

Throughout the year he will also value his close circle of friends. Not only can they support one another but much fun can be had by sharing interests and going out together. Water Roosters who move during the year, possibly as a result of their education, will also find this gives them the opportunity to meet others. The Water Rooster selects his friends with care and the camaraderie he enjoys can bring him a great deal of pleasure this year. For some there could also be the chance of romance but, as many may find, the path of true love does not always run smooth and it may be best for the Water Rooster to enjoy the present rather than look too far ahead or place high expectations on new-found love. As has often been said, 'What will be will be.'

In view of his many interests and busy social life, the Water Rooster should keep a close watch on his spending over the year. Rabbit years tend to be expensive and in order to do all he wants, the Water Rooster should avoid too many impulse buys. Also, with the mixed aspects concerning finance, should he have any problems with financial matters, whether over grants, benefits or other transactions, he should seek advice.

For Water Roosters in work, the Rabbit year can be challenging. The Water Rooster may feel he is not always using his abilities to their best advantage or that certain aspects of his work are unsatisfactory. However while sometimes frustrated, by doing his best and gaining experience, he will often be in a much stronger position to apply when other opportunities become available.

Similarly, for Water Roosters seeking work, their quest may not be easy, but positions they obtain can not only give them valuable working experience but also be a stepping-stone to other possibilities. Some may be offered an apprenticeship or work-release scheme or have the chance to learn a new skill or trade, and again should follow this up. Positive action the Water Rooster takes in the Rabbit year can often have long-term value. April, May, October and November could see some interesting openings to pursue.

In his home life the Water Rooster should be open and communicative. Although sometimes different outlooks and a gap in years may cause problems, by talking about his current activities and discussing decisions and any concerns, the Water Rooster will find others will not only be better able to support and advise him but that home life in general will benefit. Also, by playing a full part in family plans and activities, including a possible break or holiday, the Water Rooster will often enjoy what he gets to do. Domestically, this is a year for openness and participation.

Overall, the Year of the Rabbit will be an important and personally valuable one for the Water Rooster. He will not only further his education and experience (sometimes quite substantially), but also have an excellent chance to develop other personal qualities and strengths. And while he will have to work hard for success, what he accomplishes this year can give him the skills and qualifications necessary for later progress. The benefits of the Rabbit year can be considerable *and* far-reaching.

TIP FOR THE YEAR

As a Water Rooster you have many abilities. In the Rabbit year let these emerge and make the most of your opportunities. The next few years hold great promise and what you do now can have future significance.

The Wood Rooster

This will be a quiet and generally pleasant year for the Wood Rooster. Being the keen planner that he is, he will draw satisfaction from being better able to concentrate on the things he wants and seeing many of his plans and ideas take shape.

One of the most pleasing aspects of the year will be the time the Wood Rooster is able to spend developing certain interests. He may have had some of these for a long time and this year he could find his often extensive knowledge opening up new possibilities. He may choose to share his thoughts with other enthusiasts, write about his experiences or explore a particular idea, but by using his knowledge in ways he enjoys, he can find this a personally rewarding time.

However, it is not just existing interests that are likely to appeal to him over the year. Sometimes his partner or a close friend may encourage him to join them in something they do or he may find himself becoming more involved in another activity. Alternatively, by following up something in his area that he may hear about, whether a local group, project, campaign or course, he will find the Rabbit year can open up some interesting possibilities. The key is to remain aware and act on ideas.

The Rooster has an affinity for the land and many Wood Roosters will also take considerable pleasure over the year in being out of doors. If they have a garden or allotment these Wood Roosters could spending many a happy hour tending their plot and enjoying what they grow, whether plants to admire or produce to eat. Alternatively, others may appreciate local amenities, including parks or places of interest.

In addition, many Wood Roosters will give some thought to their well-being during the year and here again could be helped by local facilities. Whether going to swimming pools or keep fit classes or undertaking exercise initiatives or other measures themselves, they will find that with proper guidance their activities can be fun and often beneficial. Joining others can also bring a certain amount of mutual encouragement and good humour to what they do. Generally, the possibilities for the Wood Rooster are many and varied this year, but to benefit, it is a case of following up those that interest him.

Although many Wood Roosters will have retired from work or decide to do so soon, quite a few will be keen to continue working in some capacity or to put an interest or skill to profitable use. Free from some of the pressures of previous years, these Wood Roosters can take satisfaction in what they do as well as supplementing their income.

In matters of finance, Rabbit years can be expensive and in addition to their usual outgoings, many Wood Roosters could have increased accommodation costs, including repairs, maintenance or replacing equipment. At such times the Wood Rooster should keep a close check on costs, obtaining and comparing quotations and, when making purchases, being prepared to wait for favourable buying opportunities. This is a year to be thorough and cautious. The Wood Rooster should also attend to financial paperwork carefully and seek clarification if he has any concerns.

Although he will need to keep watch on his outgoings, whenever possible he should also try to make provision for a holiday. A rest and change of location can be refreshing and beneficial. There could be some good travel possibilities towards the end of the year.

The Wood Rooster will also enjoy meeting up with his friends, and his interests, both existing and new, will offer excellent social possibilities. Any Wood Rooster who would welcome more companionship will find that joining an interest group or becoming more active in some aspect of his community (many Wood Roosters are public spirited) could be an excellent way to meet others. The Rabbit year favours positive action and March, May, September and December could see the most social activity.

Over the year the Wood Rooster will be encouraged by the support of family members. Interests and projects that can be shared can be especially gratifying, as this is a year which favours joint undertakings. The Wood Rooster will also be active in helping others and will take great interest in family activities and news. Although this is an encouraging year, if at any time he has any concerns or worries, it is important that he speaks out. This is no time to deal with matters single-handedly or keep concerns hidden from others. With openness, help can be given more easily and worries defused.

Overall, the Year of the Rabbit will give the Wood Rooster the chance to make more of his interests and proceed with his plans. This is a constructive year and with willingness and enterprise, the Wood Rooster can take a great deal of pleasure from his activities.

TIP FOR THE YEAR
Spend time enjoying your talents and interests. These can bring you pleasure, often have a fine social element and

will also open up other possibilities. With positive action, this can be a fulfilling year.

The Fire Rooster

The Fire Rooster is strong-willed and over the years his resolve and determination will have allowed him to achieve a great deal. While the Rabbit year will bring some interesting opportunities, he could find he does better this year by modifying his approach. Rather than relentlessly pursuing certain objectives, he should aim to show greater flexibility and make the most of situations *as they are*. With care and consideration, he can make this an important and personally valuable year, but should he be dogmatic or inflexible, disappointments could loom.

In his work the Fire Rooster will generally fare best by concentrating on his present role rather than looking to make major advances. By focusing on the areas he knows, he will not only have the chance to put his experience and specialist knowledge to good use but also be better able to work on certain ideas or objectives. The skills he demonstrates now can not only help his present standing but also his future prospects, especially in the auspicious Dragon year that follows.

Also, while the Fire Rooster may be experienced in his present area of work, he should keep himself informed of developments in his company and industry as well as take advantage of any training offered. By being prepared to build on his knowledge, he will again help his present situation as well as open up future possibilities. Chances for progress could be limited this year, but if any openings arise which appeal to him, the Fire Rooster should be swift to apply.

Fire Roosters who are seeking work or keen to move on from their current situation will often fare best by looking for positions where they can use or adapt existing skills rather than trying for something totally different. They can also make their applications that much stronger by emphasizing to prospective employers their experience and skills. Once they secure a position, they could find their new duties a refreshing change and interesting new challenge. Again, experience gained now can be an important stepping-stone to some of the opportunities that await in 2012. April, May, October and November could see some important developments.

With this a year favouring personal development, if there are activities or recreational pursuits that appeal to him, the Fire Rooster should waste no time in making enquiries. He can get much value from what he does. Some Fire Roosters may decide to set themselves specific projects or personal goals for the year, and by focusing on these and using their knowledge, can make this a satisfying time.

Financially, Rabbit years can be expensive and the Fire Rooster is likely to have many demands on his resources. Over the year he should remain disciplined and keep careful track of his outgoings as well as avoid too much impulse buying. This is a year for discipline and, where possible, making advance provision for outgoings, including travel.

With his existing commitments and the various activities he is involved with, the Fire Rooster may decide to keep his social life relatively low key this year. However, if he receives invitations or sees events that appeal to him, he should try to go. Not only can such occasions be fun but they can also help keep his lifestyle in balance. He will also particularly value the support, trust and 'listening ear' of some of his close friends. Socially, this may be a quieter year than some, but March, May, September, December and early January could see some interesting and pleasurable times.

In his domestic life the Fire Rooster will often be kept busy. Not only will he be keen to deal with some practical projects and possibly spend time gardening, but he will also be instrumental in making plans and will do much to help others. Over the year his careful, methodical and thoughtful approach will be appreciated. At all times he should be mindful of the views of others and discuss his hopes and plans as well as allow time for certain projects to be completed, but domestically this can be a pleasant and meaningful year. It will also contain some memorable moments and celebrations.

Overall, by moderating his expectations and concentrating on specific activities rather than setting his sights too high, the Fire Rooster can not only get greater satisfaction from what he does but ultimately stand to benefit more too. Next year is a particularly encouraging one and the experience he can gain now can prepare him well for the possibilities soon to emerge. In the meantime, this is a year to focus on the present and to enjoy time spent with loved ones, pursuing interests and following up plans and ideas.

TIP FOR THE YEAR

Use your strengths and look to build on them. By broadening your experience, you can not only get more satisfaction from the present time but also find your actions leading on to other possibilities.

The Earth Rooster

The element of Earth can make a sign more focused, practical and realistic, and these qualities are very evident in the Earth Rooster. While he likes to plan and look ahead he also accepts what is possible at any time and adapts well to prevailing conditions. In the Rabbit year he will often feel that more can be gained by concentrating on his present position and commitments rather than looking to make major changes. While his actual progress may be modest this year, his activities can not only be personally satisfying but also of later value.

Throughout the year the Earth Rooster will be particularly helped by the advice and support of friends and loved ones. In his home life, joint undertakings are especially well aspected and whether undertaking projects in the home or garden or sharing interests, the Earth Rooster will find that spending time with his loved ones can make his home life all the more rewarding. They will often seek his advice on various matters – younger relations in particular could have decisions to make regarding their education, while his partner or more senior relations may be keen to get his thoughts on plans they are considering. By providing first a listening ear and then giving his opinion or offering help, the Earth Rooster can make a positive difference and will play a key role in his domestic life this year.

Although he will have many expenses and financial commitments this year, he should also try to make provision for a holiday or short break or, if this is not possible, make sure there are some family treats for all to look forward to. Time spent with his loved ones can lead to some pleasurable occasions.

In view of his other commitments, the Earth Rooster may decide to cut back on his socializing this year, but should not deny himself the chance to go to events that appeal to him. These are not only good ways for him to relax and enjoy himself but also give him the opportunity to meet others. Any Earth Rooster who would welcome new friendships could find certain interests they have offering good social possibilities. March, May September and December could see the most social activity.

With his keen and interested nature, the Earth Rooster is also likely to give some consideration to his own personal development over the year. Some Earth Roosters could decide to enrol on courses or set time aside for study and research. By furthering their knowledge and skills in ways they feel could be helpful, they will not only take much satisfaction in what they do but also find their new knowledge giving them the scope to do more. For personal development and advancing skills and interests, this is an encouraging time.

In their work many Earth Roosters will also have more opportunity to concentrate on the areas where they are most skilled. Those who have been involved in recent change in particular will have an excellent chance to get more established as well as learn about other aspects of their work and industry. The main benefits for the Earth Rooster this year can come from building on his present position and adding to his skills. Throughout the year he should also work closely with colleagues and, when appropriate, use his chances to network and get himself better known. His efforts and conscientious nature will impress many and prepare him for future opportunities, particularly in 2012.

For Earth Roosters who are keen to move on from what they currently do as well as those seeking work, the Rabbit year can be significant. Obtaining a position will not be easy and many Earth Roosters will face disappointments and some unhelpful bureaucratic obstacles or delays in their quest. However, the Earth Rooster is a realist and retaining his self-belief and remaining persistent, he may well prevail and secure an interesting new position. This may not always be in the exact area he was hoping for and could involve quite a bit of learning and adjusting to, but it can nevertheless be a springboard to future success. Mid-March to May, October and November could see some encouraging work developments.

This can be an expensive year, however, and the Earth Rooster should keep track of his outgoings and check the terms and conditions of any new agreement he may enter into. This is no time to make assumptions, take risks or succumb to too many impulse buys. Earth Roosters, take note and remain disciplined in your spending.

Overall, this will be a pleasant and constructive year for the Earth Rooster and making the most of his chances, especially to develop his skills, will reward him well. With his prospects set to improve next year, significant chances await. In the meantime, by devoting time to his loved ones and interests, he will be able to appreciate this year all the more.

Be active and involved. Whether in your home life, work or other interests, by making the most of the present, you will find your actions can bring you both benefit and pleasure. As an Earth Rooster you have much to give, and the Rabbit year will offer you the chance to appreciate *and* be appreciated.

FAMOUS ROOSTERS

Mohamed al Fayed, Fernando Alonso, Beyoncé, Cate Blanchett, Barbara Taylor Bradford, Sir Michael Caine, Enrico Caruso, Christopher Cazenove, Eric Clapton, Joan Collins, Rita Coolidge, Daniel Day Lewis, Minnie Driver, the Duke of Edinburgh, Gloria Estefan, Roger Federer, Errol Flynn, Benjamin Franklin, Dawn French, Stephen Fry, Melanie Griffith, Josh Groban, Deborah Harry, Goldie Hawn, Katharine Hepburn, Paris Hilton, Jay-Z, Catherine Zeta Jones, Quincy Jones, Diane Keaton, Søren Kierkegaard, D. H. Lawrence, David Livingstone, Ken Livingstone, Jayne Mansfield, Steve Martin, James Mason, W. Somerset Maugham, Paul Merton, Kate Middleton, Bette Midler, Van Morrison, Willie Nelson, Kim Novak, Yoko Ono, Dolly Parton, Matthew Perry, Michelle Pfeiffer, Priscilla Presley, Joan Rivers, Kelly Rowland, Kevin Rudd, Jenny Seagrove, George Segal, Carly Simon, Britney Spears, Johann Strauss, Verdi, Richard Wagner, Serena Williams, Neil Young, Renée Zellweger.

28 JANUARY 1922 ⌣ 15 FEBRUARY 1923   *Water Dog*

14 FEBRUARY 1934 ⌣ 3 FEBRUARY 1935   *Wood Dog*

2 FEBRUARY 1946 ⌣ 21 JANUARY 1947   *Fire Dog*

18 FEBRUARY 1958 ⌣ 7 FEBRUARY 1959   *Earth Dog*

6 FEBRUARY 1970 ⌣ 26 JANUARY 1971   *Metal Dog*

25 JANUARY 1982 ⌣ 12 FEBRUARY 1983   *Water Dog*

10 FEBRUARY 1994 ⌣ 30 JANUARY 1995   *Wood Dog*

29 JANUARY 2006 ⌣ 17 FEBRUARY 2007   *Fire Dog*

THE
DOG

THE PERSONALITY OF THE DOG

I have my values
and beliefs.
These are my beacon
in an ever-changing world.

The Dog is born under the signs of loyalty and anxiety. He usually holds very firm views and beliefs and is the champion of good causes. He hates any sort of injustice or unfair treatment and will do all in his power to help those less fortunate than himself. He has a strong sense of fair play and will be honourable and open in all his dealings.

The Dog is very direct and straightforward. He is never one to skirt round issues and speaks frankly and to the point. He can be stubborn, but he is prepared to listen to the views of others and will try to be as fair as possible in coming to his decisions. He will readily give advice where it is needed and will be the first to offer assistance when things go wrong.

The Dog instils confidence wherever he goes and there are many who admire him for his integrity and resolute manner. He is a very good judge of character and can often form an accurate impression of someone very shortly after meeting them. He is also very intuitive and can frequently sense how things are going to work out long in advance.

Despite his friendly and amiable manner, the Dog is not a big socializer. He dislikes having to attend large functions or parties and much prefers a quiet meal with friends or a chat by the fire. He is an excellent conversationalist and is often a marvellous raconteur of amusing stories and anecdotes.

The Dog is also quick-witted and his mind is always alert. He can keep calm in a crisis and although he does have a temper, his outbursts tend to be short-lived. He is loyal and trustworthy, but if he ever feels badly let down or rejected by someone, he will rarely forgive or forget.

The Dog usually has very set interests. He prefers to specialize and become an expert in a chosen area rather than dabble in a variety of different activities. He usually does well in jobs where he feels that he is being of service to others and is often suited to careers in the social services, the medical and legal professions and teaching. He does, however, need to feel motivated in his work. He has to have a sense of purpose and if ever this is lacking he can quite often drift through life without ever achieving very much. Once he has the motivation, however, very little can prevent him from securing his objective.

Another characteristic of the Dog is his tendency to worry and to view things rather pessimistically. Quite often his worries are totally unnecessary and are of his own making. Although it may be difficult, worrying is a habit that all Dogs should try to overcome.

The Dog is not materialistic or particularly bothered about accumulating great wealth. As long as he has the money necessary to support his family and to spend on the occasional luxury, he is more than happy. However, when he does have any spare money he tends to be rather a spendthrift and does not always put it to its best use. He is also not a very good speculator and would be advised to get professional advice before entering into any major long-term investment.

The Dog will rarely be short of admirers, but he is not an easy person to live with. His moods are changeable and his standards high, but he will be loyal and protective to his partner and will do all in his power to provide a comfortable home. He can get on extremely well with those born under the signs of the Horse, Pig, Tiger and Monkey, and can also establish a sound and stable relationship with the Rat, Ox, Rabbit, Snake and another Dog, but will find the Dragon a bit too flamboyant for his liking. He will also find it difficult to understand the imaginative Goat and is likely to be highly irritated by the candid Rooster.

The female Dog is renowned for her beauty. She has a warm and caring nature, although until she knows someone well she can be both secretive and very guarded. She is highly intelligent and despite her calm and tranquil appearance can be extremely ambitious. She enjoys sport and other outdoor activities and has a happy knack of finding bargains in the most unlikely of places. She can also get rather impatient when things do not work out as she would like.

The Dog usually has a very good way with children and can be a doting parent. He will rarely be happier than when he is helping someone or doing something that will benefit others. Providing he can cure himself of his tendency to worry, he will lead a very full and active life, and in that life he will make many friends and do a tremendous amount of good.

THE FIVE DIFFERENT TYPES OF DOG

In addition to the 12 signs of the Chinese zodiac there are five elements and these have a strengthening or moderating influence on the signs. The effects of the five elements on the Dog are described below, together with the years in which they were exercising their influence. Therefore those Dogs born in 1970 are Metal Dogs, those born in 1922 and 1982 are Water Dogs, and so on.

Metal Dog: 1970

The Metal Dog is bold, confident and forthright and sets about everything he does in a resolute and determined manner. He has a great belief in his abilities and no hesitation about speaking his mind or devoting himself to some just cause. He can be rather serious at times and can become anxious and irritable when things are not going according to plan. He tends to have very specific interests and it would certainly help him if he were to broaden his outlook and become more involved in group activities. He is extremely loyal and faithful to his friends.

Water Dog: 1922, 1982

The Water Dog has a very direct and outgoing personality. He is an excellent communicator and has little trouble in persuading others to fall in with his plans. He does, however, have a somewhat carefree nature and is not as disciplined or as thorough as he should be in certain matters. Neither does he keep as much control over his finances as he should, but he can be most generous to his family and friends and will make sure that they want for nothing. He is usually very good with children and has a wide circle of friends.

Wood Dog: 1934, 1994

This Dog is a hard and conscientious worker and will usually make a favourable impression wherever he goes. He is less independent than some of the other types of Dog and prefers to work in a group rather than on his own. He is popular, has a good sense of humour and takes a keen interest in the activities of the various members of his family. He is often attracted to the finer things in life and can obtain much pleasure from collecting items of interest, beauty or antiquity. He prefers to live in the country rather than the town.

Fire Dog: 1946, 2006

This Dog has a lively, outgoing personality and is able to establish friendships with remarkable ease. He is an honest and conscientious worker and likes to take an active part in all that is going on around him. He also likes to explore new ideas and providing he can get the necessary support and advice, he can often succeed where others have failed. He does, however, have a tendency to be stubborn. Providing he can overcome this, he can often achieve considerable fame and fortune.

Earth Dog: 1958

The Earth Dog is very talented and astute. He is methodical and efficient and is capable of going far in his chosen profession. He tends to be rather quiet and reserved, but has a very persuasive manner and usually secures his objectives without too much opposition. He is generous and kind and always ready to lend a helping hand when it is needed. He is also held in very high esteem by his friends and colleagues and is usually most dignified in his appearance.

PROSPECTS FOR THE DOG IN 2011

The Year of the Tiger (14 February 2010–2 February 2011) will have been a busy and interesting one for the Dog, but to get the most from what remains of it, he will need to act determinedly. It is a time to be active and bold.

His personal life is especially well aspected, and for the unattached, romance can bring much happiness. As the Tiger year draws to a close, the Dog can also look forward to an increasing number of social occasions. The final weeks of the year could give many Dogs the chance to meet someone they have not seen for some considerable time.

The Dog's home life is also set to become busier and at all times he needs to liaise closely with others. If anything is concerning him or he would welcome additional help, he should let others know. In Tiger years it is important for Dogs to be forthcoming.

In work matters, Tiger years can be fast moving, and to do well the Dog will need to be adaptable and act quickly when he sees opportunities. September and November could be particularly active and potentially rewarding months.

In money matters the Dog could enjoy some good fortune, perhaps receiving a gift or some additional payment. By keeping alert, he could be fortunate in obtaining some items at very advantageous prices. As with so much in the Tiger year, it will reward him to remain aware and act quickly when the time is right.

The Rabbit year starts on 3 February and its message for the Dog is simple: build on your strengths and move forward. This is a positive time for him and a lot can go in his favour.

His personal life is particularly well aspected, with his relations with others both meaningful and positive. For those Dogs who are enjoying romance, perhaps with someone met in the Tiger year, the indications are encouraging, and many will find their relationship growing ever stronger. For those currently unattached, the Rabbit year is superbly aspected. A chance meeting could be significant and while Dogs like to take their time in forming friendships, someone special could quickly add a new dimension to their life. Over the year quite a few Dogs will decide to settle down with a partner or marry.

During the year the Dog should also take advantage of the social opportunities that come his way. By adding to his contacts, he could find himself benefiting from suggestions or just enjoying the chance to talk, socialize and enjoy shared interests. March to mid-April, June, August and October could see the most social activity, while for the unattached, Cupid's arrow could strike at any time and possibly unexpectedly.

The positive aspects are not just restricted to the Dog's social life, for many Dogs will also have excellent cause for some domestic celebrations during the year. This could be an addition to their family or some other gratifying news. In addition, with the Dog sensing that this is a year for making things happen, he may be tempted to move to accommodation more suited to his present needs. A lot is set to happen this year and although this can put additional pressure on the Dog, he will often delight in his achievements.

Throughout the year it is important that he is forthcoming and talks about his ideas and hopes, as that will give others the chance to assist as well as address any concerns he may have. Also, with some of the major developments of the year, this is very much a time for pooling energies and acting together. While the Dog will be eager for certain plans to go ahead, he will need, however, to show patience. The Rabbit year is not as fast paced as some, although when things do happen, they can be very much to his benefit. Domestically, this will be an eventful and significant year.

The aspects are also promising as far as work prospects are concerned. For many Dogs there will now be excellent opportunity to build on their current position and secure a greater role. Skills they have recently demonstrated and successes they have enjoyed can be important factors, and when promotion opportunities occur or the Dog sees a vacancy that interests him, he will often be well placed to apply. Some Dogs could also be assisted by more senior colleagues who are keen for them to make more of their potential. March, June, July and September to mid-October could see some good opportunities, but throughout the year it would benefit the Dog to have self-belief and put himself forward. Fortune will favour the bold Dog this year.

With the Rabbit year such an exciting and progressive time, there will also be some Dogs who are tempted to become self-employed or start a business. In either case they should take full advantage of the information available to them. The better their support and preparation, the better their prospects. As the Chinese proverb states, 'Well begun is half done.'

For Dogs seeking work, the Rabbit year can again offer exciting possibilities. Some may be keen to take on a totally different position or start a new career, while others will consider other ways in which they could use their experience. By remaining alert and having a determined 'can do' attitude, the Dog will find doors opening for him and his redoubtable spirit will shine through. The Rabbit year is an encouraging one for him and his qualities and strengths will be recognized and rewarded.

His progress at work will also help him financially and some Dogs may be able to supplement their income through a hobby or interest. However, with some of the exciting plans the Dog may have, as well as his existing commitments, he will need to remain disciplined and budget carefully. This is a time favouring personal development, however, and if there is some equipment he needs for a hobby, a course that could be useful to him or a trip he would like to take, he should make allowance for this. Financially, this can be an improved year and with planning and some good decisions, the Dog will often be delighted with what he is able to do.

The Year of the Rabbit is an encouraging one for the Dog, although it does require him to act positively. The progress he makes will be down to his own efforts and his willingness to put himself forward. There will be exciting developments in many a Dog's personal life, however, with his relations with others and the realization of certain hopes making this a special year. Overall, a time of considerable possibility and promise.

The Metal Dog

The Metal Dog has great willpower and determination and once he has set his sights on an objective, he will work tirelessly to achieve his aim. He has commitment and tremendous strength of character, and these quantities will serve him well in this year of opportunity.

Although the Metal Dog tends to be self-reliant, it is important that he does not act too independently this year or without sufficient consultation. With advice and the support of others, he will fare much better. Also, as with other Dogs, the Metal Dog can be guarded when he first meets someone and, whether in social or work situations, he should try to lose some of his reserve. With a good early impression, he can make some firm friends and valuable contacts. It is possible that some of those he meets this year will be particularly helpful to him, and many Metal Dogs will find that the more people they know, the more possibilities open up for them. March to mid-April, June, August and October could be the busiest months socially, and whenever the Metal Dog has invitations to go out or sees events that appeal to him, he should try to go. Many Metal

Dogs will also find their personal interests leading to some social opportunities and will enjoy some rewarding times and new friendships with fellow enthusiasts.

For Metal Dogs who would welcome a more fulfilling social life, this is a year to involve themselves more fully in their interests and community and enjoy the opportunities these bring. Affairs of the heart are well aspected and some unattached Metal Dogs could meet someone who will in time become very special to them. As far as the Metal Dog's relations with others are concerned, this can be an important and positive year.

His domestic life will also see much activity. With change in the air, sometimes routines will need altering and adjustments will need to be made. However, with support and co-operation, these will soon fall into place and some unexpected benefits may arise. Similarly, with some of the family activities that take place, the earlier that these can be talked through, the more that can be arranged. Whether a holiday, some trips and treats out or home improvements, there will be much for the Metal Dog to appreciate.

The aspects are also encouraging as far as his work prospects are concerned. With his determination and the experience he has behind him, he will be well placed to make progress. The Rabbit year will also bring some important new possibilities. Often these will arise in the Metal Dog's current place of work and senior colleagues will be keen for him to make more of his particular strengths. Whether being offered the chance to concentrate on a more specific area, take on new objectives or move to a different role, many Metal Dogs will have the opportunity to take their career to a new level this year.

With this also an excellent year as far as the Metal Dog's relations with others are concerned, he should again make every effort to work closely with colleagues, become better known and use his chances to network.

For Metal Dogs who feel they have accomplished all they can with their present employer and are keen to move on, as well as those seeking work, the Rabbit year can open some significant doors. By widening the scope of what they are prepared to consider and remaining resolute in their quest, many Metal Dogs will find their tenacity rewarded with an important new position. While this may involve considerable readjustment, these Metal Dogs will often revel in the chance they have been given and be keen to make their mark. March, June, July and September to mid-October could see some important developments, but the Rabbit year is an encouraging one and the Metal Dog's drive, commitment and reputation will serve him well throughout.

His progress at work can also help him financially, but to get the full benefit from this he will need to keep tabs on his spending and ideally set funds aside for certain plans and purchases. The more control he has, the more likely certain plans are to be realized. He should also be careful when attending to financial paperwork. A delay, misplaced document or oversight could be to his detriment. Metal Dogs, take note.

With the progressive nature of the year it is also important that the Metal Dog keeps his lifestyle in balance and takes good care of himself. If sedentary for much of the day, he should consider ways in which he could exercise, and if reliant on convenience foods, he could find changes to his diet making a difference. Preserving quality time for loved ones and personal interests can also help to make his year more gratifying.

Overall, the Year of the Rabbit offers great scope for the Metal Dog, and with his earnest nature and desire to move his situation forward, he can make this an important and personally successful time. And throughout the year he will be well supported, with his relations with others helping him both personally and professionally.

TIP FOR THE YEAR

Although you may value a certain independence and like to set about your activities in your own way, this is a year to join forces with others. Raise your profile and let others see your fine qualities and potential. With determination, much is now possible, but you can't do it all singlehandedly.

The Water Dog

One of the great strengths of the Water Dog is his ability to communicate. He expresses himself well, is able to relate and empathize and is very clear thinking. And these abilities will be of great value to him in the Rabbit year. Not only will his manner and talents impress many, but with his desire to progress, a lot can open up for him. This is a positive and constructive year and one which can contain some very special moments.

The Water Dog's relations with others will be especially meaningful, and for those with a partner, this can be an exciting year. Some will decide to start a family and/or move and enjoy setting up a new home. This is a year when great plans can be set in motion and hopes realized. Water Dogs who are already parents will take particular delight in watching and encouraging their child's development. Domestically, this can be an exciting and often happy time.

For many unattached Water Dogs the Rabbit year can also see significant developments. Affairs of the heart are prominent, with the chance of an existing friendship suddenly becoming much more serious or the Water Dog meeting someone in chance circumstances. This is also a year when many Water Dogs will settle down with a partner or marry. On a personal level, the Rabbit year can often be special.

For any Water Dog starting the Rabbit year in low spirits, this is a good time to draw a line under what has happened and look forward. With a positive and willing approach, he can see new chances opening up and his determination to 'turn the corner' paying off. The Water Dog knows deep down that, despite any personal or professional knocks he may have had, he has the abilities to triumph, and his resolve and character will see him through. In the Rabbit year the aspects are firmly on his side.

A further factor in the Water Dog's favour will be the positive relations he enjoys with so many. Friends can be especially helpful and if the Water Dog mentions certain hopes or plans, some may be able to advise or assist in unexpected ways. Throughout the year the Water Dog should make the most of his chances to meet others and, whether socially or in connection with his personal interests or work, he will often impress and make some useful contacts. March to mid-April, June, August and mid-September to October could see the most social activity, although at most times during the year the Water Dog will have things to enjoy.

The Rabbit year favours culture, learning and creativity, and here again the Water Dog can benefit from the prevailing aspects. For those Water Dogs who enjoy creative pursuits, this is an excellent year for making more of their talents. It can be an inspiring time. Also, if the Water Dog becomes interested in a new subject or would like to obtain a further skill or qualification, this would be an excellent year to follow this up. Positive action on his part can not only benefit him in the present but also give rise to some future possibilities. The value of the Rabbit year should not be underestimated.

The Water Dog will also see important developments in his career, but while he can make good progress this year, he will need to remain alert and be prepared to adapt. Although he may have certain notions about how he would like his career to develop, sometimes events can take a curious course. It could be that openings in his present place of work give him the chance to progress but involve a change of duties, or new objectives mean a shift in role. The Rabbit year will bring change, but by being willing, working well with his colleagues and making the most of his chances, the Water Dog can not only accomplish a great deal but also demonstrate his future potential. His opportunities this year may not be what he was expecting, but can nevertheless be far-reaching.

Although many Water Dogs will remain with their present employer this year, for those who feel it is now right to move on, as well as those seeking work, the Rabbit year can be a time of encouraging developments. Not only should the Water Dog consider ways in which he would like to use certain strengths but also contact professional organizations, companies and employment agencies for advice and to see what possibilities are on offer. By seeking information and keeping alert, he can uncover opportunities, and once in a new position, can find it a useful platform on which to build in the future. Again, work developments may not always be as anticipated, but what happens over the year can give the Water Dog important new experience. March, June, July and September to mid-October could see some good opportunities.

The Water Dog's progress at work can also lead to an increase in income, but with exciting developments in his personal life and a possible change of accommodation, this can be an expensive year. As a result the Water Dog will need to watch his spending and plan ahead. Also, when entering into any agreement, he needs to check the terms, make comparisons and, when necessary, seek further advice. In matters of finance, this is a year to be thorough.

Although the aspects are generally favourable for the Water Dog this year, as with any year problems will arise and sometimes these will not be helped by tiredness, the pressures of particularly long days or uncertainties over some plans. At all times the Water Dog should remember that there are people that he can talk to and professionals or help centres that can advise. This is no year to keep his anxieties to himself. As he will find, the very process of taking action can ease problems or set significant wheels in motion.

Overall, the Year of the Rabbit is a promising one for the Water Dog. In his work and interests there will be excellent chances to gain experience, while personally, the love, support and assistance of others can be instrumental in some of the developments he will enjoy over the year. The Rabbit year can also give rise to some personal celebrations. In many ways this will be a pleasing and often special year for the Water Dog.

TIP FOR THE YEAR
Make the most of your people skills. By meeting others, getting support and asking for advice you can be helped in some significant ways. Also, value your relations with those who are special to you. They are treasures in your life. Treasure them.

The Wood Dog

This will be a year of considerable scope for the Wood Dog and with a willing attitude he can make good progress and enjoy some fine success.

In his education the pressures could well increase. With exams and coursework to prepare for and more complex topics to study, the Wood Dog will need to remain focused and put in the time and effort. Although he may feel uncomfortable with the amount he has to do, it is by being challenged that he will learn more. The Rabbit year will test his capabilities but, in the process, show his aptitude in certain areas. Also, as he gets to do more, he will often feel himself to be making progress and this will encourage him on.

There will also be more chance for the Wood Dog to spend time on activities he enjoys. Again, by developing knowledge and skills and exploring his talents, he can gain a lot from what he does as well as often have fun. His activities could include sport, music, drama or other creative pursuits, but for the keen, the Rabbit year is one of possibility.

In all he does, the young Wood Dog does need to be open to instruction. In some cases certain skills or techniques may seem difficult or the Wood Dog may have developed bad habits. By listening carefully to what is said and making an effort to correct what he is doing, he can not only help his present situation but also his future progress. This year can have long-term value and with a willing attitude, the Wood Dog will acquit himself well.

Throughout the year it is also important that he is forthcoming and talks about his current activities as well as any choices he may need to make. Some Wood Dogs may be required to select subjects for further study or have the chance to talk to advisors about career or further education choices. At such times the Wood Dog should make his views known but also listen carefully to advice given. Some of what he may now decide can shape the next few years and it is important that he thinks carefully about what feels right for him.

Similarly, if at any time he is worried over his work or any other matter, he should again speak to those who are in a position to help, whether family, tutors or other professionals. By being forthcoming, he will find that difficulties can often be eased, support given and solutions found. The Wood Dog does have a very responsible attitude, but over the year he should not keep any anxieties to himself.

In his home life, although he will often be busy with his studies and other pursuits, he should also involve himself in joint activities as well as help others. His participation and involvement will not only be appreciated but also help general understanding. And again he should be open to the assistance and advice family members are able to give.

The Wood Dog will value his friendships over the year and can have a lot of fun sharing interests, talking and just being with others. As a result of certain activities, he will also have the chance to meet new people, and while, in typical Dog fashion, he does take some time to lower his reserve and build up friendships, some of those he meets will in time become part of his social circle. The Rabbit year favours the Dog's relations with others, and family, friends and acquaintances can all be supportive and encouraging.

For Wood Dogs in work or seeking work, the Rabbit year can see some interesting developments. Those currently in work will often be encouraged to extend their role where they are, although some will decide to build on what they have been doing and try for a better position elsewhere. For those seeking work, the Rabbit year can open up some important possibilities, including, for some, the chance to combine work with learning. By taking advantage of such opportunities, including apprenticeship schemes, these Wood Dogs can gain a solid base on which to build. March, mid-May to July and September to mid-October could see some interesting possibilities, but the emphasis this year is very much on personal development and gaining skills.

With all the various items the Wood Dog will want to buy, together with recreation costs, he will need to manage his money well. With certain purchases, if he is prepared to

wait he could benefit from some favourable buying opportunities and save himself considerable outlay. Financially,
this is a year that rewards patience and good control.

Overall, the importance of the Rabbit year should not be
underestimated. By using his chances to learn and add to
his skills, the Wood Dog will not only be pleased with the
headway he makes but also the opportunities that the
results of his efforts bring. With his resolve and character,
the Wood Dog has a great future ahead of him and his
achievements in the Rabbit year can prepare him for the
exciting times ahead.

TIP FOR THE YEAR
Take your opportunities. By adding to your knowledge and
skills, you will find more becoming possible for you. Also,
be forthcoming. Tell others of your hopes and concerns and
listen to their advice. You have much in your favour this
year and your accomplishments can have far-reaching
value.

The Fire Dog

One of the benefits of the Rabbit year is that it can usher
in more settled times, allowing many to set about their
activities in a more considered and measured way. The Fire
Dog will appreciate this and can enjoy some pleasing
personal developments.

A further feature of the year will be the excellent
support – and affection – the Fire Dog will receive and at all
times he should be open and forthcoming. Considering
ideas and possibilities with others can take many of his

plans further. His thinking could relate to accommodation matters, his interests or his work situation, but no matter what the area, the more discussion and consideration, the better the outcome. Also, as many Fire Dogs will discover, once plans are set in motion they could enjoy an unexpected impetus. Luck can play a part this year.

Accommodation plans will figure prominently for many Fire Dogs, with some deciding to move, perhaps to an area they have long favoured, or, if they remain where they are, adding improvements to their home and making changes. Either way, the Fire Dog will often feel excited by how his ideas and plans take shape and his care and judgement will reward him well. Events do not always move swiftly in the Rabbit year, so time should be allowed for decisions and choices to be made. In addition, where purchases are concerned, by biding his time the Fire Dog could benefit from some good buying opportunities or find something ideal by chance. His eye for quality and suitability will serve him well this year.

The Fire Dog will also enjoy the chance to spend time with others. Whether involved with household tasks and plans, helping younger family members, spending time with grandchildren or enjoying shared activities, he will find the Rabbit year containing some fine family moments.

In addition, travel could appeal to many Fire Dogs, and by making enquiries and keeping alert for offers and opportunities, they will particularly enjoy some of the interesting things they do and see. This is a year for acting on ideas.

This also applies to the Fire Dog's personal interests. With his passion for certain activities, if there are events that appeal to him, he should try to go. In addition a new interest or activity could catch his attention and be something he will enjoy finding out more about.

For Fire Dogs in work this can be an eventful year. Some will retire or reduce their working commitments and while this will involve considerable readjustment, it will give the Fire Dog the chance to follow up long-held ideas. With these being times of change, he should talk over his options with others and listen carefully to what is suggested. With support and careful thought, important decisions can be made.

In matters of finance, he can fare well and be fortunate in some transactions. By taking his time in making choices, he will be pleased with what he does. If at any time he has problems or uncertainties over forms, benefits or other important matters, it is important that he seeks advice rather than worries over what could be a complex situation.

He will appreciate the social opportunities that arise this year and new interests can introduce him to a new set of people. March to mid-April, June, August and October could see the most social activity.

Overall, the Rabbit year is a promising one for the Fire Dog and will allow him to further his ideas and enjoy the benefits that can so often follow on. He will be well supported by those around him, with his family and social life bringing him much pleasure. Generally, with initiative, willingness and support, a lot can go in his favour this year.

TIP FOR THE YEAR
Be forthcoming and talk over ideas, hopes and plans. By involving others, you can not only enjoy greater support

but also find combined talents adding momentum to what you do. Also, spend time enjoying and exploring your interests, whether existing or new.

The Earth Dog

The Earth Dog has a careful and disciplined nature. He is not one who favours rush or acting on impulse. Instead he prefers a more considered approach and also pays great attention to his instincts. He has remarkably good judgement and is able to gauge situations well. And his talents will be of considerable help to him in the Rabbit year.

In his work this can prove an important year. Although many Earth Dogs will have seen changes in their role in recent years, quite a few will not feel entirely fulfilled. They may consider they are not using their skills or experience to best advantage or may have become staid and disenchanted with what they are doing. Rather than remain in an unsatisfactory situation, these Earth Dogs should realize that change rests with them and the Rabbit year can present some interesting possibilities. Those well established in a particular company will benefit from keeping alert for internal vacancies, while others may decide to make enquiries elsewhere, but, as many will find, once they start to explore options, interesting developments can quickly follow on. The Rabbit year has an element of luck to it and the Earth Dog's instincts and drive can serve him well.

Another helpful feature of the Rabbit year will be the opportunities it brings to develop certain strengths. Sometimes these will come as a result of new duties the

Earth Dog takes on, but if he has the chance of training or can set time aside for research and keeping up to date with developments in his industry, he will strengthen his position. As the Chinese proverb states, 'Diligence leads to riches,' and the Earth Dog's diligence this year can lead to some significant developments.

It is also important that he talks to others about his situation and hopes. Sometimes more senior colleagues or contacts could prove especially helpful, either in suggesting ways forward, providing references or being instrumental in giving the Earth Dog the chance he needs. He will have much in his favour this year, but he does need to be forthcoming and be prepared to add to his skills.

This also applies to Earth Dogs who are seeking work. Although they may face considerable competition, this is a time for self-belief and determination. By exploring ways in which they can use or adapt their skills, many will secure an excellent new position, often as a direct result of their initiative and enterprise. The Rabbit year can open up possibilities, but it does call on the Earth Dog to act. March, June, July and September to mid-October could see the best work opportunities.

Another rewarding aspect of the year will be the pleasure the Earth Dog's personal interests bring him. This is a time for developing ideas and starting projects. Some Earth Dogs may decide to join local groups or enrol on courses, and any Earth Dog who, because of pressures or concerns, has neglected his interests of late or let his life get out of balance should aim to rectify this during the Rabbit year.

There will also be some good travel possibilities, sometimes related to the Earth Dog's interests or an invitation to visit family or friends. Again the Rabbit year is one for making the most of opportunities and following up ideas.

The Earth Dog's progress at work can also lead to an improvement in his earnings and some Earth Dogs may be able to supplement this through an additional activity. However, to benefit from any upturn, the Earth Dog will need to manage his resources and, if possible, look to reduce his borrowings as well as make provision for his outgoings. He will find that good financial control can make a substantial difference to his position.

The Rabbit year will also see an increase in social activity and the Earth Dog will enjoy the conversations and laughs he has as well as the opportunity to unwind, be entertained or just do something different. March to mid-April, June, August and October could see much social activity, and for unattached Dogs, the aspects are promising for new friends or romance.

The Earth Dog's home life will also be active and throughout the year he will play an important and very appreciated role in the lives of those close to him. In addition there could be some far-reaching decisions to be made. Time needs to be given for these to be fully discussed and the financial implications considered, and here again the Earth Dog's judgement and instinct will be on good form. There could also be family news to celebrate, possibly including the birth of a grandchild. Domestically, this can be a rewarding and pleasurable year.

Overall, the Rabbit year holds good prospects for the Earth Dog, and his resolve and determined character will stand him in excellent stead. This is a year for him to take action as well as enjoy his interests, family and social life and the opportunities that are opening up for him. An important and often fortuitous year.

TIP FOR THE YEAR
Seize your opportunities to develop your skills and interests. Furthering your knowledge will allow other possibilities to arise. This will be an interesting year. Do make the most of it, for you can gain a lot from it.

FAMOUS DOGS

King Albert II of Belgium, Brigitte Bardot, Candice Bergen, Andrea Bocelli, David Bowie, George W. Bush, Naomi Campbell, Fabio Capello, Mariah Carey, King Carl Gustaf XVI of Sweden, José Carreras, Paul Cézanne, Cher, Sir Winston Churchill, Bill Clinton, Leonard Cohen, Jamie Lee Curtis, Matt Damon, Charles Dance, Claude Debussy, Dame Judi Dench, Joseph Fiennes, Robert Frost, Ava Gardner, Judy Garland, George Gershwin, Anne Hathaway, Lenny Henry, O. Henry, Victor Hugo, Barry Humphries, Holly Hunter, Michael Jackson, Al Jolson, Jennifer Lopez, Sophia Loren, Joanna Lumley, Shirley MacLaine, Andie McDowell, Madonna, Norman Mailer, Barry Manilow, Freddie Mercury, Liza Minelli, Simon Pegg, Sydney Pollack, Elvis Presley, Tim Robbins, Paul Robeson, Andy Roddick, Susan Sarandon, Claudia Schiffer, Dr Albert Schweitzer, Sylvester Stallone, Robert Louis Stevenson, Sharon Stone, Donald Sutherland, Chris Tarrant, Mother Teresa, Uma Thurman, Donald Trump, Voltaire, Prince William, Shelley Winters.

16 FEBRUARY 1923 ⌢ 4 FEBRUARY 1924   *Water Pig*

4 FEBRUARY 1935 ⌢ 23 JANUARY 1936   *Wood Pig*

22 JANUARY 1947 ⌢ 9 FEBRUARY 1948   *Fire Pig*

8 FEBRUARY 1959 ⌢ 27 JANUARY 1960   *Earth Pig*

27 JANUARY 1971 ⌢ 14 FEBRUARY 1972   *Metal Pig*

13 FEBRUARY 1983 ⌢ 1 FEBRUARY 1984   *Water Pig*

31 JANUARY 1995 ⌢ 18 FEBRUARY 1996   *Wood Pig*

18 FEBRUARY 2007 ⌢ 6 FEBRUARY 2008   *Fire Pig*

THE
PIG

THE PERSONALITY OF THE PIG

It's the doing,
the giving,
the playing the part,
that makes life what it is.
And what it can be.

The Pig is born under the sign of honesty. He has a kind and understanding nature and is well known for his abilities as a peacemaker. He hates any sort of discord or unpleasantness and will do everything in his power to sort out differences of opinion or bring opposing factions together.

He is also an excellent conversationalist and speaks truthfully and to the point. He dislikes any form of falsehood or hypocrisy and is a firm believer in justice and the maintenance of law and order. In spite of these beliefs, however, he is reasonably tolerant and often prepared to forgive others for their wrongdoings. He rarely harbours grudges and is never vindictive.

The Pig is usually very popular. He enjoys other people's company and likes to be involved in joint or group activities. He will be a loyal member of any club or society and can be relied upon to lend a helping hand at functions. He is also an excellent fundraiser for charities and is often a great supporter of humanitarian causes.

The Pig is a hard and conscientious worker and is particularly respected for his reliability and integrity. In his early years he will try his hand at several different jobs, but he is usually happiest where he feels that he is being of service to others. He will unselfishly give up his time for the common good and is highly valued by his colleagues and employers.

The Pig has a good sense of humour and invariably has a smile, joke or some whimsical remark at the ready. He loves to entertain and to please others, and there are many Pigs who have been attracted to careers in show business or who enjoy following the careers of famous stars and personalities.

There are, unfortunately, some who take advantage of the Pig's good nature and impose upon his generosity. The Pig has great difficulty in saying 'no', and although he may dislike being firm, it would be in his own interests to say occasionally, 'Enough is enough.' He can also be rather naïve and gullible; however, if at any stage in his life he feels that he has been badly let down, he will try to become self-reliant. There are many Pigs who have become entre-preneurs or forged a successful career on their own after some early disappointment in life. Although the Pig tends to spend his money quite freely, he is usually very astute in financial matters and there are many Pigs who have become wealthy.

Another characteristic of the Pig is his ability to recover from setbacks reasonably quickly. His faith and his strength of character keep him going. If he thinks that there is a job he can do or there is something that he wants to achieve, he will pursue it with dogged determination. He can also be stubborn and no matter how many may plead with him, once he has made his mind up he will rarely change his views.

Although the Pig may work hard, he also knows how to enjoy himself. He is a great pleasure-seeker and will quite happily spend his hard-earned money on a lavish holiday or an expensive meal – for the Pig is a connoisseur of good food and wine – or a variety of recreational activities. He also enjoys small social gatherings and if he is in company he likes he can very easily become the life and soul of the party. He does, however, tend to become rather withdrawn at larger functions or when among strangers.

The Pig is a creature of comfort and his home will usually be fitted with the latest in luxury appliances. Where possible, he will prefer to live in the country rather than the town and will opt to have a big garden, for the Pig is usually a keen and successful gardener.

The Pig is very popular with others and will often have numerous romances before he settles down. Once settled, however, he will be loyal to his partner and he will find that he is especially well suited to those born under the signs of the Goat, Rabbit, Dog and Tiger and also to another Pig. Due to his affable and easy-going nature he can also establish a satisfactory relationship with all the remaining signs of the Chinese zodiac, with the exception of the Snake. The Snake tends to be wily, secretive and very guarded, and this can be intensely irritating to the honest and open-hearted Pig.

The female Pig will devote all her energies to the needs of her children and her partner. She will try to ensure that they want for nothing and their pleasure is very much her pleasure. She can be a caring and conscientious parent and has very good taste in clothes. Her home will either be very clean and orderly or hopelessly untidy. Strangely, there seems to be no in between with Pigs – they either love housework or detest it! The female Pig does, however, have considerable talents as an organizer and this, combined with her friendly and open manner, enables her to secure many of her objectives.

The Pig is usually lucky in life and will rarely want for anything. Provided he does not let others take advantage of his good nature and is not afraid of asserting himself, he will go through life making friends, helping others and winning the admiration of many.

THE FIVE DIFFERENT TYPES OF PIG

In addition to the 12 signs of the Chinese zodiac there are five elements and these have a strengthening or moderating influence on the signs. The effects of the five elements on the Pig are described below, together with the years in which they were exercising their influence. Therefore those Pigs born in 1971 are Metal Pigs, those born in 1923 and 1983 are Water Pigs, and so on.

Metal Pig: 1971
The Metal Pig is more ambitious and determined than some of the other types of Pig. He is strong, energetic and likes to be involved in a wide variety of different activities. He is very open and forthright in his views, although he can be a little too trusting at times and has a tendency to accept things at face value. He has a good sense of humour and loves to attend parties and other social gatherings. He has a warm, outgoing nature and usually has a large circle of friends.

Water Pig: 1923, 1983

The Water Pig has a heart of gold. He is generous and loyal and tries to remain on good terms with everyone. He will do his utmost to help others, but sadly there are some who will take advantage of his kind nature and he should, in his own interests, be a little more discriminating and be prepared to stand firm against anything that he does not like. Although he prefers the quieter things in life, he has a wide range of interests. He particularly enjoys outdoor pursuits and attending parties and social occasions. He is a hard and conscientious worker and invariably does well in his chosen profession. He is also gifted in the art of communication.

Wood Pig: 1935, 1995

This Pig has a friendly, persuasive manner and is easily able to gain the confidence of others. He likes to be involved in all that is going on around him but can sometimes take on more responsibility than he can properly handle. He is loyal to his family and friends and derives much pleasure from helping those less fortunate than himself. He is usually an optimist and leads a very full, enjoyable and satisfying life. He also has a good sense of humour.

Fire Pig: 1947, 2007

The Fire Pig is both energetic and adventurous and sets about everything he does in a confident and resolute manner. He is very forthright in his views and does not mind taking risks in order to achieve his objectives. He can, however, get carried away by the excitement of the moment and ought to exercise more caution in some of the enterprises in which he gets involved. He is usually lucky in money matters and is well known for his generosity. He is also very caring towards the members of his family.

Earth Pig: 1959

This Pig has a kindly nature. He is sensible and realistic and will go to great lengths in order to please his employers and to secure his aims and ambitions. He is an excellent organizer and is particularly astute in business and financial matters. He has a good sense of humour and a wide circle of friends. He also likes to lead an active social life, although he does sometimes have a tendency to eat and drink more than is good for him.

PROSPECTS FOR THE PIG IN 2011

Tiger years are fast moving and often leave the Pig feeling uneasy about the speed with which things happen. He may have found parts of this Tiger year (14 February 2010–2 February 2011) frustrating. Despite his efforts, his plans may not always have proceeded in the way he wanted. However, the aspects are changing and the closing months of the year will bring improvement as well as prepare the way for the next, more favourable Chinese year.

In what remains of the Tiger year the Pig will need to remain attentive and aware. This is particularly the case in matters of finance, and with the closing months of the year traditionally more expensive, he will need to watch his spending and avoid risks. Also, paperwork and matters with financial implications need close attention.

Many Pigs will see an increase in their workload at this time as well as have some awkward work issues to deal with. However, by concentrating on what needs to be done and using their experience well, they can help their reputation and prospects. With this a year of fast-moving developments, mid-October to early December and January could see interesting opportunities for some.

With his agreeable nature the Pig enjoys good relations with many and can look forward to some fine social occasions in the closing months of the year. However, while he will enjoy himself, when in company he should be careful not to say things he may later regret. As the saying goes, 'Walls have ears,' and an indiscretion could be embarrassing.

The Pig's home life will also see much activity and he will often do much to help others as well as enjoy any get-togethers and visits to friends and relations. There will be a lot to fit in in the last few Tiger weeks.

The Pig has a great appetite for life. He likes his indulgences but is also prepared to work hard and takes his responsibilities seriously. And he will find the Rabbit year an encouraging one. It will bring the chance for his efforts to reap considerable rewards.

The Rabbit year begins on 3 February and as it starts, if not shortly before, the Pig would do well to give some thought to his hopes for the year, particularly any work aspirations. This is a time for moving forward and with thoughts in mind, he will become more aware of certain opportunities to follow. There is an element of good fortune and synchronicity in the Rabbit year and this can help the Pig in several different ways.

For Pigs who are well established in their career, there will be an excellent chance to progress to a new level and often secure responsibilities they have been working towards for some time. When promotion opportunities arise or they see suitable vacancies, these Pigs should be swift to apply. Speed is of the essence, but with their experience, determination and personable manner, they have a lot in their favour this year.

For Pigs who feel unfulfilled in their present position and are keen to move on, as well as those seeking work, the Rabbit year can again bring some encouraging developments. By making enquiries, considering various possibilities and taking advantage of the support, training and advice available, many Pigs will secure a position that is different from what they have previously been doing but offers an interesting new challenge. And, as the Pig has so often demonstrated, once he has the motivation, he often distinguishes himself. February, March and late August to early October could see the best work opportunities, but throughout the Rabbit year the Pig should keep alert and act quickly when chances arise.

The progress he makes can also lead to an increase in income, and financially this is an improved year. As a result the Pig will often be tempted to go ahead with plans and purchases both for himself and his home. However, while he will enjoy the rewards his efforts will bring, when possible he should consider reducing any borrowings as well as take advantage of tax incentives to save or perhaps supplement a pension policy. With good decisions, he could benefit from his actions in years to come. However, should any Pig find himself in a complex or troubling situation, it would be worth him seeking professional advice. Fortunately this will only apply to a small minority, but matters which could have important implications need to be dealt with effectively and, when appropriate, with expert guidance.

The Pig is a keen socializer and over the year can look forward to a pleasing social life. Some long-standing friends could be particularly helpful regarding certain decisions he has to make. His interests can also bring him into contact with others and his social circle is set to increase quite substantially during the year. April to June, August and December could see the most social activity but, with his kindly and outgoing nature, the Pig will often find himself in demand. For any Pig who starts the year in low spirits or has had some recent adversity to bear, the Rabbit year will see a brightening in his situation, with new activities, friendships and possibly love bringing new joy into his life.

The Pig always attaches great importance to his home life and again this will mean a lot to him over the year. With his enthusiastic nature he will often be the driving force behind many activities, with his care, thoughtfulness and optimism bringing many plans to successful fruition. However, he should try to avoid having too much happen at once. This is a year when there will be a lot to do, and it will be best for events to happen at a measured rather than hurried pace.

Overall, the Year of the Rabbit is an encouraging one for the Pig and by keeping alert for opportunities and making the most of his talents and ideas he will be able to make good headway. His enthusiasm and wonderful personal manner will again be great assets and this will be an active and personally rewarding year.

The Metal Pig

The Metal Pig has resolve, spirit and flair. And as the Rabbit year starts he will be more determined than ever to make the most of the next 12 months. Not only does this mark the start of a new decade in his life but after recent events he will feel the time is now right to pursue his objectives. And his positive actions can reward him well this year.

Any Metal Pig who may start the year discontented will soon find the tide beginning to turn. Some may even experience positive developments in the first few weeks of 2011 or be feeling more optimistic in themselves. For these Metal Pigs it could also be helpful to draw a line under previous disappointments and focus their attention firmly on the present.

The Metal Pig's work situation can take a particularly interesting course during the year. Many Metal Pigs will be well established in a certain career and there will be an excellent chance for them to secure promotion and take on greater responsibilities. Their experience, backed by their contacts and reputation, can now reward them well, and whether staying with their current employer or moving elsewhere, this is a year for some well-deserved (and sometimes overdue) success.

The Rabbit year also holds excellent prospects for Metal Pigs who are disenchanted with their present position or keen to take their career in a new direction. By keeping alert and persisting in their quest, they will see opportunities coming their way, sometimes with responsibilities that are very different from their previous roles. What happens over the year will allow virtually all Metal Pigs to master new skills and, while initially challenging, this can give them the motivation they may have been lacking for some time.

The same is true for Metal Pigs seeking work. By being willing to learn and adapt, they can be rewarded with some significant opportunities. Events can happen quickly, with February, March and late August to early October seeing some important developments.

Another valuable aspect of the year concerns the Metal Pig's personal development. Not only will he add considerably to his working knowledge but may also be keen to use some of his free time to develop his skills in some way. This could be by enrolling on a course, whether for interest or a possible qualification, or by setting himself a new challenge or research project. By deciding on something he will enjoy and which could be of possible use to him, he can reinforce the progressive nature of the year. For the keen, this can be an inspiring time.

The Metal Pig's success at work can also lead to an increase in income. However, he does need to manage his outgoings well. With his existing commitments and plans for the year, his spending could quickly mount up. Also, should he have any financial concerns or find himself in a difficult situation at any time, he should seek professional guidance. Problems do need to be dealt with promptly and effectively, otherwise they could worsen. Metal Pigs, do take note.

Socially, the Metal Pig will find himself in demand during the year and should take advantage of any chances to meet others. With his engaging and empathetic manner, he will often be in impressive form. Late March to June, August and December could see the most social activity. For the unattached a certain friendship could suddenly become more meaningful and quite a few Metal Pigs will find themselves enjoying romance or a busier and more rewarding social life.

The Metal Pig's home life will also be busy, and domestic routines may need altering due to work changes. Those close to the Metal Pig could have important decisions to make and this will call for consultation and co-operation. The progress made, however, can enhance the positive nature of the year. In addition, loved ones will often be keen to celebrate the Metal Pig's fortieth birthday in style and their affection and some surprises they have planned will mean a great deal to him.

The Metal Pig will also spend some time during the year on home improvements and some may actually move. However, with the busy nature of the year, sometimes practical plans will take longer than envisaged and the Metal Pig will need to be patient and allow ample time for their completion. Rabbit years do not favour rush.

Overall, the Year of the Rabbit will be a significant one for the Metal Pig. Not only does it mark the start of a new decade in his life but he will feel readier to build on his strengths and move forward. This is a progressive time for him and can bring some important opportunities and well-deserved success.

TIP FOR THE YEAR
Set yourself some goals for the year and take action. With good use of your time and opportunities, you can achieve a great deal. Your fortieth year can be a personally very special one. Use it well.

The Water Pig

The Water Pig has a great many quantities. He is loyal, kindly and diligent, and over the year he can not only look forward to pleasing developments in his personal life but his skills and enterprise rewarding him well. This is a progressive and often lucky year.

Relations with others are especially favoured and for those Water Pigs with a partner, 2011 can bring some special times. Quite a few could start or see an addition to their family and will enjoy encouraging the development of babies or young children. The Water Pig has a loving and responsive nature and will often form a strong bond with those around him.

Another cause for excitement will be accommodation. Some Water Pigs will decide to move to somewhere that better meets their needs, and while the moving process may be protracted (the Rabbit year does not favour rush), they will be excited by the possibilities that lie ahead. Water Pigs who remain where they are will also often spend time deciding on improvements and stamping their home with their own personality. Whether changing décor and furnishings or updating equipment, the Water Pig will have a lot of fun making plans and considering choices.

Throughout the year he will also value the love and support he is given. Water Pigs with a partner will feel particularly buoyed up by the care shown to them. Many will enjoy a special holiday or more spontaneous chances to go away. The Rabbit year will contain quite a few highlights.

For Water Pigs who are alone, the Rabbit year can bring a transformation, giving these Water Pigs – particularly any who have had their confidence or personal esteem knocked – the tonic they need and the chance to move on to better times. Affairs of the heart are excellently aspected and a friendship could become more special as the year progresses. Quite a few Water Pigs who are alone at the start of the year will find love, settle down with a partner or marry, such are the encouraging aspects of the Rabbit year.

With his friendly and outgoing nature, the Water Pig enjoys his social life and will again value meeting up with his friends and attending events. Several times over the year friends will be particularly grateful for his insights and advice. April to June, August and December could see the most social activity.

Although the Water Pig will be kept busy with his various commitments, it is also important that he does not allow his recreational pursuits to suffer as a result. Not only can these sometimes give him the chance of additional exercise or be an outlet for his ideas, but they can also keep his lifestyle in balance. Any Water Pigs who are sedentary for much of the day or rely a lot on convenience foods should consider ways in which they can get more exercise and improve their diet. With this a promising year, the Water Pig does need to keep himself in good form.

In his work this can be a year of important developments. With his experience, including some of the recent challenges he has had to meet, he will often feel ready to take on a greater role. This could be through promotion in his existing place of work or by applying elsewhere, but this is a time to seize the initiative. The momentum is with the Water Pig this year and by putting himself forward, he will find doors opening for him.

For Water Pigs who are keen to make a more substantial career change or are seeking work, again the Rabbit year can open up excellent possibilities. Making a change will take considerable effort, but by showing initiative and remaining alert, many Water Pigs will be offered a new position which will allow them to develop particular strengths. February, March and late August to early October could see some encouraging developments.

The Water Pig's progress at work will also help him financially, but this will be an expensive year and the Water Pig will need to be disciplined in his spending and manage his resources well. When entering into new agreements he also needs to compare and check the terms and obligations.

Although this is a favourable year, there is also the possibility that some Water Pigs may find themselves in a contentious or difficult situation. Rather than deal with this alone, these Water Pigs should draw on the advice of those who are qualified to help. Disagreements and problems need to be resolved quickly. Water Pigs, take note and *do* seek advice if necessary.

Overall, the Rabbit year will be an exciting and promising one for the Water Pig. On a personal level, he can look forward to some great times and in his work he will often have the chance to find greater fulfilment in new responsibilities. This is a positive year offering considerable scope.

TIP FOR THE YEAR

Believe in yourself and go forward. Keep alert for chances to build on your talents. With determination and willingness, you can achieve a lot this year. Also, enjoy the love and special relations you have with those around you. These are precious and can add a lot to your year.

The Wood Pig

This will be a year of far-reaching significance for the Wood Pig, with his decisions often helping to shape the next few years.

In his education he will be reaching what can be a pivotal stage, and with exams to sit and coursework to prepare, he will need to remain disciplined and show commitment. A lot will hinge on how he fares this year, including his possible choice of subjects for later study and ultimately even his career choice. This is no year for slacking, and by working consistently and well, many Wood Pigs will not only be pleased with their progress but also feel more inspired and confident in themselves. Many will also be pleased with the way they are encouraged to develop certain strengths.

However, while this is an encouraging year, it will not be entirely problem free. Sometimes the Wood Pig's confidence may be knocked when certain work does not get the marks or response he was hoping for. Although disappointing, a great quality of Pigs is that they are resilient and after setbacks they do bounce back. If the Wood Pig should experience any disappointment this year, he should look at the reason why it has occurred and what he can learn from it. In this respect, any reversals suffered now can be constructive and, for some, be a wake-up call indicating the effort now required. The Rabbit year can be wonderfully instructive, but for any Wood Pigs who slack or do not give their best, it is capable of producing some timely reminders.

During the year the Wood Pig will get much pleasure from his personal interests and by spending time on these will not only have a lot of fun but also welcome the chance to extend his knowledge and try out ideas. This is an encouraging year and one for seizing opportunities.

In a lot of what he does the Wood Pig will also value the support and camaraderie of his friends, and as he extends his interests and gets to do more, he will often have good opportunities to meet others. April to June, August and December will be particularly active months.

In his home life he should be open and forthcoming. Being prepared to talk about what he is doing and share any concerns will not only lead to better understanding but also guidance. Family members will also take delight in his achievements and his home life is likely to be marked by some fine moments. Throughout the year, the Wood Pig should remember that those close to him are always keen to support him and should he have any worries or difficulties it is important that he talks about these rather than keeps matters to himself. A worry shared will so often be a worry halved.

During the year the Wood Pig will often be tempted by various purchases, and to buy or do all he wants will require good control and planning.

For Wood Pigs who decide to seek work, the Rabbit year can be illuminating. These Wood Pigs will need to remain persistent and be ready to demonstrate their willingness to learn and adapt. Any position, however routine, can provide experience and be something they can build on in the future. For some there could be the chance to take on an apprenticeship and so combine work with education. Here again, what the Wood Pig can achieve this year can be far-reaching.

For Wood Pigs born in 1935 this can also be a satisfying year and during it they should make the most of their ideas and opportunities. Whether enjoying personal interests, joining community groups or following the activities of family members, they will find the Rabbit year can contain some special occasions. Some will particularly delight in the places they visit. During the year these Wood Pigs will often have much of interest to do.

Overall, the Rabbit year can be a pleasing one for the Wood Pig but it is a case of making the most of his opportunities. With willingness and action, important headway can be made and, for the younger Wood Pig, valuable skills learned and qualifications gained. And all Wood Pigs will enjoy spending time on their personal interests and be grateful for the support of their family and friends. A pleasant and positive year.

TIP FOR THE YEAR

Use your strengths and opportunities. With a keen, determined attitude you will not only achieve a great deal but also find other possibilities opening up. The rewards of this year can be far-reaching.

The Fire Pig

The Fire Pig has an amiable nature, enjoys wide interests and busies himself with many activities. The Rabbit year can give him the chance to set plans in motion and obtain some significant results.

To help make the most of this encouraging year, the Fire Pig would do well to give careful thought to what he would like to accomplish over the next 12 months. With some ideas in mind, he will not only have something to work towards but also be more alert for specific opportunities. As many Fire Pigs will discover, once plans start to take shape, further possibilities can quickly follow on. The Fire Pig's ideas can concern almost any area of his life, but as the Chinese proverb states, 'Well begun is half done,' and good planning at the start of the Rabbit year can do much to shape the next 12 months.

For Fire Pigs who have been considering moving for some time, perhaps to a new area or to accommodation that better suits their requirements, this will be a good year to start looking at possibilities and begin sorting through items in preparation for a move. As many will find, once they start to act, plans can take on a momentum of their own and there can be some exciting and busy months ahead. This will be the year when many Fire Pigs will see their hopes of a new home realized.

Fire Pigs who remain where they are could also become occupied with accommodation matters. Whether making repairs, having alterations carried out or enhancing certain living areas, they may be involved in a lot of practical (and occasionally exhausting) activity. The Fire Pig will be the instigator of much of it and will enjoy making choices and, in some cases, being lucky with certain purchases.

With considerable spending on accommodation likely, together with the Fire Pig's other plans, he will need to be careful in financial matters. This includes keeping account of his spending, making provision for large outgoings and checking the terms and obligations when entering into any agreement. Although the Fire Pig is usually careful in such matters, this is not a year to be lax or make assumptions. He also needs to be thorough with paperwork and attend to forms and correspondence promptly. With the busy nature of the year, sometimes he may be tempted to put these to one side, but delay or an oversight could have repercussions. Fire Pigs, do take note. Also, should the Fire Pig find himself involved in a difficult or complex matter, it is important that he seeks professional advice. Problems need to be dealt with promptly *and* decisively.

With all the practical activities likely to be going on in the Fire Pig's home, it is important that there is good co-operation and communication. A pooling of ideas can lead to more being decided upon and more satisfactory results being obtained. The activity and excitement of the year need not be restricted to just accommodation plans. Some Fire Pigs may decide to treat themselves and their loved ones to a special holiday and a destination that has been tempting them for some time. Rabbit years favour the realization of hopes. In addition, the year will be marked by some family achievements which will make many a Fire Pig feel proud and special.

Another satisfying area of the year will be the Fire Pig's personal interests. Here again, by deciding on his objectives, he can get a lot of pleasure from what he does. This is a year for him to set time aside to enjoy his interests and make more of his ideas, particularly if he is creative or enjoys the arts. Any Fire Pigs who have become intrigued by a certain interest or recreational pursuit should aim to find out more. Other benefits may well follow on.

The Fire Pig's social life is also encouragingly aspected. Not only can he look forward to spending time with his friends but also going to a variety of social occasions. With his wide interests, capacity for fun and ability to relate to others, he will thoroughly enjoy himself. Fire Pigs who move will have excellent opportunities to meet new people as well as discover amenities in their new area. Socially, the Rabbit year is one of great possibility, with late March to June, August and December being particularly busy months. For the unattached Fire Pig who would welcome more company, there will be excellent opportunities to meet others and, for some, romance can be a distinct possibility.

For Fire Pigs in work this will be an important year and many will be able to make greater use of their talents and experience. Whether working on particular objectives, overseeing projects or assisting with training, they are likely to be kept busy. Some Fire Pigs will, though, choose to retire or alter their working commitments to allow more time for other activities. The Rabbit year will present some interesting options. Fire Pigs who retire or have retired might decide to use their skills in other ways, perhaps, with the Pig's strong humanitarian leanings, giving time to charity or community work or helping a person in need.

Overall, the Year of the Rabbit can be both instructive and satisfying. It is a time for setting plans in motion. The Fire Pig will be encouraged by the support of those around him and this, along with his own enterprising nature, can lead to him accomplishing a great deal. Purposeful action can reward him well.

TIP FOR THE YEAR
The Rabbit year is full of possibility but it does require action. Do not let your hopes come to nothing. Seize the initiative, make enquiries and set the ball rolling. With enthusiasm and support, you will find a lot can open up for you this year.

The Earth Pig
The Earth Pig is set to do well in the Rabbit year. With his amiable, conscientious nature he can look forward to making important progress as well as reaping the rewards of some earlier efforts. In 2011 he will have much going his way.

One reassuring aspect of the Rabbit year is that it is a more settled time than previous years and the Earth Pig will be able to determine the course of events rather than be buffeted by outside pressures. This is a time when many Earth Pigs will be able to take stock of their situation and decide on objectives to pursue. And by considering ideas and thinking about the potential benefits, the Earth Pig will start to feel more inspired than he has for some time.

He will also be helped by the support of family and friends, and by talking over his thoughts will not only receive useful advice but also possibly other suggestions. In so much that he does this year it will be in his interests to consult others *and* listen closely to them.

In his work the aspects are encouraging. After the pressures and often difficult working situations many Earth Pigs will have had to cope with in recent years, this will be a time when their efforts will be recognized and there will be chances to progress. If promotion opportunities become available or the Earth Pig sees a suitable position, he should put himself forward. This is a year for taking on new challenges, and even if some applications the Earth Pig makes do not go his way, by indicating his desire to move forward and remaining persistent, he will find that doors will open for him.

Over the year contacts and senior colleagues can also be helpful, whether in alerting him to new possibilities or being willing to put in a good word or a reference on his behalf. In 2011 the Earth Pig will have many rooting for him and his experience and reputation will stand him in good stead.

There will, though, be some Earth Pigs who are feeling disillusioned with their current type of work and would welcome a new challenge. For these Earth Pigs, as well as those seeking a position, the Rabbit year can be a time of exciting possibility. By keeping alert and widening the scope of positions they are prepared to consider, many will be successful in securing a new role and with it a fascinating personal challenge. This could include learning new duties and getting used to a different working pattern, but many will revel in this new chapter in their working lives. The Rabbit year is encouraging and with determination and willingness, the Earth Pig can see a lot open up for him. February, March and late August to early October could see some important work developments.

The progress the Earth Pig makes at work can also help him financially. However, to benefit he will need to manage his situation well and monitor his outgoings. If he is able, taking steps to reduce any borrowings and setting funds aside for specific requirements will be helpful. Financially, this is a year for sensible management.

Also, should the Earth Pig find himself in a difficult situation at any time, he does need to seek professional guidance. These words only apply to a minority of Earth Pigs, but if problems arise, the Earth Pig *does* need to be on his guard.

A feature of the Rabbit year is that it favours personal development and not only will many Earth Pigs have a good chance to further their professional knowledge, but also develop their personal interests. Many will enjoy the social element some of these have and any who have neglected their interests in recent years will find the Rabbit year is an ideal time to get their lifestyle back into balance.

The year can also see an increase in social activity and the Earth Pig will often enjoy the chance to go out and meet others. April to June, August and December could be the busiest months and, with the prevailing aspects, Earth Pigs who are currently unattached could find affairs of the heart adding excitement to this already full and interesting year.

The Earth Pig's home life will also see much activity, with possible celebrations in store. Whether these are marking his own progress or another's personal news, the Earth Pig can enjoy some memorable family events. His organizational talents will be particularly appreciated, with some months busy but personally rewarding. Not only will the Earth Pig value the support he receives, but over the year will reciprocate by helping loved ones in turn, including assisting in what can be an unexpected and generous fashion. His family and home life always mean a lot to him and will be particularly special this year.

Overall, the Year of the Rabbit is an important one for the Earth Pig and will give him the opportunity to progress. Whether in his work or personal interests, this is a time for adding to his skills as well as developing his ideas. With willingness and positive action, much can now be achieved. The support and encouragement of others, backed by the Earth Pig's own desire for progress, can make this a successful and personally rewarding year.

TIP FOR THE YEAR

Your experience and personal qualities can be well rewarded this year. Be active and make the most of your opportunities, ideas and strengths. This is a positive time that will not only provide you with some important opportunities but also some pleasurable and often heartening personal times. Use it well.

FAMOUS PIGS

Bryan Adams, Woody Allen, Julie Andrews, Marie Antoinette, Fred Astaire, Humphrey Bogart, James Cagney, Maria Callas, Hillary Rodham Clinton, Glenn Close, Sacha Baron Cohen, Cheryl Cole, Alice Cooper, the Duchess of Cornwall, Noël Coward, Simon Cowell, Oliver Cromwell, Billy Crystal, the Dalai Lama, Ted Danson, Richard Dreyfuss, Ben Elton, Ralph Waldo Emerson, Henry Ford, Stephen Harper, Emmylou Harris, Ernest Hemingway, Henry VIII, Conrad Hilton, Alfred Hitchcock, Sir Elton John, Tommy Lee Jones, Carl Gustav Jung, Stephen King, Kevin Kline, Hugh Laurie, Nigella Lawson, David Letterman, Jerry Lee Lewis, Meat Loaf, Ewan McGregor, Ricky Martin, Johnny Mathis, Dannii Minogue, Morrissey, Wolfgang Amadeus Mozart, George Osborne, Sir Michael Parkinson, James Patterson, Luciano Pavarotti, Iggy Pop, Maurice Ravel, Ronald Reagan, Ginger Rogers, Winona Ryder, Françoise Sagan, Carlos Santana, Arnold Schwarzenegger, Kevin Spacey, Steven Spielberg, Sir Alan Sugar, David Tennant, Emma Thompson, Herman Van Rompuy, Jules Verne, David Walliams, Amy Winehouse, Michael Winner, the Duchess of York.

APPENDIX

———◦◆◦———

The relationships between the 12 animal signs, both on a personal level and business level, are an important aspect of Chinese horoscopes and in this appendix the compatibility between the signs is shown in the two tables that follow.

Also included are the names of the signs ruling the hours of the day and from this it is possible to find your ascendant and discover yet another aspect of your personality.

Finally, to supplement the earlier chapters on the personality and horoscope of the signs, I have included a guide on how you can get the best out of your sign and the year.

RELATIONSHIPS BETWEEN THE SIGNS

Personal Relationships

KEY

1 Excellent. Great rapport.
2 A successful relationship. Many interests in common.
3 Mutual respect and understanding. A good relationship.
4 Fair. Needs care and some willingness to compromise in order for the relationship to work.
5 Awkward. Possible difficulties in communication with few interests in common.
6 A clash of personalities. Very difficult.

	Rat	Ox	Tiger	Rabbit	Dragon	Snake	Horse	Goat	Monkey	Rooster	Dog	Pig
Rat	1											
Ox	1	3										
Tiger	4	6	5									
Rabbit	5	2	3	2								
Dragon	1	5	4	3	2							
Snake	3	1	6	2	1	5						
Horse	6	5	1	5	3	4	2					
Goat	5	5	3	1	4	3	2	2				
Monkey	1	3	6	3	1	3	5	3	1			
Rooster	5	1	5	6	2	1	2	5	5	5		
Dog	3	4	1	2	6	3	1	5	3	5	2	
Pig	2	3	2	2	2	6	3	2	2	3	1	2

Business Relationships

KEY

1 Excellent. Marvellous understanding and rapport.
2 Very good. Complement each other well.
3 A good working relationship and understanding can be developed.
4 Fair, but compromise and a common objective are often needed to make this relationship work.
5 Awkward. Unlikely to work, either through lack of trust, understanding or the competitiveness of the signs.
6 Mistrust. Difficult. To be avoided.

	Rat	Ox	Tiger	Rabbit	Dragon	Snake	Horse	Goat	Monkey	Rooster	Dog	Pig
Rat	2											
Ox	1	3										
Tiger	3	6	5									
Rabbit	4	3	3	3								
Dragon	1	4	3	3	3							
Snake	3	2	6	4	1	5						
Horse	6	5	1	5	3	4	4					
Goat	5	5	3	1	4	3	3	2				
Monkey	2	3	4	5	1	5	4	4	3			
Rooster	5	1	5	5	2	1	2	5	5	6		
Dog	4	5	2	3	6	4	2	5	3	5	4	
Pig	3	3	3	2	3	5	4	2	3	4	3	1

YOUR ASCENDANT

The ascendant has a very strong influence on your personality and will help you gain an even greater insight into your true personality according to Chinese horoscopes.

The hours of the day are named after the 12 animal signs and the sign governing the time you were born is your ascendant. To find your ascendant, look up the time of your birth in the table below, bearing in mind any local time differences in the place you were born.

11 p.m.	to	1 a.m.	The hours of the Rat
1 a.m.	to	3 a.m.	The hours of the Ox
3 a.m.	to	5 a.m.	The hours of the Tiger
5 a.m.	to	7 a.m.	The hours of the Rabbit
7 a.m.	to	9 a.m.	The hours of the Dragon
9 a.m.	to	11 a.m.	The hours of the Snake
11 a.m.	to	1 p.m.	The hours of the Horse
1 p.m.	to	3 p.m.	The hours of the Goat
3 p.m.	to	5 p.m.	The hours of the Monkey
5 p.m.	to	7 p.m.	The hours of the Rooster
7 p.m.	to	9 p.m.	The hours of the Dog
9 p.m.	to	11 p.m.	The hours of the Pig

RAT

The Rat ascendant is likely to make the sign more outgoing, sociable and careful with money. A particularly beneficial influence for those born under the signs of the Rabbit, Horse, Monkey and Pig.

OX

The Ox ascendant has a restraining, cautionary and steadying influence that many signs will benefit from. This ascendant also promotes self-confidence and willpower and is especially good for those born under the signs of the Tiger, Rabbit and Goat.

TIGER

The Tiger ascendant is a dynamic and stirring influence that makes the sign more outgoing, action-orientated and impulsive. A generally favourable ascendant for the Ox, Tiger, Snake and Horse.

RABBIT

The Rabbit ascendant has a moderating influence, making the sign more reflective, serene and discreet. A particularly beneficial influence for the Rat, Dragon, Monkey and Rooster.

DRAGON

The Dragon ascendant gives strength, determination and ambition to the sign. A favourable influence for those born under the signs of the Rabbit, Goat, Monkey and Dog.

SNAKE

The Snake ascendant can make the sign more reflective, intuitive and self-reliant. A good influence for the Tiger, Goat and Pig.

HORSE

The Horse ascendant will make the sign more adventurous, daring and on some occasions fickle. Generally a beneficial influence for the Rabbit, Snake, Dog and Pig.

GOAT

The Goat ascendant will make the sign more tolerant, easy-going and receptive. It could also impart some creative and artistic qualities. An especially good influence for the Ox, Dragon, Snake and Rooster.

MONKEY

The Monkey ascendant is likely to impart a delicious sense of humour and fun to the sign. It will make the sign more enterprising and outgoing – a particularly good influence for the Rat, Ox, Snake and Goat.

ROOSTER

The Rooster ascendant helps to give the sign a lively, outgoing and very methodical manner. Its influence will increase efficiency and is good for the Ox, Tiger, Rabbit and Horse.

DOG

The Dog ascendant makes the sign more reasonable and fair-minded and gives an added sense of loyalty. A very good ascendant for the Tiger, Dragon and Goat.

PIG

The Pig ascendant can make the sign more sociable and self-indulgent. It is also a caring influence and one that can make the sign want to help others. A good ascendant for the Dragon and Monkey.

HOW TO GET THE BEST FROM YOUR CHINESE SIGN AND THE YEAR

Each of the 12 Chinese signs possesses its own unique strengths and by identifying them you can use them to your advantage. Similarly, by becoming aware of possible weaknesses you can do much to rectify them and in this respect I hope the following sections will be useful. Also included are some tips on how you can get the best from the Year of the Rabbit.

The Rat

The Rat is blessed with many fine talents, but his undoubted strength lies in his ability to get on with others. He is sociable, charming and a good judge of character. He also possesses a shrewd mind and is good at spotting opportunities.

However, to make the most of his abilities, he does need to impose some discipline upon himself. He should resist the (sometimes very great) temptation of getting involved in too many activities all at the same time and should decide upon his priorities and objectives. By concentrating his energies on specific matters he will fare much better. Also, given his personable manner, he should seek out positions where he can use his personal relations skills to good effect. For a career, sales and marketing could prove ideal.

The Rat is astute in dealing with finance, but while often thrifty, he can sometimes give way to moments of indulgence. Although he deserves to enjoy the money he has so carefully earned, it would sometimes be in his interests to exercise restraint when tempted to satisfy too many expensive whims!

The Rat's family and friends are important to him and while he is loyal and protective towards them, he does tend to keep his worries and concerns to himself and would be helped if he were more willing to discuss his anxieties. Others think highly of him and are prepared to do a lot to help him, but for them to do so the Rat does need to be less guarded.

With his sharp mind, keen imagination and sociable manner, he does, however, have much in his favour. When he has commitment, he can be irrepressible and, given his considerable charm, often irresistible as well! Provided he channels his energies wisely, he can make much of his life.

Advice for the Rat's Year Ahead

GENERAL PROSPECTS

The Rat likes to be busy and active, but the pace of the Rabbit year can be slow. However, by adjusting and showing patience, he can usefully add to his skills and his achievements can pave the way for some important successes in 2012.

CAREER PROSPECTS

One of the Rat's greatest strengths is his ability to relate to people, and he should work closely with others and make the most of any chances to network. Over the year he can impress many. If seeking work, he should seek out those who are able to advise as well as be open to different possibilities. A positive approach can bring useful progress and those Rats whose work or interests involve creativity should actively promote their ideas.

FINANCE

A year for care and keeping track of outgoings. Any new agreements need to be checked, and if problems arise, the Rat would do well to seek advice. Financially, a year to be vigilant and thorough.

RELATIONS WITH OTHERS

The Rat places much value on his relations with others and over the year these can go well. Family, friends and colleagues will be supportive and give useful assistance. Many Rats can also look forward to some important personal developments, with some seeing an addition to their family. However, at all times the Rat needs to be mindful of the views of others. The greater his awareness, the better.

The Ox

Strong-willed, determined and resolute, the Ox certainly has a mind of his own! He is persistent and sets about achieving his objectives with dogged determination. In addition he is reliable and tenacious and is often a source of inspiration to others. He is an achiever, and he often achieves a great deal. However, to really excel, he would do well to try and correct some of his weaknesses.

Being so resolute and having such a strong sense of purpose, the Ox can be inflexible and narrow-minded. He can be resistant to change and prefers to set about his activities in his own way rather than be dependent on others. His dislike of change can sometimes be to his detriment and if he were prepared to be more adaptable and adventurous he would find his progress easier.

The Ox would also be helped if he were to broaden his range of interests and become more relaxed in his approach. At times he can be so preoccupied with his own activities that he is not always as mindful of others as he should be, and his demeanour can sometimes be studious and serious. There are times when he would benefit from a lighter touch.

However, the Ox is true to his word and loyal to his family and friends. He is admired and respected by others and his tremendous willpower usually enables him to achieve a great deal in life.

Advice for the Ox's Year Ahead

GENERAL PROSPECTS

A promising and often lucky year, but to benefit the Ox will need to act determinedly. With action and commitment, a lot can become possible. Fortune will very much favour the bold.

CAREER PROSPECTS

Some interesting opportunities can arise this year, either for the Ox to make progress where he is or to switch to a new area of work. To benefit, he will need to keep alert and be adaptable in approach. With the willingness to move his situation forward, he can make this a successful year.

FINANCE

Although income may improve, spending needs to be watched and, where possible, the Ox should make early provision for certain plans and more expensive outgoings. He should also be careful if lending to others.

RELATIONS WITH OTHERS

A very positive year, with the Ox often helped by the support, encouragement and advice of those around him. Interests can often lead to new friendships and romance can become more meaningful. The Ox should be open, communicative and value those who are special to him in this personally rewarding year.

The Tiger

Lively, innovative and enterprising, the Tiger enjoys an active lifestyle. He has a wide range of interests, an alert mind and a genuine liking of others. He loves to live life to the full. However, despite his enthusiastic and well-meaning ways, he does not always make the most of his considerable potential.

Being so versatile, the Tiger does have a tendency to jump from one activity to another or dissipate his energies by trying to do too much at the same time. To make the most of himself he should try to exercise a certain amount of self-discipline. Ideally, he should decide how best he can use his abilities, give himself some objectives and then stick to them. If he can overcome his restless tendencies, he will find he will accomplish far more as a result.

Also, in spite of his sociable manner, the Tiger likes to retain a certain independence in his actions, and while few begrudge him this, he would sometimes find life easier if he were more prepared to work in conjunction with others. His reliance on his own judgement does sometimes mean that he excludes the views and advice of those around him, and this can be to his detriment. He may possess an independent spirit, but he must not let it go too far!

The Tiger does, however, have much in his favour. He is bold, original and quick-witted. If he can keep his restless nature in check, he can enjoy considerable success. In addition, with his engaging personality, he is well liked and much admired.

Advice for the Tiger's Year Ahead

GENERAL PROSPECTS

A constructive and satisfying year. However, to get the best from it, the Tiger will need to be disciplined and use his time and opportunities to advantage. This is a year for effort, planning and focus.

CAREER PROSPECTS

There will be some excellent chances for the Tiger to add to his knowledge, skills and contacts. Although the headway he makes may be more modest than major, what he achieves now can be to his long-term benefit. This can be a valuable and encouraging year with interesting possibilities to explore.

FINANCE

Many Tigers will enjoy an increase in earnings, but with much spending likely on accommodation and other activities, they will need to remain disciplined and keep watch on their outgoings. A year for careful control.

RELATIONS WITH OTHERS

With his amiable nature, many interests and often active lifestyle, the Tiger invariably knows a lot of people and this year will find himself in demand, with the possibility of new friendships and romance. His interests and work can also bring him into contact with others. This is a year to be active and use his people skills well. In return, he can greatly benefit from the support and goodwill of others.

The Rabbit

The Rabbit is certainly one who appreciates the finer things in life. With his good taste, companionable nature and wide range of interests, he knows how to live well – and usually does!

However, for all his finesse and style, the Rabbit does possess traits he would do well to watch. His desire for a settled lifestyle makes him err on the side of caution. He dislikes change and as a consequence can miss out on opportunities. Also, there are many Rabbits who will go to great lengths to avoid difficult and fraught situations, and again, while few may relish these, sometimes in life it is necessary to take risks or stand your ground. At times it would certainly be in the Rabbit's interests to be bolder and more assertive in going after what he desires.

The Rabbit also attaches great importance to his relations with others and while he has a happy knack of getting on with most people, he can be sensitive to criticism. Difficult though it may be, he should really try to develop a thicker skin and recognize that criticism can provide valuable learning opportunities, as can some of the problems he strives so hard to avoid.

However, with his agreeable manner, keen intellect and shrewd judgement, the Rabbit does have a lot in his favour and invariably makes much of his life – and enjoys it too!

Advice for the Rabbit's Year Ahead

GENERAL PROSPECTS

A year of great potential, but it does call on the Rabbit to act. This is not a time for him to feel fettered by past disappointments or regrets but to show his true spirit and talents. By seizing his opportunities, he can make this a successful and personally rewarding time.

CAREER PROSPECTS

Great possibilities beckon, and by keeping alert and being willing to put himself forward, the Rabbit may well secure promotion or obtain a more fulfilling position. He should also take full advantage of opportunities to add to his skills. For the willing, this is an important and progressive year.

FINANCE

Many Rabbits will enjoy a rise in income or receive something extra this year. However, major purchases and plans will need to be considered carefully. This is a time for good management, but the Rabbit's naturally astute manner will help. The year can also bring some moments of luck and if a competition interests him, the Rabbit would do well to enter it.

RELATIONS WITH OTHERS

The Rabbit values his relations with others and over the year these can bring him great happiness. In his home life, shared plans and activities and some family successes, including his own, will mean a lot, while socially, new interests can often bring new friendships. For the unattached, affairs of the heart can help make their own year special.

The Dragon

Enthusiastic, enterprising and honourable, the Dragon possesses many admirable qualities and his life is often full and varied. He always gives his best and even though not all his endeavours meet with success, he is nonetheless resilient and hardy, and is much admired and respected.

However, for all his qualities, the Dragon can be blunt and forthright and, through sheer strength of character, sometimes domineering. It would certainly be in his interests to listen more closely to others rather than be so self-reliant. Also, his enthusiasm can sometimes get the better of him and he can be impulsive. To make the most of his abilities, he should give himself priorities and set about his activities in a disciplined and systematic way. More tact and diplomacy might not come amiss either!

However, with his lively and outgoing manner, the Dragon is popular and well liked. With good fortune on his side (and the Dragon is often lucky), his life is almost certain to be eventful and fulfilling. He has many talents, and if he uses them wisely he will enjoy much success.

Advice for the Dragon's Year Ahead

GENERAL PROSPECTS
Dragons like to keep themselves active, but even they need time to recharge their batteries and the Rabbit year will give them the chance to do so. This will be an ideal time for the Dragon to take stock and consider ways in which he could develop in the future. While a slow-moving year, its significance can be considerable.

CAREER PROSPECTS
Modest progress is possible, but the real value of the year will be the experience the Dragon can gain and the strengths he can demonstrate. With commitment and willingness, he can do his prospects considerable good and prepare himself for the more substantial success he will enjoy in following years.

FINANCE
Earnings may increase, but with some expensive plans and purchases in mind, the Dragon will need to remain disciplined and budget ahead. This is not a year favouring rush or risk.

RELATIONS WITH OTHERS

Family and friends will give the Dragon great support this year and he does need to consult them and listen carefully to what they have to say. This is not a time for being too independent-minded. His interests can have a pleasing social element and in almost all his activities he can benefit from joining with others and being open and forthcoming. And both his domestic and social life can bring him great pleasure.

The Snake

The Snake is blessed with a keen intellect. He has wide interests, an enquiring mind and good judgement. He tends to be quiet and thoughtful and plan his activities with considerable care. With his fine abilities he often does well in life, but he does possess traits which can undermine his progress.

The Snake is often guarded in his actions and sometimes loses out to those who are more action-oriented and assertive. He also likes to retain a certain independence in his actions and this too can hamper his progress. It would be in his interests to be more forthcoming and involve others more readily in his plans. The Snake has many talents and possesses a warm and rich personality, but there is a danger that this can remain concealed behind his often quiet and reserved manner. He would fare better if he were more outgoing and showed others his true worth.

However, the Snake is very much his own master. He invariably knows what he wants in life and is often prepared to journey long and hard to achieve his objectives. He does, though, have it in his power to make that journey easier. Lose some of that reticence, Snake, be more open and assertive, and do not be afraid of the occasional risk!

Advice for the Snake's Year Ahead

GENERAL PROSPECTS

An encouraging but busy year. The Snake is patient and watchful and in the Rabbit year he will sense the time is right to act. By taking the initiative, he can look forward to some pleasing and deserving success. His progress will, though, bring new demands and it is important that he keeps his lifestyle in balance.

CAREER PROSPECTS

A year for learning and moving forward. By keeping alert, many Snakes can make important progress in their career or secure a new and different position. However, to do well, the Snake *will* need to put in the effort, including learning new skills, making adjustments and sometimes being prepared to undertake some additional personal study. This is a successful and progressive year, but will ask a lot of him.

FINANCE

The Snake's success at work can lead to an increase in income, but to benefit he will need to keep careful control of his budget. He could find it helpful to review his current situation and put funds aside for a holiday or break. In this active year, time away will do him good.

RELATIONS WITH OTHERS

Others can be supportive and offer the Snake good advice, particularly at challenging times. But the Snake himself will need to be open and communicative and watch his independent tendencies. He should also be careful not to become involved in any potentially difficult personal situation. Lapses and indiscretions could cause serious problems. However, with care and the willingness to involve others, this will be a generally pleasing year, with, for the unattached, encouraging romantic possibilities.

The Horse

Versatile, hardworking and sociable, the Horse makes his mark wherever he goes. He has an eloquent and engaging manner and makes friends with ease. He is quick-witted, has an alert mind and is certainly not averse to taking risks or experimenting with new ideas.

He possesses a strong and likeable personality, but he does also have his weaknesses. With his wide interests he does not always finish everything he starts and he would do well to be more persevering. He has it within him to achieve considerable success, but to make the most of his talents he does need to overcome his restless tendencies. When he has made plans, he should stick with them.

The Horse loves company and values both his family and friends. However, there will have been many a time when he will have lost his temper or spoken in haste and regretted his words later. Throughout his life he needs to keep his temper in check and be diplomatic in tense situations. If not, he could risk jeopardizing the respect and good relations he so values.

However, the Horse has a multitude of talents and a lively and outgoing personality. If he can overcome his restless and volatile nature, he can lead a rich and highly fulfilling life.

Advice for the Horse's Year Ahead

GENERAL PROSPECTS

This can be a pleasant and constructive year for the Horse, although it will require him to be flexible in attitude and make the most of situations. It is an especially good year for personal development and any skills and qualifications the Horse can gain will be to his present and future advantage.

CAREER PROSPECTS

The Rabbit year holds considerable opportunity, but to benefit the Horse will need to remain aware and adaptable. This is an excellent year for adding to his skills, gaining new experience and listening closely to the advice of others. With support and the Horse's own earnest nature, much is possible.

FINANCE

An improved year financially, but the Horse should avoid hurried decisions. This is a time for carefully considering purchases and transactions.

RELATIONS WITH OTHERS

Others will be helpful and supportive and the Horse can benefit from consulting them. Joint activities are favoured, and at work, networking and building contacts can help.

Interests and activities the Horse becomes involved with can also have a good social element and enable him to meet others, but new romances need care if they are to endure.

The Goat

The Goat has a warm, friendly and understanding manner and gets on well with most people. He is generally easy-going, has a fond appreciation of the finer things in life and possesses a rich imagination. He is often artistic and enjoys the creative arts and outdoor activities.

However, despite his engaging manner, there lurks beneath his skin a sometimes tense and pessimistic nature. The Goat can be a worrier and without the support and encouragement of others can feel insecure and be hesitant in his actions.

To make the most of himself he should aim to become more assertive and decisive as well as more at ease with himself. He has much in his favour, but he really does need to promote himself more and be bolder. He would also be helped if he were to sort out his priorities and set about his activities in an organized and disciplined manner. There are some Goats who tend to be haphazard in the way they go about things and this can hamper their progress.

Although the Goat will always value the support of others, it would also be in his interests to become more independent and not be so reticent about striking out on his own. He does, after all, possess many talents, as well as a sincere and likeable personality, and by always giving his best he can make his life rich, rewarding and enjoyable.

Advice for the Goat's Year Ahead

GENERAL PROSPECTS

A positive and encouraging year, but it does call on the Goat to act. This is a time for seizing the initiative and, if necessary, coming out of the comfort zone. As Virgil noted, 'Fortune favours the bold,' and for the bold and willing Goat, this is a year of considerable promise.

CAREER PROSPECTS

There will be good opportunities for the Goat to make headway or, if feeling staid or looking for a position, to change what he does. The year will require some adjustment and a willingness to adapt, but will give the Goat the chance to extend his experience as well as make more of his talents, including his creativity and great communication skills. This is a year for self-belief and stepping forward.

FINANCE

Many Goats will enjoy an increase in earnings this year. However, the Goat should manage his finances carefully and make early provision for more expensive plans, including travel. By keeping alert, he could benefit from some special buys. His eye for quality and style will be on fine form.

RELATIONS WITH OTHERS

With his wonderful people skills, the Goat may find himself in demand. Domestically and socially, this can be a full and personally rewarding year, with new friendships and romance favourably aspected. Some Goats could also have personal celebrations in store. Again, to benefit from these encouraging aspects, the Goat will need to be active and prepared to consult others. But personally, the Rabbit year can be a pleasing one.

The Monkey

Lively, enterprising and innovative, the Monkey certainly knows how to impress. He has wide interests, a good sense of fun and relates well to others. He also possesses a shrewd mind and often has a happy knack of turning events to his advantage.

However, despite his versatility and considerable gifts, he does have his weaknesses. He often lacks persistence, can get distracted easily and also places tremendous reliance upon his own judgement. While his belief in himself is a commendable asset, it would certainly be in his interests to be more mindful of the views of others. Also, while he likes to keep tabs on all that is going on around him, he can be evasive and secretive with regard to his own feelings and activities, and again a more forthcoming attitude would be to his advantage.

In his desire to succeed, the Monkey can also be tempted to cut corners or be crafty and he should recognize that such actions can rebound on him!

However, he is resourceful and his sheer strength of character will ensure that he has an interesting and varied life. If he can channel his considerable energies wisely and overcome his sometimes restless tendencies, his life can be crowned with success. And with his amiable personality, he will have many friends.

Advice for the Monkey's Year Ahead

GENERAL PROSPECTS

A progressive and favourable year, but to benefit the Monkey will need to be active, promote his ideas and use his strengths to advantage. For the determined, this is a year of considerable opportunity.

CAREER PROSPECTS

Born under the sign of fantasy, Monkeys have a rich imagination which can be the source of many fine ideas. They are also highly resourceful. All these talents can serve the Monkey well this year, and by following through his ideas, he can make excellent headway. The Rabbit year holds great potential for him and will reward determination and initiative.

FINANCE

Progress at work can help financially, but the Monkey will have many outgoings, especially accommodation-wise. As a result, he will need to keep tabs on his spending and budget ahead for large expenses.

RELATIONS WITH OTHERS

A year to be with others. The Monkey may well have personal or family news to celebrate as well as benefit from the support of those around him. His interests can also have a good social element and, for the unattached, new friendships and romance can considerably brighten their situation.

The Rooster

With his considerable bearing and incisive and resolute manner, the Rooster cuts an impressive figure. He has a sharp mind, is well informed on many matters and expresses himself clearly and convincingly. He is meticulous and efficient in his undertakings and commands a great deal of respect. He also has a genuine and caring interest in others.

The Rooster has much in his favour, but there are some aspects of his character that can tell against him. He can be candid in his views and over-zealous in his actions, and sometimes he can say or do things he later regrets. His high standards also make him fussy, even pedantic, and he can get diverted into relatively minor matters when in truth he could be occupying his time more profitably. This is something all Roosters would do well to watch. Also, while the Rooster is a great planner, he can sometimes be unrealistic in his expectations. In making plans – indeed, in most of his activities – he would do well to consult others. He would benefit greatly from their input.

The Rooster has many talents as well as commendable drive and commitment, but to make the most of himself he does need to channel his energies wisely and watch his candid and sometimes volatile nature. With care, however, he can make a success of his life, and with his wide interests and outgoing personality, he will enjoy the friendship and respect of many.

Advice for the Rooster's Year Ahead

GENERAL PROSPECTS

The Rooster is efficient and well organized and likes to get things done. However, he will fare best this year by accepting that it favours a more measured approach and keeping his expectations realistic. It is a time for proceeding steadily and building on skills and interests. What is achieved can be significant, however, particularly in the auspicious Dragon year that follows.

CAREER PROSPECTS

Many Roosters will be content to remain in their present position and add to their knowledge and reputation. This is also an excellent year to work closely with others and, if appropriate, join a professional organization. For Roosters seeking a position, an initial opening can often lead on to other possibilities. What is achieved this year can have long-term significance.

FINANCE

An expensive year and the Rooster will need to keep strict control over his outgoings. Budgeting ahead will help.

RELATIONS WITH OTHERS

The Rooster's opinions and insights are highly regarded and others will often be glad of his help. However, while he has his own views, it is important he consults others over his plans and ideas as well as joins them in his various activities. This is a year favouring joint undertakings and spending quality time with loved ones.

The Dog

Loyal, dependable and with a good understanding of human nature, the Dog is well placed to win respect and admiration. He is a no-nonsense sort of person and hates any sort of hypocrisy and falsehood. With the Dog you know where you stand and, given his direct manner, where he stands on any issue. He also has a strong humanitarian nature and often champions good causes.

The Dog has many fine attributes, although there are certain traits that can prevent him from either enjoying or making the most of his life. He is a great worrier and can get anxious over all manner of things. Whenever he is tense or concerned, he should be prepared to speak to others rather than shoulder his worries all by himself. In some cases, they could even be of his own making! Also, he has a tendency to look on the pessimistic side and it would help to view his undertakings more optimistically. He possesses many skills and should have faith in his abilities. Another weakness is his tendency to be stubborn over certain issues. If he is not careful, at times this could undermine his position.

If the Dog can reduce the pessimistic side of his nature, he will not only enjoy life more but also find he is achieving more. He possesses a truly admirable character and his loyalty, reliability and sincerity are appreciated by all he meets. In his life he will do much good and befriend many people – and he owes it to himself to enjoy life too. Sometimes it might help him to recall the words of another Dog, Sir Winston Churchill: 'When I look back on all these worries I remember the story of the old man who said on his deathbed that he had had a lot of trouble in his life, most of which never happened.'

Advice for the Dog's Year Ahead

GENERAL PROSPECTS

The Dog can get a lot out of the Rabbit year and will find his plans now easier to advance. It is a year for positive and considered action, and the support of others will help.

CAREER PROSPECTS

A progressive year, but one which can also hold surprising developments. New opportunities may arise or the Dog may be involved in a change of duties. However, this can be a refreshing change for him. This is a year to keep alert, be adaptable and add to skills. What is achieved now can have long-term significance.

FINANCE

The Dog's progress at work can lead to an increase in income and with good control over his outgoings and taking the time to reflect on his decisions and purchases, he will fare well. However, should he be involved in any complex transaction or faced with a decision with important implications, he should seek professional advice.

RELATIONS WITH OTHERS

The Dog can really benefit from the support and encouragement of others this year, but he does need to be forthcoming and, when meeting people for the first time, try to lose some of his Dog reserve. New friends and contacts could come to be important and, with the affairs of the heart especially well aspected, this can be a personally special year.

The Pig

Genial, sincere and trusting, the Pig gets on well with most people. He has a kind and caring nature, a dislike of discord and often a good sense of humour. In addition, he has a fondness for socializing and enjoying the good life!

The Pig possesses a shrewd mind, is particularly adept at dealing with business and financial matters and has a robust and resilient nature. Although not all his plans may work out as he would like, he is tenacious and will often rise up and succeed after experiencing setbacks and difficulties. In his often active and varied life he can accomplish a great deal, although there are certain aspects of his character that can tell against him. If he can modify these or keep them in check then his life will certainly be easier and possibly even more successful.

In his activities the Pig can sometimes over-commit himself and while he does not want to disappoint, it would help if he were to set about his activities in an organized and systematic manner and give himself priorities at busy times. He should also not allow others to take advantage of his good nature. There will have been times when he has been gullible and naïve; fortunately, though, he quickly learns from his mistakes. However, he possesses a stubborn streak and if new situations do not fit in with his line of thinking, he can be inflexible.

The Pig is a great pleasure-seeker and while he should enjoy the fruits of his labours, he can sometimes be self-indulgent and extravagant. Though he may possess some faults, those who come into contact with him are invariably impressed by his integrity, amiable manner and intelligence. If he uses his talents wisely, his life can be crowned with considerable achievement and he will be loved and respected by many.

Advice for the Pig's Year Ahead

GENERAL PROSPECTS

The Pig will set about his aims with considerable determination, and his resolve and enterprise will serve him well in this year of progress and good fortune. With commitment, a lot can be achieved.

CAREER PROSPECTS

The Pig has considerable drive and is sometimes blessed with entrepreneurial flair. In 2011 he can make his experience and qualities count. This is a year of progress and some important new personal challenges, and the Pig's determination will allow him to make excellent headway.

FINANCE

The Pig's finances can improve, but spending does need to be watched. Home expenses can be substantial this year. Also, if any Pigs find themselves in a potentially difficult situation, it is important that they seek professional guidance and get the matter dealt with effectively.

RELATIONS WITH OTHERS

The Pig can look forward to many happy times this year. Plans shared with loved ones can be meaningful, while his personal interests can have a good social element and, for the unattached, romance can add a sparkle to this promising year.